Episkope

Episkope

The Theory and Practice of Translocal Oversight

Edited by

Roger Standing
Paul Goodliff

scm press

© Editors and Contributors 2020

Published in 2020 by SCM Press
Editorial office
3rd Floor, Invicta House,
108–114 Golden Lane,
London EC1Y 0TG, UK
www.scmpress.co.uk

SCM Press is an imprint of Hymns Ancient & Modern Ltd
(a registered charity)

Hymns Ancient & Modern® is a registered trademark of
Hymns Ancient & Modern Ltd
13A Hellesdon Park Road, Norwich,
Norfolk NR6 5DR, UK

All rights reserved. No part of this publication may be reproduced,
stored in a retrieval system, or transmitted,
in any form or by any means, electronic, mechanical,
photocopying or otherwise, without the prior permission of
the publisher, SCM Press.

The Authors have asserted their right under the Copyright, Designs and
Patents Act 1988 to be identified as the Authors of this Work

British Library Cataloguing in Publication data

A catalogue record for this book is available
from the British Library

978-0-334-05938-7

Typeset by Regent Typesetting
Printed and bound by
CPI Group (UK) Ltd

*With gratitude to God
and to the memory of our friend Douglas McBain,
our elder brother in Christ, who mentored,
encouraged and exemplified a gospel-centred
translocal ministry with both of us.*

Contents

Acknowledgements	xi
Contributors	xiii
Foreword: Bishop Joe Aldred	xix
Foreword: Rt Revd Rowan Williams	xxi
Introduction	xxiii

Part 1 Foundations

1 Beyond the Household: The Emergence of Translocal Ministry in the New Testament   3
Sean F. Winter

2 Theological Issues: Constants in Context   14
Roger Standing

3 Contemporary Models of Translocal Ministry: Ecumenical Landscapes   44
Paul Goodliff

Part 2 Experience

4 Anglican Episcopacy
The Ministry of Bishops in the Church of England   61
Paul Avis

Church of England Bishops as Pastor and Evangelist   71
Stephen Cottrell

Church of England Bishops as Religious and Civic Leaders   81
James Jones

	Translocal Ministries in the Church of England as Institutional Leadership *Julian Hubbard*	93
5	The Roman Catholic Church Theological Dynamics for Understanding the Roman Catholic Episcopate in Britain *Jacob Phillips*	103
6	The Methodist Church A Connexion of Translocal Ministry, Oversight and *Episkope* *Martyn Atkins*	116
7	The Baptist Union of Great Britain The Theory and Practice of Translocal Oversight in a Baptist Context *Dianne Tidball*	125
8	The United Reformed Church Synod Moderators *Roberta Rominger*	136
9	The Salvation Army Territorial Command Structures *Mike Parker*	145
10	Pentecostalism Translocal Leadership in UK Pentecostal Churches *William K. Kay*	155
11	Apostolic Ministry in the New Church Streams Personal Reflections from Newfrontiers *Terry Virgo*	164
	Personal Reflections from Pioneer *Gerald Coates*	169
12	The Black Church and Episcopacy *R. David Muir*	175

13 Oversight and the New Monasticism
   Episkope and Being a Leader in the New Monasticism in
   the Church of England   184
   Ian Mobsby

   Episkope and the New Monasticism in the Celtic
   Tradition: The Northumbria Community   192
   Roy Searle

Part 3 Practice

14 *Episkope*, Identity and Personhood   203
   Roger Standing

15 The Shape of Translocal Oversight   213
   Roger Standing

16 Translocal Ministry and Scholarship   225
   Paul Goodliff

17 *Episkope* and Gender: An Anglican Case Study   232
   Anne Hollinghurst

18 *Episkope* and Supervision   244
   Paul Goodliff

19 Translocal Ministry in Post-Christendom   254
   Stuart Murray

20 Conclusion: The Future Trajectory of Translocal Ministry 267
   Paul Butler

Index   273

Acknowledgements

Unless otherwise indicated, Scripture quotations are from The New Revised Standard Version of the Bible, Anglicized Edition, copyright © 1989, 1995 by the Division of Christian Education of the National Council of the Churches of Christ in the United States of America, and are used by permission. All rights reserved.

Scripture quotations marked KJV are from the Authorized Version of the Bible (The King James Bible), the rights in which are vested in the Crown, and are reproduced by permission of the Crown's Patentee, Cambridge University Press.

The Scripture quotation marked ESV is from The ESV® Bible (The Holy Bible, English Standard Version®), copyright © 2001 by Crossway, a publishing ministry of Good News Publishers. Used by permission. All rights reserved.

The Scripture quotation marked NASB is taken from the New American Standard Bible®, Copyright © 1960, 1962, 1963, 1968, 1971, 1972, 1973, 1975, 1977, 1995 by The Lockman Foundation. Used by permission.

Contributors

Revd Dr Martyn Atkins is a Methodist Minister who has served as postgraduate tutor and Principal at Cliff College and General Secretary of the Methodist Church of Great Britain. He was elected President of the Methodist Conference in 2007 and is currently Superintendent Minister and Team Leader at Methodist Central Hall Westminster. Martyn has written several books, focusing on mission, Fresh Expressions of church and Christian discipleship in the Methodist/Wesleyan tradition. He is married, has adult children and a growing number of grandchildren.

Revd Prof. Paul Avis was in parish ministry for 23 years before serving as the General Secretary of the Council for Christian Unity (1998–2012). He has been a member of international ecumenical dialogues and serves on the Inter-Anglican Standing Commission for Unity, Faith and Order. Paul was Chaplain to HM Queen Elizabeth II (2008–17), Canon Theologian of Exeter Cathedral (2008–15) and Honorary Visiting Professor at the University of Exeter (2008–17), where he is currently an honorary Research Fellow. He holds an honorary chair of theology at Durham University. He is the editor of *The Oxford Handbook of Ecclesiology* (2018) and of the journal *Ecclesiology*.

Rt Revd Paul Butler is the Church of England Bishop of Durham. He has previously served as Bishop of Southampton and Bishop of Southwell and Nottingham. He is still surprised and humbled to be a bishop and is a member of the House of Lords. Paul came to faith in Jesus as a teenager through his school Christian Union and a great Free Church youth group. His ministry passions are children and young people, social justice for the poor, especially children, asylum seekers and refugees. He regularly visits Burundi and Rwanda. He is married, has four grown-up children and is a proud grandad.

Gerald Coates is married with three adult sons and lives in Surrey. He is one of the founders of the House Church Movement that began in 1970 – he later renamed it the New Church Movement. He has authored nine books, the last being *Sexual Healing* (2013). Ralph Turner has written his biography, *Gerald Coates: Pioneer* (2015). He began the Pioneer network of churches and several related training courses.

Most Revd Stephen Cottrell is the Archbishop of York and formerly the Bishop of Chelmsford. He is a member of the House of Lords and is on the Select Committee for Communication. He is a well-known writer and speaker on evangelism, spirituality and catechesis. He is married to Rebecca, who is a potter, and they have three boys. His most recent books are *The Sleepy Shepherd* (2018) and *Striking Out: Poems and Stories from the Camino* (2018).

Revd Dr Paul Goodliff is a Baptist minister, currently serving as General Secretary of Churches Together in England. He has pastored churches in Streatham, Stevenage and Abingdon, and from 1999 to 2004 was General Superintendent for the Baptist Union of Great Britain's Central Area, and then for ten years its Head of Ministry. He is a pastoral and systematic theologian and has written widely about pastoral care and ministry, including *Care in a Confused Climate* (1998) and *Shaped for Service* (2017). He co-founded the Order for Baptist Ministry in 2010 and is a part-time tutor at Spurgeon's College. He loves art, writes a little poetry and is married to Gill, a retired university lecturer.

Rt Revd Anne Hollinghurst has been Suffragan Bishop of Aston in the Diocese of Birmingham since 2015 and was among the first women to be consecrated as a bishop in the Church of England. Ordained in 1996, she has held a variety of roles parish ministry, higher education chaplaincy, lecturing on gender and religious studies and cathedral ministry. She is a member of the Faith and Order Commission and of the Implementation and Dialogue Group tasked with reviewing how the House of Bishops' Declaration and the Five Guiding Principles, as part of the settlement that made possible the admission of women to the episcopate, are being understood, implemented and received in the Church. She is married to Steve, who is also ordained and has held a range of roles focusing on mission and evangelism in contemporary culture.

Venerable Julian Hubbard is a priest of the Church of England who has served as a vicar, area dean, chaplain in healthcare and education, tutor at a theological college and as a director of ministerial training in a diocese. He was Archdeacon of Oxford and Canon of Christ Church from 2005 to 2011 before becoming Director of Ministry at the Archbishops' Council of the Church of England from 2011 to 2018. Much of his ministry has been exercised through institutions and his academic interests include institutionalism and the future of the Church of England and its role in society.

Rt Revd James Jones became Bishop of Hull in 1994 and Bishop of Liverpool in 1998. He was deeply involved in the regeneration of both cities, understanding that a bishop in the established Church is a civic as well as a religious leader. He saw too that a bishop was a pastor not just to members of the church but to the whole community. His theological convictions about the environment, truth and justice led him to chair the Independent Panel on Forestry, the Hillsborough Independent Panel and the Gosport Independent Panel. He sat in the House of Lords for ten years and in 2017 was awarded a KBE for services to the bereaved and to justice.

Prof. William Kay is Emeritus Professor of Theology at Wrexham Glyndŵr University and Honorary Professor of Pentecostal Studies at the University of Chester. He was also the founding director of the Centre for Pentecostal and Charismatic Studies at Bangor University. He edits the *Journal of the European Pentecostal Theological Association* and has authored *Pentecostals in Britain* (2000) and *Apostolic Networks in Britain* (2007). His most recent books are *Pentecostalism: A very short introduction* (2012) and *George Jeffreys: Pentecostal Apostle and Revivalist* (2017). He is co-editor of Brill's *Global and Pentecostal Studies* series. He is married to Anthea and they have two grown-up sons and five grandchildren.

Revd Ian Mobsby is an author, speaker, missioner, Church of England priest and enthusiast of New Monasticism. He is currently the Woolwich Episcopal Area Mission Enabler in the Diocese of Southwark, Priest in Charge of St Luke Camberwell and Prior to the Wellspring New Monastic Community. In Spring 2019, Ian was awarded the St Dunstan Award by the Archbishop of Canterbury for his service to the religious life and prayer in the development of New Monastic communities. He was a founding member of Moot, a New Monastic community in London, and has also been elected Guardian of the Society of the Holy Trinity, which seeks to promote the support and development of New Monastic communities.

Dr R. David Muir is Senior Lecturer in Ministerial Theology and Public Theology at Roehampton University. His research interests include the intersection of theology and politics, and the role of African and Caribbean churches in society. Previously executive director of Public Policy and Public Theology at the Evangelical Alliance, he was also an adviser to the Home Secretary (2002–08). Recent publications include *Pentecostalism and Political Engagement* (2019), *London's Burning: Riots, Gangs, and the Moral Formation of Young People* (2014), *Theology and the Black Church* (2010). David is a member of the Kirby Laing Institute for Christian Ethics at Cambridge University and the European convener for the Transatlantic Roundtable on Religion and Race.

Dr Stuart Murray was a church planter in East London and then Director of Church Planting and Evangelism at Spurgeon's College. He founded Urban Expression, a pioneering mission agency. Since 2001, he has worked under the auspices of the Anabaptist Network as a trainer and consultant with a particular interest in urban mission, church planting and emerging forms of church. In 2014 he became the Director of the Centre for Anabaptist Studies at Bristol Baptist College. He has written several books on church planting, urban mission, emerging church, the challenge of post-Christendom and the contribution of the Anabaptist tradition to contemporary missiology.

Commissioner Mike Parker has served as a Salvation Army Officer for 42 years, rising to the rank of Commissioner. Together with his wife Joan, he was a Corps Officer in Wales, Carlisle and London, followed by five years at the Training College and service as Divisional Leader in Wales and London. At Territorial Headquarters he was for six years the Secretary for Personnel and subsequently Secretary for Administrative Review. In 2011 he was appointed as Chief Secretary in Indonesia, with his final appointment before retirement being its Territorial Commander. He has been married for 48 years and has three children and eight grandchildren.

Dr Jacob Phillips is Director of the Institute of Theology at St Mary's University, Twickenham. He works across various areas in systematic and philosophical theology, and is particularly concerned with issues of human self-understanding, conscience and obedience, as well as the interrelations of theology and culture. He is author of *Mary, Star of Evangelization: Tilling the Soil and Sowing the Seed* (2018) and *Human Subjectivity 'in Christ' in the Theology of Dietrich Bonhoeffer* (2019).

Revd Roberta Rominger served as moderator of the Thames North Synod of the United Reformed Church from 1998 to 2008, overseeing churches and ministers in North London and the surrounding area. She then became General Secretary of the denomination. In 2015 she returned to the United Church of Christ USA, the church in which she was ordained. She now serves as pastor at the Congregational Church on Mercer Island, Washington and brings her translocal experience to her role as a director of the Church Council of Greater Seattle. She is an environmental activist and a keen amateur cellist.

Revd Roy Searle is one of the founders of the Northumbria Community, serving now on its Council of Elders. A former President of the Baptist Union, Roy is one of the denomination's Pioneer Ambassadors. He is a part-time Free Church Tutor at Cranmer Hall, Durham, Associate Tutor at Spurgeon's College, London and a member of the Renovaré Board. A popular speaker, writer and blogger, Roy's ministry is about encouraging people to love God and live generously. He is married and now lives in North Yorkshire, where he relaxes with family and friends and also enjoys sailing, playing tennis, badminton and curling.

Revd Dr Roger Standing has served as the minister of local churches in Yorkshire and London, as a Regional Minister/Team Leader with the Baptist Union of Great Britain and in theological education at Spurgeon's College, where he taught missiology and practical theology, holding various responsibilities including that of Principal. Having begun his ministry as an evangelist in Liverpool, he has written several books focusing on preaching as well as mission and evangelism, including *Finding the Plot* (2004), *Re-emerging Church* (2008) and *As A Fire By Burning...* (2013). He is married to Marion, who works with the Oxford Diocese as an education adviser, and together they have three children and five grandchildren. Roger loves jazz and is a shareholder and lifelong supporter of Norwich City FC.

Revd Dianne Tidball has been the minister of Baptist churches in Ruislip and North Bushey and was the Regional Minister/Team Leader of the East Midlands Baptist Association for nine years. Her passion is for healthy churches and Holy Spirit-enabled discipleship. As President of the Baptist Union 2017–18, she served the churches of the Union by encouraging and inspiring them to be faithful to God and his mission. She studied and trained at the London School of Theology and was a teacher of Business Studies and Economics before being full-time in church leadership. She has written four books: *Esther: A true first lady* (2001), *Discovering John's Letters* (2002), *Discovering Peter and Jude* (2007) and *The Message of Women: Creation, Grace and Gender* (2012).

Terry Virgo is married to Wendy and they have five married children. He founded the Newfrontiers family of churches, which now includes over 2,000 churches in 72 nations. Having transitioned the leadership of Newfrontiers to the next generation with approximately 20 teams scattered around the world, he continues travelling and preaching and has written a number of books, such as *God's Lavish Grace* (2004), *The Spirit-Filled Church* (2011) and his autobiography, *No Well-Worn Paths* (2001).

Revd Prof. Sean F. Winter is an ordained Baptist Minister, the Principal of Pilgrim Theological College and an Associate Professor within the University of Divinity in Melbourne, Australia. He was educated at the Universities of Bristol and Oxford and received his DPhil for a thesis on Paul's Letter to the Philippians. He is completing a major study on the theme of friendship in that letter and is the author of numerous essays on Pauline literature and theology, the theology and hermeneutics of Dietrich Bonhoeffer and theological hermeneutics.

Foreword

BISHOP DR JOE ALDRED
Church of God of Prophecy

The Church of Jesus Christ has needed oversight from the beginning. Today, in this ecumenical age, its variety and character are diverse. In my own tradition, oversight by bishops is foundational to the life of the Church, as it is for the Roman Catholics, Anglicans and others. For those with more congregational ecclesiologies – such as the Baptists, representing the tradition of the two editors of this collection, Roger Standing and Paul Goodliff – oversight offered from beyond the congregation is often welcomed, but is not of the essence of the Church, so cannot be insisted upon. Whether that oversight is essential, or simply beneficial, it often fulfils similar roles in the rich diversity of church order represented in today's ecumenical world.

For those beginning such roles – be they a Catholic or Anglican Bishop, Methodist District Chair, Salvation Army Divisional Commander, Baptist Regional Minister or the many different roles within Free Church, New Church or Pentecostal churches – understanding what ecumenical colleagues do and how they relate to their churches can initially be bewildering. This collection offers insights into these roles in their similarity and diversity. Throughout Britain, meetings of those church leaders exercising oversight soon demonstrate how similar are many of the tasks before them: pastoral care of clergy and their families; leadership in mission; proclaiming, teaching and defending the 'faith once given'; administration of a diocese, Salvation Army division, United Reformed Church synod, Methodist District or Baptist Association and participating in the public life of the area they cover. This book will act as a primer for those who serve in such capacities. It will also help to distinguish those roles that are very specific to some traditions, and absent in others. Anglican bishops regularly preside at services of confirmation, while Baptist Regional Ministers have no such role.

Preparing for such a translocal role, and then serving effectively and faithfully in it, requires significant adjustments for those whose experience hitherto has been confined to parish or congregational life. The sense of loss of local community that results can seem like a bereavement, the workload overwhelming and the context unforgiving – making unjustified criticisms of those in authority is found as readily in the Church as in any other sphere. It helps to be aware of those changes and to begin to prepare for the demanding role that translocal oversight represents and the broader canvas upon which this Christian ministry is exercised. This collection reflects helpfully on aspects of that adjustment for those preparing to take up office.

If the Church rises or falls according to the calibre of its clergy, then translocal oversight offers one of the most valuable – indeed, essential – ways of encouraging the best from those who serve a local parish or congregation. In their collegial roles, those in the translocal ministry of oversight offer leadership to the tradition or denomination they serve, and in ecumenical aspects, to the whole Church. The better-prepared men and women are to understand the demands of translocal oversight, and the greater the awareness of how others practise this ministry, the more competent will be the oversight of the Church, and the more effective will be the participation in the *missio Dei* to which all are called.

Foreword

RT REVD DR ROWAN WILLIAMS
Master of Magdalene College Cambridge and formerly Archbishop of Canterbury

Traditionally, bishops have been understood as a kind of focus for claims about the 'apostolic' character of ministry in various churches. In the first Christian centuries, the bishop became the visible sign of continuity in teaching, guaranteeing that the Church remained accountable to the primary creative witness of the apostles. Like the canon of Scripture, the existence of a ministerial presence connecting the congregation here and now to the beginnings of faith was a reminder that the congregation did not set its own standards of belief but needed to be guided back towards the mystery at its origins, to the Word made flesh, crucified and risen. For all the complex and fussy ways the Church has developed of securing continuity, the heart of the idea lies here: the Church is always being made contemporary with the incarnation, cross and resurrection of Christ as the present act of God in judgement, mercy and promise. The Holy Spirit, which constantly brings us back to the reality of the Word made flesh, works in both the Spirit-breathed Scripture and the Spirit-called ministry, which is authorized to interpret Scripture and open it afresh, and to connect the local church with sisters and brothers across time and space.

Perhaps one of the things we most need in today's Church is a recovery of the sense that the bishop is above all a witness to this basic accountability in the life of the Church, its willingness to stand before the mystery of God's action and be challenged and changed by it. It may sound odd, but the way in which this ministry best 'guarantees' the Church's continuity and apostolic integrity may be less by trying to keep it 'safe' than by modelling and enabling this risky encounter with God in Christ – not only by teaching but by pastoral presence and fidelity to those who share public ministry and those who are finding and sustaining faith. In this sense, the bishop is very much a giver of permission to those seeking new ways of sharing the Good News – alert and sympathetic to what is happening at what we think of as the 'edges' as well as the historic and administrative 'centre' of the Church.

Presence and fidelity: just as the Church declares in every community that it is there to stay, ready to share the struggles and perils of all human neighbours, so the ministry of oversight, simply by being there, declares that Christian ministry is meant to be shared; that no pastor should be struggling alone and unsupported; that the well-being of every community is of equal importance. When the episcopal ministry fails, as it does, it is when the needs of an abstract institution prevail over this kind of faithful attention – whether in the shameful confusions and collusions around abuse that have come so unmercifully to light in recent years, or in a bureaucratic and insensitive implementing of discipline, or in a preoccupied distance from the pressures and anxieties and hopes of actual believers. The bishop is there to connect – to connect with the apostolic witness and bring alive its scriptural testimony, and to connect with the reality of the body of Christ as it concretely is in this place and time, in these variously sinful, confused, hopeful, generous, timid or ecstatic worshippers.

The Church always needs to refresh its sense of what this ministry most fundamentally is, and the contributions to this book offer just such reflection for our day. Churches may realize the episcopal ministry in a number of diverse ways – we have discovered in the last century or so that we must move beyond mechanical notions of succession – but it is a remarkable grace that so many Christian traditions have begun to look at the heart and energy of the episcopal idea – as a ministry of connection, a ministry of resurrection testimony, most fully itself at the Lord's table, a ministry of ministerial formation and encouragement and faithful solidarity. And because resurrection testimony, eucharistic sharing, learning in the communion of the Spirit and faithful presence are all fundamental to a living Church, we may hope to see better how clarity about the episcopal calling clarifies the gift and calling of all believers.

Introduction

Bishops, moderators, apostles, regional ministers ... the range of titles given to those who exercise some form of translocal oversight of Christian communities in contemporary Britain is wide indeed. Together they represent a spectrum of response to a range of dynamics drawing on biblical foundations, received church tradition, present felt needs and the demands of the contemporary cultural context. This book seeks to establish the common ground to inform our conversations about translocal ministry and map the present-day models and experience of ecclesial oversight. Building on these shared insights a variety of themes are explored that we hope will contribute to helping translocal ministry be fit for purpose.

The idea behind this book has been in gestation for more than a decade. Previously, as Area Superintendents in the Baptist Union of Great Britain (BUGB), we had both straddled the organizational changes that saw an old regime of centrally appointed and accountable translocal leaders become a decentralized system of Regional Ministers devolved among 13 Associations. Both of us then later moved into new roles as Paul became Head of Ministry at BUGB and Roger moved to teach missiology at Spurgeon's College in London. Together we were invited to deliver training for newly appointed Baptist Regional Ministers as part of a proposed in-service master's degree, and we set about the task convinced that it should be set and delivered within an ecumenical context.

We were both aware of how little preparation there had been for our respective moves from local pastorates to translocal posts. Outside of some helpful denominational orientation over a couple of days at our national headquarters alongside the provision of a 'field manual', there was a notable absence of time to reflect and grapple with the responsibilities we were to carry, the tasks we were expected to undertake and the Baptist and ecumenical contexts in which we were to minister. We also quickly discovered how little there was in print about the task of *episkope*. In fact, what there was tended to be solely related to a particular denomination or theological conviction. Interestingly, Malcolm Grundy makes the same observation as a more recent writer on the subject in an Anglican context following his own postgraduate research (2011, pp. 3–4).

Our vision was for a book that met this felt need – a volume that might have helped us gain a better grasp of the theological and practical issues we had faced. More than that, the ecumenical space we now moved in presented a bemusing array of ecclesiologies, and their organizational expressions, inhabited by our colleagues from other denominations and networks. The surprising degree of translocal ecumenical interaction and cooperation made this a particularly immediate and pressing need.

Over the years we sought to recruit potential contributors to the writing project and found an amazing degree of excitement and willingness to be involved from church leaders of all varieties. Despite busyness keeping the venture from moving much beyond second base, we never stopped believing that the need for the book was compelling and we were determined to give it one last try. In that final push we are grateful to David Shervington at SCM Press for his encouragement and giving us the impetus to get it over the line. We are grateful too for the contributions of our 21 translocal leaders who have taken the time to reflect on their own experience and write pertinent and insightful pieces. All have come in on time, and the sum total of what the book contains greatly exceeds what we hoped we might achieve.

As will be readily obvious, the book itself is written unashamedly from an ecumenical commitment: a perspective rooted in the conviction that, though our practice of *episkope* can appear to be very different, there is no doubt that such differences can be both authentically Christian and practised with integrity. Having immersed ourselves in the subject, the picture that comes to mind is of the Holy Spirit's action on the Day of Pentecost. The creative Spirit of God enabled everyone to speak in their own tongue, rather than endorse a single divine language at the birth of the Church. Indeed, the whole of creation speaks of a God who delights in creative diversity. We wonder whether God may also rejoice in the variety of ecclesiastical solutions that the good news of the kingdom of God has seeded: a true unity in diversity.

For the purposes of this volume it is important to state at the outset that we have adopted a working definition of translocal oversight as relating to those working at a diocesan or regional level. In several places some contributors move beyond this narrow definition to provide a fuller picture and necessary context to understand *episkope* in their tradition. A second thing to note is that we consistently use the Greek word *episkope* to mean 'oversight', though we were taken with a Methodist document that reported it as used in the Bible to describe God visiting people and 'keeping an eye' on what is happening (Methodist Conference, 2005, p. 1).

The book itself falls into three distinct parts. In the first we explore some of the foundational issues of biblical and ecclesiological theory

INTRODUCTION

from which the rest of the book flows. As Baptists, our tradition inclines us to begin with the Scriptures, and Professor Sean Winter from Australia opens up contemporary insights into the relevant biblical material. This is then followed by some extended theological and ecumenical groundwork that underpins our overall approach.

The second part explores the wide variety of practice and experience in translocal ministry across the denominations. It is perhaps no surprise that common themes begin to emerge from across the contributors' experience. Given the significance of Anglicanism within these shores, we have solicited four contributions to this part to enable a fuller picture to be painted for the benefit of us all.

The third part covers the practice of translocal ministry and includes a personal reflection and case study from Anne Hollinghurst on gender and *episkope* in the Church of England to illustrate the debate and experience of this controversial dimension of church life. This third part, and the book itself, is then drawn to a close as the Bishop of Durham, Paul Butler, explores what might lay ahead for those exercising *episkope* in the British churches.

Our hope is that this book will broaden our shared understanding, deepen our theological and ecclesiological thinking and provide insights for our mutual benefit regarding the practice of *episkope*. Indeed, we are convinced that this is vital in enabling the ministry of the churches to be the best that it can be for the kingdom of God and the flourishing of its mission in Christ.

Amid the challenges presented by the retreating certainties of Christendom and the opportunities presented by an emerging post-secular world, the task of *episkope* is as important as ever, if not more so. As we reflect on our experience and drawing this volume together, we find ourselves very much in agreement with Martyn Percy, the Dean of Christ Church, Oxford, when he writes of his own denomination what could also be said of all:

> the early church, by appealing to ideas of 'family', 'household', 'marriage' and 'body', emphasised the intricate, organic and intimate bonds forming this complex institution. That is why our bishops are mothers or fathers in God, not managers. They are chief pastors, not our chief executives. Like a family, the church exists for love, formation and growth; 'a bodie mysticall', as Hooker would say. (Percy, 2017, p. 66)

Roger Standing
Paul Goodliff
Epiphany 2020

References

Grundy, Malcolm, 2011, *Leadership and Oversight: New Models for Episcopal Ministry*, London: Mowbray.

Methodist Conference, 2005, *The Nature of Oversight: Leadership, Management and Governance in the Methodist Church in Great Britain*, www.methodist.org.uk/about-us/the-methodist-conference/conference-reports/conference-reports-2005/ (accessed 17.10.2019).

Percy, Martyn, 2017, *The Future Shapes of Anglicanism: Currents, Contours, Charts*, London: Routledge.

PART I

Foundations

I

Beyond the Household: The Emergence of Translocal Ministry in the New Testament[1]

SEAN F. WINTER

Introduction

There are plenty of books available that provide historical and theological insights into the development of early Christian ministry insofar as that development is visible to us in the writings of the New Testament and related early Christian texts.[2] This chapter will not go back over that ground, but instead pursue a specific question. It now seems likely that, around the turn of the third century CE, the Church developed explicit structures whereby 'bishops' (*episkopoi*) exercised their ministry across a wider geographical area and offered authoritative oversight of multiple local assemblies. Given that this state of affairs is not likely to have developed out of thin air, we can ask: where in the New Testament do we see trajectories of church order and ministry that contributed to the emergence of that arrangement?[3] In short, we are looking for whatever happened in the first two or three generations of the early Christian movement that contributed to the rise of the classic episcopal structures that continue to shape, through adoption or antipathy, ecclesial organization today.

As we search for an answer to that question, we should bear in mind that it is impossible to recover a comprehensive picture of the earliest understanding, practice and organization of Christian leadership and ministry. The evidence we have is fragmentary and therefore partial. It is dominated by texts directly from, or reflecting upon, the experience of Paul and his churches.[4] While a number of Gospel texts attribute sayings to Jesus that undoubtedly shaped the self-understanding of his followers (e.g. Mark 10.42–45; John 20.21–23), we cannot expect the Gospel tradition to provide insight into Jesus' understanding of 'ministry' beyond the basic notion that he called followers and expected them to share in his mission of proclamation of the reign of God.[5] While it is true that texts referring to the setting apart of the Twelve and the commissioning of Peter are read within many traditions as providing dominical instructions relating to priestly and apostolic office, we should be cautious in drawing the connecting line between first-century Jesus traditions and later ecclesial practices too confidently.[6] There are other relevant texts (e.g. 1 Pet. 4.10–11; Heb. 13.7), but they are isolated textual fragments that suggest the existence of, but provide little access to, the specific social and historical realities of the earliest forms of Christian ministry.

The evidence we do have is also diverse. Titles, roles and implied relationships between individuals and communities seem to differ from one locality to the next, indicating the lack of a single framework for understanding ministry and church order. There is nothing to suggest that, for example, the presence of 'overseers and deacons' in Philippi (Phil. 1.1, NASB) extended to other Pauline congregations. Other letters refer to those who lead or teach without the mention of any specific title (1 Thess. 5.12–13; 1 Cor. 16.15–18; Gal. 6.6). Luke mentions apostles in the Jerusalem church in the early chapters of Acts (Acts 1.2; 2.37, 42–43; 4.33, 35; 5.2, 12, 18, 29, 40; 6.6; 8.1, 18; 9.27; 11.1), but also 'elders' (Acts 11.30; 15.2, 4, 6, 22–23; 16.4; 21.18). The relationship between these two groups is far from clear.[7]

This diversity is explained by several aspects of the earliest period that are now clear to the majority of scholars. First, early Christian ministry was not straightforwardly the product of clear instruction or teaching from Jesus, nor of any identifiable line of 'succession' whereby the office and roles given to the Twelve, for example, were handed down to subsequent generations in a linear chain of apostolic transmission. Instead, and second, both role and office were the result of various kinds of cultural, social and theological negotiation with the emerging tradition, contextual demands and the cultural milieu of the Jewish and Greco-Roman world. While it seems clear that there was a trajectory towards a greater degree of institutionalization in the post-apostolic period, the evidence does not allow us to assume that we have the complete picture. Third, an understanding of these various forms of negotiation serves to challenge easy assumptions about what we are actually seeing when we look at the New Testament texts, and in particular reminds us of the danger of anachronism. It is unwise to interpret the New Testament use of the term 'elder' (*presbuteros*) in the light of later taxonomies of a threefold order of ministry, because the term probably emerged within the household structures of early Christianity as an honorific term, denoting the character of those who exercised oversight in the early assemblies (Campbell, 1994, pp. 236–60). Likewise, our understanding of the meaning of the term 'servant/minister/deacon' (*diakonos*) should not be overly determined by the recent history of the renewal of the diaconate in some Christian traditions (Collins, 2014).

In relation to our topic, these introductory remarks serve to remind us that we simply will not find the third-century *monepiskopos* (a single figure exercising translocal oversight for multiple congregations in a particular city or region) in the pages of the New Testament.[8] Instead, we must go looking for something more nuanced.

What are we searching for?

I suggest that the phenomenon of 'translocal' ministry is reflected in New Testament texts in ways that relate to three possible models of the relationship between the ministry 'agent' and early Christian communities. In each case we encounter a relationship beyond that established within a local Christian community. These more 'local' forms of ministry quite clearly drew on models of oversight and authority relating to the household and/or religious or civic associations (Giles, 1989, pp. 27–48; Clarke, 2000, pp. 59–141). In some sense the move towards more regional forms of oversight are little more than an extension of these local models over a wider area: ministry beyond the household. There are, however, additional trajectories present in the evidence of the New Testament that help us to see where the impulse for these wider forms of leadership came from. The models I propose here are heuristic categories that can help us understand the shifting patterns of ministry that emerged in the early period of the Church's life. It is preferable to look for such patterns, rather than for evidence of specific 'offices of ministry', because of the ambiguity of our evidence. Overall, these patterns suggest that the earliest forms of ministry, including any translocal variations, reflect the emergence of certain kinds of 'relationship between churches', rather than the occupation of clearly identified and pre-existing offices or roles. I propose that we think of three such models, described initially in more abstract terms, and then explored in relation to the key terms for translocal ministry that we find in the early period.

First, we see evidence of an 'itinerant' model of translocal ministry. This term describes ministry that is offered to local communities or assemblies across a geographical region, but where the individual offering ministry is not explicitly identified with or located in any one of them. We might take the commissioning text in Matthew 10 as a template for this model. There Jesus instructs the Twelve to enter the towns and villages of Galilee and (presumably) Judea, but only to 'stay there until you leave' (Matt. 10.11). 'Ministry' is here offered across a wide territory, and its itinerant nature arguably preserves a model that was prevalent in the first century and continued well into the second. Evidence for such itinerant movements within the Jesus movement in Galilee, and for the possible conflicts that arose as a result of this activity, can be found in Matthew 7.15–23; 10.5–23, 40–42; Mark 13.5–6/Matthew 24.5/Luke 21.7–8; Luke 9.1–6; 10.1–12. In some cases itinerants are likely to have been somehow appointed by another community, although our texts make it difficult to determine who the authorizing community might have been.[9] Less ambiguous is the evidence of the Johannine epistles, where we are offered a glimpse into the doctrinal battles fought between different groups of itinerants. We read there of a group who have 'gone out' from the community (1 John 2.19; 2 John 7) but who, it seems, now seek to be welcomed back. The church is warned not to welcome such people (2 John 10–11) for their intention is to deceive (1 John 2.26; 3.7). Instead, a welcome is to be offered to the 'brothers' who visit the church, but who are on a journey for the sake of Christ, and who thus seek no support from unbelievers. The church has a responsibility to such strangers (3 John 5–10).

The impression given by these texts is that some forms of translocal ministry in the New Testament disturbed local unity, obscured doctrinal clarity and hampered missionary progress: translocal itinerants could be as much a hindrance as they were a help. This impression is confirmed by the evidence of the *Didache*. This instruction manual for early Christian communities offers clear advice for handling such people. If they teach a different doctrine they are not to be listened to (11.1–2) and if an apostle or prophet outstays their welcome (i.e. stays more than two nights) or asks for money, then they are a false prophet and should be rejected (11.3–6 cf. 13.1–7). For this reason, congregations are advised to appoint local bishops and deacons who will 'minister to you the ministry of the prophets and teachers' (15.1–2).

Once the notion of an authorizing community comes to the fore, we move to what might be called the 'envoy' model. The key idea here is that translocal ministry is the product of one local community delegating or setting apart one of its own members, who exercises ministry in another locality or community. Thus, Barnabas and Saul are set apart by the church at Antioch and embark upon what is usually referred to as Paul's first missionary journey (Acts 13.1–3), although of course the work assigned to them is initially that of proclamation of the gospel and the initial formation of churches, rather than that of continued oversight.[10] The Pauline letters refer to these 'envoys', delegated by one assembly to travel and somehow offer ministry in another. The 'brothers' of 2 Corinthians 8.23 and Epaphroditus (Phil. 2.25) come into this category. At a number of places Paul seems to suggest that preachers from 'outside' of the community to which he is writing have infiltrated those congregations (see most clearly 2 Cor. 11.1–29; Gal. 2.12; 3.1; 6.12–13; Phil. 1.15–18), and many have understood Paul's opponents here as itinerant teachers, perhaps sent under the auspices of the increasingly conservative Jerusalem Church under the leadership of James.

It is likely that the 'envoy' model accounts for the initial use of the term 'apostle' within the early Christian movement: a delegate from one church to another (see below). But 'apostle' in the New Testament is used more broadly than this, which suggests the presence of a third model. In this model, translocal ministry consists of the exercise of authority over a network or group of churches without the direct need for delegation from elsewhere. In contrast to the 'itinerant' model, ministry is not equated with the particular encounter between visitor and community, but is enduring, stable, even permanent. In contrast to the 'envoy' model, legitimation comes not from a sending church but from the receiving churches who recognize divine authorization of the leader. Here, ministry and authority extend over time and across space to establish what we might call the 'governance' model of translocal ministry. At times, this form of oversight may be collective (the Jerusalem elders, or Paul and his co-workers), but at other times and perhaps inevitably, individual figures come to assume forms of governmental oversight in relation to a network of churches or a geographical region. In the immediate post-apostolic period we see clear evidence of claims that such authority endures over time (beyond the death of the apostles, thus setting up the notion of 'succession') and across space (establishing the notion that the apostolic witness is the foundation of the universal Church) (Flett, 2016). It is this third model, present in the witness of the New Testament, that in my view undergirds the otherwise surprising emergence of the mono-episcopate.

It is tempting to interpret the relationship between these three models (which, again, are schematic impositions on the evidence for the sake of clarity, not the terms in which the New Testament writers thought) as one of linear development: from unauthorized itinerancy, to legitimated delegation, to settled governance. In some accounts of the development of ministry these ideas are aligned to a scheme that revolves around the shift from Spirit-endowed 'charisma' to permanent 'office'.[11] But Spirit endowment and institutional office are not so easily distinguished in our sources, and the co-existence of these models partially explains the existence of conflict between rival sources of translocal oversight in the early period.[12] These two models can also help us to understand the way that the New Testament uses two key terms: apostle and overseer.

Apostles and apostleship

The origin, character and significance of the term *apostolos* continue to be debated in New Testament scholarship. The term is clearly used to connote an appointed delegate or envoy, dispatched by a local assembly for a specific purpose. Paul's description of Epaphroditus (Phil. 2.25) is the most obvious example of this, but Luke also uses the term in this way to refer to Paul and Barnabas, as delegates of the church in Antioch (Acts 14.4, 6). This usage most closely aligns with proposed Jewish and Greco-Roman backgrounds to the term.[13] The more common usage reflects the notion of divine authorization. The 'apostles', often simply identified with the 'Twelve', are commissioned by Jesus (Matt. 10.2; Luke 6.13; Acts 1.2, 26), or by the 'Wisdom of God' (Luke 11.49), and this status endures after Easter within the Jerusalem community.[14] It seems to have been Paul who took this emphasis on direct authorization and elevated it to the point where he could make a distinction between the Twelve and the apostles, including himself (see 1 Cor. 15.3–9).[15] The post-apostolic generation looked back on this authoritative commissioning, and particularly the 'teaching' that emerged from it, and came to regard it as the foundation upon which the Church's ongoing witness should be based (see Eph. 2.20; 2 Pet. 3.2, cf. 3.15–16; Jude 17; Rev. 21.14).

The transition that seems to have taken place in the development of the notion of apostleship conforms in broad terms to the shift between the 'envoy' model and the 'governance' model as outlined above. In both cases we have a version of translocal ministry, but the understanding of the source of authority and the nature of the relationship between the one authorized and commissioned and the assemblies in a particular region or network changes. In the post-apostolic period, the term 'apostle' contracts to refer to the first-generation leaders, at first a larger group, and eventually limited to the Twelve and Paul (Giles, 1989, pp. 168–9). At the same time it expands to become a key component in the development of ideas about the Church's universal scope and historical continuity.

Overseers/*Episkopoi*

The term *episkopos* is used quite rarely within the New Testament. In Acts 1.20, Peter cites Psalm 109.8 (LXX) in support of the need for a replacement for Judas among the Twelve. In describing things this way, Luke associates the term with the apostolic office and the role of the Twelve. In the other Acts reference, however, it is clear that the overseers are those who have been set apart by the Spirit as leaders and pastors within a local congregation (Acts 20.28). Their role is to pay attention to themselves and the flock of God and to be alert, on the lookout for false teaching (Acts 20.28–31).[16] The reference in Philippians 1.1 is so oblique as to be almost indecipherable. We simply have no way of knowing who those denoted *hoi episkopoi* were, whether they are the same group of people as the 'deacons' of the same verse, or why Paul singles them out for mention at the start of this letter. In any case, the ministry they offer seems to be located within the Philippian church and thus adds little to our enquiry.

It is only when we reach the Pastoral epistles (which in the view of the present author represent a situation after the death of Paul and the other apostles) that the role of the *episkopos* is firmly established and carefully described (1 Tim. 3.1–7; Titus 1.7). However, there is little to suggest that the person so described has any responsibility beyond the local church. Indeed, the nature of the language used to describe the bishop's role suggests that the focus of oversight is a house church within a given city (Verner, 1983). The same impression is given by the other relevant New Testament text in 1 Peter 5.2, where, in any case, the word *episkopountes* is missing from several manuscripts.

It would appear, then, that the New Testament offers little direct support for the development of a translocal episcopate. 'Bishops', it seems, were locally appointed and locally accountable leaders. Alister Stewart has made a careful case in support of the view that their primary responsibility related to the kinds of economic tasks that enabled association, the sharing of a common meal, and care for the poor (Stewart, 2014, pp. 55–119).

And yet, as is well known, by the third, or possibly as early as the mid-second century, this model of the local *episkopos*, integrated into the household structure of early Christian assemblies and concerned with regulating economic affairs, had given way to the translocal 'office' of the *monepiskopos*, now ruling over multiple assemblies within a broader geographical region (thus, an example of the 'governance' model).[17]

Conclusion

At the risk of oversimplification, the evidence suggests that translocal ministry emerges out of two trajectories. The first, evident within the New Testament itself, is the move from itinerancy and local, delegated authority to notions of divine authorization and the need for historical and regional continuity. The second, which extends beyond the first and into the second century, is the move from local forms of oversight related to individual assemblies, to translocal oversight, focused on the individual *episkopos*. These two trajectories blend into the fully-fledged account of episcopacy, and the associated notions of apostolic continuity, that are familiar today.

The reasons for these historical developments are difficult to discern with accuracy. Suggestions include the growing institutionalization (in the sociological sense) of the early Christian movement as well as the emergence of heterodoxy and the need for the defence of orthodoxy. It is more likely, however, that the trajectories I have pointed to were responses to the simple fact that as Christian assemblies grew larger and developed relationships with each other, new forms of translocal ministry emerged in response. Stewart refers to the 'associational aspect' of the early Christian movement, which might, in a given city, turn into a 'federation'. As ecclesial structures shifted beyond the household, so did the structures of ministry related to them, as well as the focus of oversight (from financial considerations, to doctrinal and educational concerns) (Stewart, 2014, pp. 300–1).

The value of this analysis for understanding contemporary forms of translocal ministry is a matter of discernment rather than of implementing a New Testament model. If the fragmentary evidence of the biblical texts suggests that forms of ministry (local and translocal) were responsive to historical and ecclesial developments, and embedded in recognizable social and cultural norms, this might indicate that there is no single contemporary model that can claim exclusive scriptural legitimation. How are local assemblies relating to each other? What are the practical, educational and theological needs of the Church that are best dealt with beyond the local gathering? What is the nature of the Church's mission in this social and cultural moment? These seem to be the questions that generated the earliest forms of translocal ministry and should perhaps continue to provoke both continuity and change.

Notes

1 This chapter draws on earlier arguments made in Sean Winter, 2004, 'Translocal Ministry: New Testament Perspectives', in Stuart Murray (ed.), *Translocal Ministry: 'Equipping the Churches for Mission'*, Didcot: Baptist Union of Great Britain, pp. 14–23. In certain respects it develops, and in one or two cases disputes, the arguments and assumptions of that earlier discussion.

2 Standard English-speaking discussions include Colin G. Kruse, 1983, *New Testament Foundations of Ministry*, London: Marshall, Morgan & Scott; C. K. Barrett, 1985, *Church, Ministry, and Sacraments in the New Testament*, Exeter: Paternoster Press; Kevin Giles, 1989, *Patterns of Ministry Among the First Christians*, North Blackburn: CollinsDove; John N. Collins, 1990, *Diakonia: Re-interpreting the Ancient Sources*, New York: Oxford University Press; J. T. Forrestell, 1991, *As Ministers of Christ: The Christological Dimension of Ministry in the New Testament: An Exegetical and Theological Study*, New York: Paulist Press; David L. Bartlett, 1993, *Ministry in the New Testament*, Minneapolis, MN: Fortress Press; R. Alastair Campbell, 1994, *The Elders: Seniority Within Earliest Christianity*, Edinburgh: T & T Clark; Andrew D. Clarke, 2000, *Serve the Community of the Church: Christians as Leaders and Ministers*, Grand Rapids, MI/Cambridge: Eerdmans. In writing this chapter I have been heavily influenced by Alistair C. Stewart, 2014, *The Original Bishops: Office and Order in the First Christian Community*, Grand Rapids, MI: Baker Academic, whose work is part of an emerging 'new consensus' (p. 6, n. 24) on the historical emergence of 'translocal' ministry.

3 Stewart, pp. 2–3, argues that evidence for the 'phenomenon of a sole bishop within a city of multiple congregations ... is entirely lacking' any earlier than the late second century CE.

4 This covers Paul's authentic letters, letters written in Paul's name, and the Acts of the Apostles.

5 David Bartlett's *Ministry in the New Testament* surveys the Pauline and Gospel evidence alone. Colin Kruse is confident that we can get a sense of 'Jesus' understanding of ministry' through using criteria to determine the authenticity of relevant gospel traditions. See Kruse, pp. 9–12.

6 Three factors support the need for such caution. First, Jesus was a Jew and so insofar as such texts preserve authentic memories of his words or practice, we are dealing with 'ministry' within and for Judaism. Second, the calling of the Twelve, and arguably of Peter, was understood as representative of the calling of Israel as a whole, not a particular group of leaders within Israel. The line of connection to such traditions is ecclesial, rather than strictly ministerial. Finally, these remembered traditions are already shaped by the development of the early Christian movement and its conflicts, and so do not provide us with straightforward access to Jesus' 'view of ministry'.

7 In my view Campbell makes a convincing case to the effect that the title 'elder' in Acts does not refer to a separate office of ministry but is instead 'an alternative term for the leaders whom we meet under other titles' (he has in mind 'apostles' and 'overseers'); see Campbell, p. 173.

8 I prefer Stewart's use of the term *monepiskopos* to the older term 'monarchical overseer/bishop'.

9 For example, are the prophets of Acts 11.27–28 delegates of the Jerusalem church? The evidence is unclear. Or again, the 'strangers' spoken about in 3 John

5–10 are otherwise unidentified, and so we cannot connect them to a 'sending' community. Note also the instructions given in the *Didache* 11.1–6. Concern about the possible influence of itinerants leads the author of the *Didache* to 'elect for yourselves bishops and deacons who are worthy of the Lord ... for these conduct the ministry of the prophets and teachers among you' (*Didache* 15.1–2, translation by Ehrman).

10 In one sense the notion of translocal ministry begins at the point where Paul decides to re-visit the communities that he and Barnabas have founded (see Acts 14.21–28). The notion of repeated visits (by Paul and co-workers) and, of course, ongoing communication via letter, suggests that Paul understood apostolic ministry not simply as a responsibility for the initial formation of Christian assemblies but also for ensuring adequate oversight of their ongoing growth and well-being.

11 Note the way that this notion is preserved in Bible translations. The NRSV continues the tradition (since at least Tyndale and the KJV) of rendering 1 Tim. 3.1 as 'whoever aspires to the office of a bishop'.

12 Most obviously that between Paul and some factions within the Jerusalem church. See Holmberg.

13 Classically, of course, Rengstorf's notion of the apostle as *shaliach*. See Rengstorf, 1967.

14 The likely original significance of the 'Twelve' was symbolic (of Israel's twelve tribes) and therefore representative of a renewed Israel. At the foundational level, the notion of 'twelve apostles' is a Jewish concept relating to the kind of intra-Jewish debates that characterized the early Jesus movement.

15 For Paul himself as Apostle to the Gentiles, see Rom. 1.1; 11.13; 1 Cor. 1.1; 9.1; 15.9; 2 Cor. 1.1; Gal. 1.1. For others as apostles in this technical sense (i.e. as Christ-commissioned), see Rom. 16.7 (Andronicus and Junia); 1 Cor. 4.9 (general reference); 1 Cor. 9.5 (general reference but with the 'brothers of the Lord' and Cephas singled out); 1 Cor. 12.28–29 (general reference); 1 Cor. 15.7 (general including James); 2 Cor. 11.5, 13; 12.11–12 (the false/super-apostles, the term here used ironically by Paul but perhaps indicating the claim to the title by other Christian missionary teachers); Gal. 1.17, 19 (the apostles in Jerusalem, including James); 1 Thess. 2.6–7 (general reference).

16 Paul's speech is directed, of course, at the Ephesian *elders* (Acts 20.17), who are then called overseers. Neither term denotes an 'office', rather the term elder denotes status, while overseer denotes function.

17 See the overview provided in Colin G. Kruse, 1997, 'Ministry', in Ralph P. Martin and Peter H. Davids (eds), *Dictionary of the Later New Testament and its Developments*, Downers Grove, IL/Leicester: IVP, p. 745. The precise dating of this development depends largely on how one understands the Ignatian epistles. For arguments for the later date, see Stewart, pp. 241–98.

References

Barrett, C. K., 1985, *Church, Ministry, and Sacraments in the New Testament*, Exeter: Paternoster Press.
Bartlett, David L., 1993, *Ministry in the New Testament*, Minneapolis, MN: Fortress Press.
Campbell, R. Alastair, 1994, *The Elders: Seniority Within Earliest Christianity*, Edinburgh: T & T Clark.
Clarke, Andrew D., 2000, *Serve the Community of the Church: Christians as Leaders and Ministers*, Grand Rapids, MI/Cambridge: Eerdmans.
Collins, John N., 1990, *Diakonia: Re-interpreting the Ancient Sources*, New York: Oxford University Press.
Collins, John N., 2014, *Diakonia Studies: Critical Issues in Ministry*, Oxford: Oxford University Press.
Flett, John G., 2016, *Apostolicity: The Ecumenical Question in World Christian Perspective*, Downers Grove, IL: IVP Academic.
Forrestell, J. T., 1991, *As Ministers of Christ: The Christological Dimension of Ministry in the New Testament: An Exegetical and Theological Study*, New York: Paulist Press.
Giles, Kevin, 1989, *Patterns of Ministry Among the First Christians*, North Blackburn: CollinsDove.
Holmberg, Bengt, 1980, *Paul and Power: The Structure of Authority in the Primitive Church as Reflected in the Pauline Epistles*, Philadelphia, PA: Fortress Press.
Kruse, Colin G., 1983, *New Testament Foundations of Ministry*, London: Marshall, Morgan & Scott.
Martin, Ralph and Peter H. Davids (eds), 1997, *Dictionary of the Later New Testament and its Developments*, Downers Grove, IL/Leicester: IVP.
Rengstorf, Karl H., 1967, 'ἀποστέλλω, ἀπόστολος', in Gerhard Kittel (ed.), *Theological Dictionary of the New Testament*, volume 1 (Grand Rapids, MI: Eerdmans), pp. 398–448.
Stewart, Alistair C., 2014, *The Original Bishops: Office and Order in the First Christian Community*, Grand Rapids, MI: Baker Academic.
Verner, D. C., 1983, *The Household of God: The Social World of the Pastoral Epistles*, Chico, CA: Scholars Press.
Winter, Sean, 2004, 'Translocal Ministry: New Testament Perspectives', in *Translocal Ministry: 'Equipping the Churches for Mission'*, Didcot: Baptist Union of Great Britain.

2

Theological Issues: Constants in Context

ROGER STANDING

Introduction: on the importance of context

I was born and brought up in East Anglia as part of a Methodist community on the edge of the Fens. The church was literally an integral part of our day-to-day life and, as I grew, by a kind of ecclesial osmosis, I drew into my experience and understanding a comprehension of what it was all about. The biblical stories and Sunday School, the rhythm of the year with its festivals and anniversaries, the social life of our congregation and the characters it contained all knitted together into a cohesive and glorious whole, an identity that proudly proclaimed itself Methodist and celebrated its life as the spiritual offspring of the Wesley brothers and the evangelical revival of the eighteenth century. As Methodists, our church was part of a circuit of churches and chapels, our minister also acted as the Circuit Superintendent Minister and, from further afield, we were occasionally visited by the Chairman of the District, who travelled the length and breadth of Norfolk and Suffolk in the discharge of his responsibilities.

The first Chairman of District I properly knew was after I had moved, newly married, to Liverpool to work as an evangelist based at the Central Hall. He had an office with us and was a kind and considerate man who took an interest in me and my developing sense of vocation. With thoughtful creativity and graciousness, he devised unorthodox strategies to encourage and support me as I sought to explore what lay ahead in responding to God's call upon my life.

When we seek to formally understand and explore the nature of translocal leadership our personal experience is not the normal starting point. More usually it is a doctrinal treatise that, based on established theological arguments, serially draws on received tradition, the insights of the Church Fathers and Scripture to accomplish its objective. It is also usual for such a treatise to be rooted within a particular ecclesiological understanding, and insofar as other positions are referenced, it is to highlight the strengths or correctness of the writers' own convictions, or to make a more inclusive nod to the fact that 'other ecclesiologies are also available'.

In seeking to understand properly how translocal Christian ministry is conceived and practised in church settings that are different from our own, this may not be the most productive approach. Indeed, to comprehend how very different forms of translocal oversight have developed and evolved over the centuries, it is essential that we resist the urge to establish theological hegemony for our own position. A more constructive objective would be to seek to understand how such widely differing forms of ministry can have developed and be practised now with spiritual sincerity and theological integrity. To do this, the place of personal experience is a key entry point to moving beyond the arguments and disputes of dogmatics to the appreciation of the rich diversity of our ecumenical differences and significant insights and understanding that we can share with one another.

Part 2 of this volume provides a whole spectrum of first-hand experience from the contemporary church. From Roman Catholics and Anglicans to Pentecostalists and two of the newer church streams, experienced leaders and scholars share revealing insights from their respective traditions. These are personal accounts rather than official formulations. They enable us to access the theological and organizational framework within which translocal ministry is exercised, and the spiritual insight and energy that animates it.

It is hardly surprising that for most practising Christians, their understanding of the nature of translocal ministry begins with personal experience. This is almost invariably located in the context of the church to which they belong, the practice it follows and the theology to which it subscribes. It is a lived reality, albeit one that is most likely to be on the periphery of their discipleship. Only over an extended period does a picture of the who, what, when, how and why of such ministry emerge. In a very real sense this is 'belonging before believing'! If the experience of such ministry is positive and it coherently sits as an expression of the theological convictions within which it is embedded, it will be readily accepted and rarely questioned. That other Christian communities do things differently, where this is considered at all, will then be viewed as anything on a continuum from harmlessly different or quirky to dangerously heretical and manipulative.

What this demonstrates is that, while the shape of any given model of translocal ministry will be justified theologically within its own ecclesial setting, for the vast majority within that setting it will have been experientially embedded and relationally strengthened well before its theological justification is properly comprehended. A given form of translocal ministry is, therefore, rarely a matter of primary theological conviction in and of itself. Rather, it flows out of the theological framework adopted by the Church, which is itself reinforced by the other spiritual, sociological, psychological and organizational elements that contribute to the cohesion of a church community.

Context is important, then, because it provides the experiential entry point for understanding translocal ministry as well as the theological framework we deploy to accomplish that. Context is important too for historical reasons. As will be seen from the three illustrations that follow, patterns of translocal ministry are often shaped significantly by the cultural location within which they were formed, and through which they have travelled, as theological convictions interact with particular circumstances and the wider cultural landscape of the time. This mirrors Winter's observations in the preceding chapter of an emerging translocal ministry in the New Testament period that evolves in response to historical and ecclesial developments in the context of first-century social and cultural norms. So three contexts need to be held in perspective as we consider our understanding of *episkope*. First, our own as it provides the context in which we experientially engage with translocal ministry. Second, the theological context within which any given form of oversight expresses its ecclesiological convictions, and third, the impact of the social and historical context in which an understanding has been born, and through which it has travelled, to the present day.

Methodism and the significance of experience and practicality

In my own journey as a young man I grew increasingly aware of the structures of Methodism and I felt very much at home. My perception was of an ecclesial version of a representative democracy, organized geographically with a local Circuit of churches that was coordinated as part of a regional District, with authority laying with the annual, national, Conference. Indeed, the annual conference appeared in many ways to reflect those of the political parties and the Trades Union Congress that were part of the annual round of life in Britain. This enabled consultation and communication up and down the structure, with a rhythm of meetings to facilitate this throughout the year. At each level, representatives were elected to participate in the next tier of the denomination's organizational life, where discussions seemed consciously framed to reflect insights gleaned from the Bible, our Wesleyan heritage and the tradition of the wider catholic Church. While there were clear parallels with other churches as we had ordained clergy, synods and District Chairs that seemed, superficially at least, not unlike Anglican bishops, there was clearly something different about us.

What I did not know at the time was how far the Methodism I knew still reflected its beginnings under the influence of John Wesley and how well it had retained its spiritual DNA along the way. To properly comprehend Methodist ecclesiology, it has to be understood that it began as a revivalist and holiness movement rather than as a breakaway sect. At the Conference of 1763 (Jackson, 1978, p. 299) the question was asked, 'What may we reasonably believe to be God's design in raising up the Preachers called Methodists?' From the response it was clear that Wesley's intention was not to establish his own brand of church but rather 'To reform the nation, particularly the church, and to spread scriptural holiness over the land'. As an ordained priest within the Church of England, Wesley saw his work as complementary to, rather than separate from, the ecclesial structures of his day. Indeed, a little over a year before he died in 1791, with a clamour from some to fully separate themselves from the established Church, he wrote:

> at the first meeting of all our Preachers in Conference, in June 1744, I exhorted them to keep to the Church, observing that this was our peculiar glory, Not to form any new sect, but abiding in our own Church, to do to all men all the good we possibly could. ... I never had any design of separating from the Church. I have no such design now. ... I do, and will do, all that is in my power to prevent such an event. ... I declare once more, that I live and die a member of the Church of England: and that none who regard my judgment or advice, will ever separate from it. (Wesley, 1827, pp. 95–7)

The rapid growth of the movement led to its organization into local societies comprised of the smaller class and band meetings that focused their attention on the application of Wesley's holiness teaching. The societies were grouped together in circuits serviced by lay and ordained preachers 'stationed' among them by Wesley himself to superintend the work. Sensing the need to regularly meet with his preachers, Wesley instituted the annual Conference in 1744 to bring them together and secure the national cohesion of the movement. He saw this as an advisory gathering, supporting him in his ministry rather than sharing in leadership with him. Writing to his brother in 1785 he is quite candid regarding his own vocation (Telford, 1960, VII, p. 284), 'I firmly believe that I am a scriptural episkopos as much as any man in England or Europe.'

There was no doubt that, at the Conference, Wesley was the key presence as he held 'the Connexion' in his grip, but this quickly expanding network needed his presence to maintain its unity and secure its prosperity. While some accused him of ambition and the pursuit of power over the movement, a careful analysis indicates that he exercised his authority with moderation and a desire to protect the societies from the abuse of others (Rack, 1989, p. 538). The question that came to exercise him was that of succession. Who would lead the movement after his death? Having failed to identify a suitable individual to take up the mantle, Wesley had documents drawn up to invest the responsibilities of his role in the senior preachers of the movement, a group that came to be known as 'the Legal Hundred'. Thus, what had been a personal *episkope* invested in Wesley himself, became corporate by nature and exercised by the Conference.

The Conference of 1791 divided the country into 27 Districts and the following year the preachers appointed to serve the Circuits of each District were asked to choose a Chairman from among their own number. These individuals were considered to be senior figures within the Connexion, though they continued in their day-to-day ministry rather than being separated to this new task. Indeed, there was little responsibility that initially attached to the role of Chairman, though the discipline of ministers and arbitration in disputes quickly accrued to them (Methodist Conference, 2005a, p. 26).

The theological framework that underpinned Wesley's structuring of Methodism was innately Anglican. Next to the Scriptures, which he viewed as the 'oracles of God', he drew on the work of the 'Primitive Fathers' (from the first three centuries) and following them, the Church of England, 'the most scriptural, national Church in the world' (Wesley, 1827, p. 95). He often quoted the Moravian Count Zinzendorf with approval, who taught that believers encounter and are led by God through Scripture, reason and experience (Telford, 1960, VII, p. 319), though he himself confessed that it was by reason that he was chiefly led (Telford, 1960, VIII, p. 154). The American Methodist theologian Albert Outler schematized this approach, naming it 'The Wesleyan Quadrilateral'.

> Thus we can see in Wesley a distinctive theological method, with Scripture as the pre-eminent norm but interfaced with tradition, reason, and Christian experience as the dynamic and interactive aids in the interpretation of the Word of God in Scripture. (Outler, 1991, p. 77)

The evolving structures and patterns of life among Methodists since the time of Wesley bear the imprint of this theological understanding. In the organizing of his preachers into circuits and calling them together at Conference, caught up as they were in the evangelical revival, the immediacy of their experience was ordered in practical and reasonable ways. The creation of 'The Legal Hundred' to oversee the work following his death was also a sensible provision, albeit creating in the process an expression of corporate *episkope*. This may not have been an issue with an extra-ecclesial movement committed to the propagation of scriptural holiness, but as that movement separated from the Church of England and took on the more formal aspects of being a Church, it led inexorably to the pattern of church life that formed me. Through the years this has led to the incorporation of practices and insights from the wider catholic Church, at others to creative innovation in both practice and understanding.

More recently, with the advent of the Anglican Methodist Covenant in 2003 and the commitment of the two churches to work closely together on a journey towards organic unity,[1] Methodism has had to engage in serious reflection on its understanding of *episkope*. The reports *Episcopacy* (1998); *Episkopé and Episcopacy* (2000); *The Nature of Oversight* (2005a) and *What Sort of Bishops? Models of Episcopacy and British Methodism* (2005b) all reflect the wrestling that has gone on under the influence of the various component parts of the Quadrilateral. An excellent example of this is found in *What Sort of Bishops?* where 11 potential models are outlined and analysed for their strengths and weaknesses, with five commended for consideration (Methodist Conference, 2005b, paras 65–78). The experience of the deepening relationship with the Church of England meant that episcopacy needed to be explored but, practically speaking, which option most closely met the presenting needs and expressed Methodism's theological understanding? A year later, following a period of consultation with minimal and mixed results (Methodist Conference, 2006, 4.7.1), it was recommended that 'The Conference does not at this point take any steps towards embracing the historic episcopate.' It was 12 years later that this issue surfaced again with a joint Anglican/Methodist report, *Mission and Ministry in Covenant*, and the recommendation for consideration of a 'President-Bishop' who personally embodied the corporate episcopacy of the Conference (Baker and Richardson, 2017, pp. 37–44). From a Methodist perspective, in the developing ecumenical context of their relationship with the Church of England, once again experience and reason are deployed as dynamic conversation partners with Scripture and tradition in discerning the appropriate practical steps to be taken towards a significant ecclesiological development.[2]

The Church of England and the 'threefold cord': Scripture, tradition and reason

On 15 February 2012, as part of the celebrations of her Diamond Jubilee, Queen Elizabeth II gave an address to an invited group of faith leaders in her role as Supreme Governor of the Church of England (www.royal.uk/queens-speech-lambeth-palace-15-february-2012; accessed 30.10.2019):

> Here at Lambeth Palace we should remind ourselves of the significant position of the Church of England in our nation's life. The concept of our established Church is occasionally misunderstood and, I believe, commonly under-appreciated. Its role is not to defend Anglicanism to the exclusion of other religions. Instead, the Church has a duty to protect the free practice of all faiths in this country.
>
> It certainly provides an identity and spiritual dimension for its own many adherents. But also, gently and assuredly, the Church of England has created an environment for other faith communities and indeed people of no faith to live freely. Woven into the fabric of this country, the Church has helped to build a better society – more and more in active co-operation for the common good with those of other faiths.

Such an inclusive vision of the Church of England's role in society is a relatively recent development in the Church's 475-year history. That it could be articulated by the monarch at such an auspicious time and at so prestigious an event is indicative of the deeply embedded relationship that exists between the state and its established Church. While the former Archbishop of Canterbury, Rowan Williams, famously observed that 'it's by no means the end of the world if the Establishment disappears' (*New Statesman*, 18 December 2008), such a possibility appears to be far from the present epicentre of agitation for social and political reform. However, that does not mean that there has been no change over recent years. Gordon Brown's removal of the Prime Minister's role in the Crown appointment of bishops in 2008 was significant. With the diocese considered to be the basic unit of the Church of England (Cameron, 1990, p. 88) and the episcopacy as central to its ecclesiology and self-understanding (Avis, 2015, p. viii), this move implied a substantial modification in understanding of the relationship between church and state that had existed since the Reformation.

The English Reformation during the rule of Henry VIII was driven more by political expediency than theological conviction. While Henry's desire to divorce his first wife, Catherine of Aragon, may have been the presenting issue that led to the break with the Roman Catholic Church, the intellectual, social and economic climate also played its part, with growing reformist sentiments among the clergy and laity, an emerging middle class seeking to establish itself in the nation's life and Henry's own need for revenue. Ultimately, Henry was to be declared 'Supreme Head on earth of the Church of England' through a series of Acts of Parliament, pivotal among which was the Act of Supremacy. In truth, except for the new role acquired by the king, much remained the same as the Church retained its full medieval framework, including the threefold ministry of bishops, priests and deacons. The position of the bishops too was largely unchanged, though the monarch now made no reference to the Pope when an appointment was made (Grundy, 2014, p. 110).

Prior to the Reformation, the role of the bishop had evolved over the centuries, from the oversight of congregations in a particular city in the early decades after the apostolic era to the feudal barons of the medieval period. Indeed, by the time of the renaissance it was not unusual for bishops to be surrounded with wealth and mimicking their peers in exercising a semi-regal oversight of their ecclesiastical estates (Grundy, 2011, pp. 55–7; Kirk, 1946, p. 389).

The territorial nature of episcopacy had significantly developed during the later period of the Roman Empire following the conversion of Constantine *c.*312, mirroring the structure of the empire itself. The emergence of hierarchy and of a gradual pre-eminence for the bishop of Rome was probably inevitable as the role of a bishop acquired skills paralleling those of a Roman prefect or magistrate (Murray, 2004, p. 126; Tustin, 2013, p. 9).

Christianity gained its first foothold in Britain in the days of the empire, as is indicated by Tertullian and Origen in the second and third centuries respectively, and there is evidence of British bishops attending ecclesiastical gatherings on the continent, such as Restitutus of London's presence at the Synod of Arles in 314.

Significant missionary work was then led by episcopal figures in the sixth and seventh centuries. In the north, leaders in the Celtic Church like Aidan (d. 651) and Cuthbert (634–87) made significant progress, while in the south Augustine of Canterbury (d. 604) and those who followed after him under the direction of Pope Gregory the Great established the Roman Church in the Kingdom of Kent under the rule of Æthelberht. Ultimately the English Church was properly united for the first time under the leadership of Theodore of Tarsus, who had been appointed Archbishop of Canterbury by the Pope in 669. The Venerable Bede records that 'Theodore was the first archbishop whom all the English Church agreed to obey' (Williams and Ward, 2012, p. 118).

Following the Reformation, and in contrast to the situation on the continent, having replaced the Pope as the Head of the Church, Henry and his successors found that they needed the bishops to be part of the 'fabric of government'. Thus, the close English intertwining of the episcopacy and the monarchy became a political and ecclesiastical reality (Faith and Order Commission, 2015, pp. 65–6). Indeed, Grundy (2014, p. 108) sees the bishops as becoming 'part of the social and intellectual elite of an emerging property-owning aristocracy, possessing spiritual authority and social power'. However, the intertwining led to an episcopal corollary of 'the divine right of kings' that saw a 'divine right of bishops', whose authority was validated and bound up with that of the sovereign, yet looked back through history to the lineal succession of the office to that of the apostles themselves (Kirk, 1946, pp. 422, 425).

While the activities of Anglican bishops adapted with each successive period of history – Tudor civil servants; Whig landed proprietors; Victorian parliamentarians and philanthropists; present-day ecclesiastical and social entrepreneurs – the writing of Richard Hooker in the seventeenth century has proved to be a defining point in the evolution of episcopal self-understanding. In his *Seventh Book of Ecclesiastical Polity* he writes:

> The Bishop is a Minister of God, unto whom with permanent continuance, there is given not only power of administering Word and Sacraments, which power other presbyters have; but also a further power to ordain Ecclesiastical persons, and a power of Chiefty in Government over Presbyters as well as Law men, a power to be by way of jurisdiction a Pastor even to Pastors themselves. (Cameron, 1990, p. 86)

If this is the historical context that has forged Anglican episcopal understanding, what is the theological methodology that has given it birth? It is Hooker again who articulates the *via media* that the Church of England attempted theologically, steering a path between a Catholicism that placed the tradition of the Church on a par with Scripture on one side, and the Puritans on the other, who saw anything that was not authorized by Scripture as sinful (Bauckham and Drewery, 1988, p. 35):

> What Scripture doth plainly deliver, to that the first place both of credit and obedience is due; the next whereunto, is what any man can necessarily conclude by force of Reason; after these, the voice of the Church succeedeth.

This is the 'threefold cord' of Scripture, tradition and reason that informs theological reflection within the Anglican tradition (Bauckham and Drewery, p. vii), a theological methodology for interrogating theological issues, mediating disagreements and establishing a mutually agreed path for progress.[3] The primary source is the written word of God in Scripture. Reason has a derivative authority and 'the voice of the Church' or tradition, when it does not disagree with Scripture and does not contradict reason, has real authority too (Bauckham and Drewery, p. 36). As the Anglican theologian Bishop Richard Hanson was keen to point out: to take the theological stance of *Sola Scriptura* was to embrace a particular theological tradition. Indeed, to own the Scriptures as 'the Word of God' was impossible without the authority of the Church (Bauckham and Drewery, pp. 292–3).

Scripture

If Scripture is the primary source for theology it is hardly surprising that, in seeking to understand the nature and pattern of translocal ministry, the Bible should be explored as the appropriate source to provide an evidential foundation. Unfortunately, this has presented two difficulties. First, the New Testament does not describe a single pattern of ministry that might serve as a blueprint (Grundy, 2011, p. 49). While there are clearly forms of oversight being exercised and patterns of ministry being practised, both local and itinerant, the embryonic life of the followers of 'the Way' (Acts 24.14, 22) does not provide a blueprint for the subsequent development of the episcopate; rather, there are a variety of things happening, out of which the future shape of the Church emerges. Then, second, in attempting to establish a historical link of 'apostolic succession', providing a lineal 'chain' of successors from the apostle Peter to the early Church of the second and third centuries has proved impossible. Even John Wesley, writing to his brother Charles in 1785 (Telford, 1960, VII, p. 284) commented, 'the uninterrupted succession I know to be a fable, which no man ever did or can prove.' It is therefore commonly accepted that attempting to read later practice back into the New Testament itself, or the life of the Church in the first decades of its existence, is a mistaken one (Faith and Order Commission, 2015, p. 64).[4]

This biblical and historical understanding is now widely acknowledged in Anglican and ecumenical writing. In 1973 the Anglican Roman Catholic International Commission (ARCIC) articulated the broad consensus that the full emergence of the 'threefold ministry' was in the second-century post-apostolic age (Pickard, 2009, p. 191). Or again, in the influential publication of the World Council of Churches, *Baptism, Eucharist and Ministry*,[5] the role of the bishop was acknowledged as taking shape in the first 50–100 years of the Church's existence, with bishops elected by the fellow presbyters to 'see over' – the literal meaning of *epi-skopos* – their own local community (Grundy, 2014, p. 122). Stewart (2014, p. 354) is quite clear in his assessment that attempts to portray any particular model of ministry as the truly biblical one should be 'consigned to the exegetical dustbin of history'.

Tradition

R. P. C. Hanson (2010, p. 79) observes that the early Anglican apologists Jewel and Hooker make no serious attempt to establish that episcopacy is the authoritative form of church government mandated exclusively by the Scriptures, only that 'it is to be found in Scripture and is not repugnant to the Word of God'. What they do stress is the adoption of the episcopacy for well over a thousand years by the universal Church. Thus, Anglicans have looked to Christian tradition, especially as articulated by the early Church Fathers Ignatius of Antioch (d. 98/117) and Cyprian of Carthage (*c.*200/210–258), as a keystone in their understanding (Kirk, 1946, p. 422) and as models to be adopted. Indeed, denominational understanding contains elements of each, but fully replicates neither. From Ignatius comes a relational approach to ministry than relies upon a moral rather than a legal appeal between bishop and clergy, though not embracing the practice of local election to office, while from Cyprian flows the sense that the episcopal office is a whole, one and indivisible, and that each individual bishop shares a part of the whole. The incorporation of this collegial shape to episcopacy takes seriously a common responsibility yet does not go on to endorse Cyprian's notion of 'succession by consecration' that makes ordination the means of passing on episcopal authority (Hanson, 2010, p. 81; Pickard, 2009, p. 195; Kirk, 1946, p. 530). Other significant influences would include Irenaeus of Lyon (*c.*130–202) and his emphasis on apostolic preaching and teaching to guard against error and heresy, and Gregory the Great (*c.*540–604), whose *Pastoral Rule* sets out episcopal duties that are embedded in exemplary character and provided the substance behind his oft-repeated epithet that the bishop should be 'the servant of the servants of God' (Grundy, 2011, p. 52).

'The development of the episcopacy was not just a practical necessity but providential: it is a gift of God' (Mellows, 2001, p. 17). In this statement, the *Resourcing Bishops* report articulates the deeply held conviction within the Anglican tradition of the 'givenness' of the episcopacy.

From its origins in the days of the New Testament, this oversight was not a human invention but a creative act of God to provide 'guardianship of faith and order, enabling the Church to carry on the ministry of Jesus and become what God intends, in mission, unity and holiness' (Cameron, 1990, pp. 17, 158).

Reason

Hanson maintains that there is a deep-seated pragmatism in Anglican theology, especially as it relates to the episcopacy (2010, p. 79). This is formationally illustrated by the circumstances of its birth and the role of the bishops. The Church of England inherited a form of episcopal government that was adapted to the late medieval period and, because they found this form of government agreeable to the word of God and the existing bishops either supported or did not frustrate a Reformation according to the word of God, they felt they had no authority or need to change the arrangements. Yet they made it clear that this was not a matter on which a church stood or fell. If it was possible to retain episcopacy, it should be adopted. However, they recognized that in other contexts of the Reformation this was not so.

Hanson further observes that this pragmatism led to a flexibility in fresh historical contexts for the nature of the episcopate to adapt and change and thus demonstrate 'a surprising power of survival' (p. 80). From absolute monarchy, to contexts of colonialism, constitutional monarchy, disestablishment, modern democracy and third-sector volunteerism, the Anglican form of episcopacy has exhibited an inherent tenacity and durability. Davis and Guest (2007, p. 18) suggest that this is really due to an absence of a fixed theology of episcopacy. This is a harsh judgement in the light of the historical evidence. Avis (2013, p. 155) is probably closer to the mark in seeing Anglican ecclesiology as a more modest endeavour that does not construct conceptual superstructures and is at once pastoral, practical and pragmatic. In that sense it is the mature fruit of the theological dialogue of Scripture, tradition and reason.

The point that Davis and Guest sought to make was with regard to the contemporary context. They maintained that the lack of a fuller theology of the episcopate has led to contemporary church leaders basing their models of church leadership more on secular theory than theological conviction. Indeed, this has been an ongoing debate within the Church of England following the publication of a number of reports and discussion papers, but most notably *The Green Report: Talent Management for Future Leaders and Leadership Development for Bishops and Deans: A*

New Approach (2014). An animated debate ensued in the pages of the *Church Times*, online through a variety of influential blogposts and a range of other publications.[6] The issue at the heart of the debate was the dynamics of a conversation between Scripture, tradition and reason. How far should a received understanding of the office of bishop be reshaped in the light of contemporary understandings of executive leadership and the application of management theory tested in business and the third sector? In one sense it is eminently reasonable given the task to hand, as Michael Sadgrove wrote as the Dean of Durham:

> I preside over a part of the nation's heritage, a medium-sized enterprise with a multi-million pound turnover, a retail outlet and catering facility, a leisure destination, a public park, a music-and-arts centre, a place of education and a sizeable piece of estate. (http://decanalwool gatherer.blogspot.com/2014/12/equipping-tomorrows-church-leaders.html; accessed 04.11.2019)

Yet he goes on to talk about how being equipped for this role has to be balanced with his calling as a priest, as the head of a religious institution and a spiritual leader. The Green Report's proposal of a talent pool, of MBA-style qualifications and 'the brand of the Church of England' drew criticism from many observers:

> In the actual text ... it has no point of origination in theological or spiritual wisdom. Instead, on offer is a dish of basic contemporary approaches to executive management, with a little theological garnish. A total absence of ecclesiology ... it is steeped in its own uncritical use of executive management-speak. (Percy, 2017, p. 34)

Indeed, Percy raises significant issues to be considered. What is the difference between an organization that is formed to accomplish an objective and an institution that is more organic, formed as the response to prevailing needs and social pressures to promote and protect certain values? If the Church is 'the household of faith' it is more like the institution of family than a business organization (2017, p. 45). Ultimately, what is reasonable must be able to withstand the theological scrutiny of an understanding informed by Scripture and the tradition of the Church. And, of course, it is the responsibility of the bishops to be the pre-eminent guardians of the application of doctrine in the life of the Church and the community of faith's fidelity to received tradition in their ongoing life (Hanson, 2010, p. 86).

Episcopacy in the Church of England

Episcopacy in the Anglican context is clearly the mature fruit of the historical and theological context out of which it has grown. Along the way it has proved to be flexible and adaptive to successive socio-political environments, most recently entering into ecumenical dialogue to articulate a shared theological understanding of the historic episcopate. It is clear that the ministry of bishops is one of the deep structures of the faith into which the Spirit has led the Church following on from the translocal ministry of the apostles (Faith and Order Commission, 2015, p. 128). Yet this has always been a dynamic phenomenon as the episcopate has had to undergo a constant re-forming as the circumstances of society and the church change (Pickard, 2009, p. 169), what a recent report has sought to identify as the practice of 'faithful improvisation' (Faith and Order Commission, pp. 50ff.).

The historic episcopate inherited by the Church of England maintained the territorial division of the Church and the integrity of its boundaries that was established by the Council of Nicaea in 325 and more recently affirmed by the Lambeth Conference of 1888 and 1988 (Avis, 2015, pp. 116–17). The Lambeth Conference of 1888 also affirmed that the historic episcopate was not essential for being a 'true church', but that the historic episcopate could be 'locally adapted in the methods of its administration to the varying needs of the nations and peoples called of God into the Unity of His Church' (Baker and Richardson, 2017, p. 10). Of course, this allows for 'faithful improvisation' like that of the Methodists and the proposal for a 'President-Bishop' outlined above. In many ways this also illustrates the ability of the Anglican system to produce a *via media* or middle way, wonderfully expressed by Martyn Percy in the following terms:

> Indeed, is it not obvious that the Church of England is, in a profound sense, a community of practice, bound together more by manners, habits and outlooks than it is by doctrinal agreement? Indeed, one could argue that Anglicanism, at its best, is a community of civilised disagreement. (Percy, 2013, p. 138)

However, with regard to the episcopate there are things around which common agreement can and does gather. A key text is the liturgy for *The Ordination and Consecration of a Bishop* found in in *Common Worship*:

> Bishops are ordained to be shepherds of Christ's flock and guardians of the faith of the apostles, proclaiming the gospel of God's kingdom and

leading his people in mission. Obedient to the call of Christ and in the power of the Holy Spirit, they are to gather God's people and celebrate with them the sacraments of the new covenant. Thus formed into a single communion of faith and love, the Church in each place and time is united with the Church in every place and time. (www.churchofengland.org/prayer-and-worship/worship-texts-and-resources/common-worship/ministry/common-worship-ordination-services; accessed 05.11.2019)

The oversight of the Church is not solely the preserve of bishops, but there is a real sense that it is focused and exemplified in their role, and is something they share with others and promote in their dioceses through teamwork and advocacy (Mellows, 2001, p. 18; Grundy, 2011, p. 48). For Hanson (2010, p. 85), this is a central representative authority that a bishop wields and should convey no sense of hierarchy. The active participation of the whole Church, clergy and laity, in the consecration of a bishop is both symbolic and expressive of this truth.

The Cameron report, *Episcopal Ministry* (1990, pp. 21–38), helpfully visualizes the bishop's ministry of unity and continuity on three planes of the Church's life. The first plane is that of the 'local church' or diocese where the bishop is the centre and focus of its life and its representative to act on its behalf. The second plane is the wider Church and, in maintaining these relationships, demonstrates the unity of the local church with all those with whom it is in communion. The third plane is that of time, where the bishop stands in direct succession to the apostles, ensuring the continuity of the contemporary Church with their teaching and mission (House of Bishops, 2000, p. 12).

Perhaps the most influential contribution to Anglican episcopal thinking over the last generation has been the ecumenical movement, and particularly the 1982 Lima document of the World Council of Churches, *Baptism, Eucharist and Ministry* and its identification of episcopal ministry as 'personal, collegial and communal'.

Episcopacy as personal, collegial and communal

Baptism, Eucharist and Ministry (BEM) strove to express the ecumenical convergence in understanding that had developed around these three central strands of ecclesiological thinking. With regard to the episcopacy it clearly identified a common understanding of the role:

> Bishops preach the Word, preside at the sacraments, and administer discipline in such a way as to be representative pastoral ministers of

oversight, continuity and unity in the Church. They have pastoral oversight of the area to which they are called. They serve the apostolicity and unity of the Church's teaching, worship and sacramental life. They have responsibility for leadership in the Church's mission. They relate the Christian community in their area to the wider Church, and the universal Church to their community. They, in communion with the presbyters and deacons and the whole community, are responsible for the orderly transfer of ministerial authority in the Church. (World Council of Churches, 1982, p. 24)

BEM stated that episcopal succession was a sign, though not a guarantee, of the unity and continuity of the Church (p. 26) and argued that all ordained ministry should be exercised in a personal, collegial and communal manner. Personal, because the presence of Christ is most effectively mediated by the ordained person as an identified and representative figure; collegial, because of the common shared task of representing the concerns of a community; and communal, because it is rooted in the shared life of a community under the guidance of the Spirit.

This threefold statement of guiding principles was then directly taken up and related specifically to the episcopacy in *Bishops in Communion* (House of Bishops, 2000, pp. 18–32) and subsequently by Grundy (2011, pp. 177–9) and Pickard (2009, p. 198–9). As Grundy observes, the fact that *episkope* is expressed in the appointment of a person means that oversight will always be conducted by people in relationship. That bishops work collaboratively together is hardly surprising, but their collegiality is a necessary corollary of the geographical nature of their office as their parallel responsibilities lead them to work together on behalf of the whole in giving leadership, sharing in discernment, participating in consultation and jointly making decisions (House of Bishops, 2000, p. 29). The role is communally exercised from consecration onwards, as is demonstrated by, but not restricted to, the oft-quoted epithet that the Church of England is 'episcopally led and synodically governed' (Grundy, 2014, p. 20).

Other patterns have been identified in the experience and understanding of Anglican episcopacy that expand and overlap those noted above. For some the personal, historic and received nature of the office provides a helpful theological purchase on the office (Baker and Richardson, 2017, p. 23; Avis, 2015, pp. 114–15), while for others the juxtaposition of the threefold ministry of Christ as 'prophet, priest and king' can be seen as reflected in the episcopal responsibilities of proclamation, priestly intercession and governance, as was highlighted by the Roman Catholic Church in Vatican II (Mellows, 2001, pp. 220, 266). Pickard (2009, pp. 79–81) wonders whether further reflection on the insights of the

Church Fathers can provide a mode of a bishop as *alter Petrus* (Cyprian), *alter apostolos* (Irenaeus), *alter Christus* (Ignatius), while the Green Report identifies the future role of bishops as caught up in serving the mission and ministry of the Church in the ecclesial constants provided by canon law and the Ordinal[7] expressed in the alliterated schema of 'word, worship, work, world' (Green, 2014, pp. 80–1).

Once again, the significance of context cannot be overstated. The historic episcopate, as embodied in the Church of England, is clearly the child of the Anglican theological method and bears the marks of its journey through history to the present-day challenges it seeks to meet. From the Queen's address at Westminster Hall to the controversial Green Report, the Church is attempting to do just that, as it has always done. With regard to the latter, Martyn Percy (2017, p. 65) appeals for the Church to learn from Evagrius of Pontus, who argued for *nous*, a kind of spiritual intuition and intelligence that arises from a mind in communion with God. It is this kind of theological wisdom that Hanson sees as the special role of a bishop who, as guardian of the household of faith, is the one who ensures, 'that the Word of God has free course in his diocese. In this necessity both Scripture and tradition unite' (Hanson, 2010, p. 86).

'Shout to the Lord!': evangelical entrepreneurialism and networked solutions

As the pre-eminent grouping of evangelicals in the UK, the Evangelical Alliance seeks to represent a coalition consisting of hundreds of organizations and thousands of churches.[8] This membership, drawn from mainline historic denominations, newer independent charismatic churches, Pentecostalists from home-grown and overseas networks and a plethora of parachurch organizations, is illustrative of the wide diversity in the present-day evangelical community. It is both theologically and relationally segmented and fragmented, providing a landscape consisting of a matrix of networks that overlap and overlie one another. A single, coherent account of its beliefs and practices is impossible to outline as it does not exist. However, some things can be helpfully outlined in broad brush strokes, and the range and nature of translocal oversight that is exercised can be indicated by influential and high-profile examples.

Famously, David Bebbington (1989, pp. 4–17) identified a common core of characteristics that have been present among evangelicals down the centuries. Conversionism, activism, biblicism and crucicentrism are not so much a theological methodology as ecclesiological markers that identify those who belong to one of the tribes of evangelicalism. Their combination is also formative – conversionism leads to a direct engagement with wider society and those who do not share their faith in Christ; activism requires the devising and initiation of missionary endeavour; while biblicism provides the theological resources to draw upon to inspire, shape and assess their endeavours.

When considering the nature of oversight in these networks, a number of issues emerge within the present context, with apostolicity and the nature of authority possibly the most significant. It is, perhaps, no surprise that there are a variety of responses to these that range from the firm, directive authority invested in named individuals who are identified as apostles and bring directional leadership, to apostles being defined as a functional missional category and the 'soft' influential authority of a consensual and more egalitarian apostolic movement. Yet in all this it is the influence of American culture in general, and corporate America in particular, that has provided the most significant contribution in shaping the more creative and dynamic examples of evangelical expression.

While the roots of evangelicalism may be in Europe, it is in America that it discovered a context in which it could thrive. The separation of church and state guaranteed by the First Amendment of the American Constitution effectively created a religious marketplace in which churches had to compete. The success of religious bodies was thus determined by the effectiveness of their clergy, the appeal of their doctrines and the fruitfulness of their evangelistic techniques. Ecclesiastical deregulation led to religious innovation (Finke and Stark, 2014, pp. 8–12), bringing modernization, pluralism, competition and choice in its wake, an Americanization of religion that rejected hierarchy and tradition by preferring the Bible and conscience (Micklethwait and Wooldridge, 2009, pp. 23, 68).

While there has been a consistent transatlantic communication between British and American evangelicalism over the years, this intensified in the latter part of the twentieth century. The successive influence of 'pastorpreneurs'[9] like John Wimber of the Vineyard movement, Bill Hybels from the Willow Creek Association, Rick Warren and 'the purpose driven church' and Bill Johnson of Bethel Church are only the headline acts of an extensive roster of preacher-authors whose books, tapes, DVDs and TV programmes have been consumed by UK evangelical audiences. Their vitality of faith, familiarity and success in the American evangelical marketplace combine with the production quality of their resources and the wider penetration of American culture to make their pitch an attractive one. Indeed, the audience themselves are quite promiscuous consumers, blending the received insights and emphases in a multi-sourced hybrid of faith and practice.

The examples that follow demonstrate something of the roots of a range of belief and practice that is presently experienced within British evangelicalism.

Willow Creek Community Church, South Barrington, Illinois

Founded by Bill Hybels in a movie theatre in 1975, Willow Creek Community Church was to become the epicentre of the 'seeker-sensitive church' movement. The raison d'être of the church was to provide a context where the 'unchurched' could hear the Christian message in a form and a context that was relevant to them. With innovative services throughout the weekend, deploying the visual and creative arts, the church adopted the mission statement, 'to turn irreligious people into fully devoted followers of Jesus Christ', along with a seven-step strategy and a set of ten core values. After 40 years the main campus now consists of an auditorium seating 7,200, with food courts, sports halls and a car park for 3,850 vehicles (Micklethwait and Wooldridge, 2009, p. 183). Seven satellite locations are spread around the 'Chicagoland' area, each receiving a live-streamed broadcast from the main venue that is also relayed live online through Willow TV.

The quintessential megachurch, Willow Creek's ministry is much broader. Under Hybels' leadership a vast array of resources was published and marketed worldwide that expounded the church's approach and ethos. The Willow Creek Association was born in 1992 to support and resource ministers and churches in their network. Now rebranded as the Global Leadership Network, it continues its work, the highlight of which is an annual global summit that is streamed to 900+ sites in 135 countries. Past speakers have included international business leaders, politicians like Jimmy Carter and Colin Powell alongside celebrities who have included Bono and Bear Grylls. Hybels' own career path was to have taken him in his father's footsteps as a business entrepreneur, but it was into Willow Creek that the entrepreneurial spirit was poured, receiving the ultimate accolade of a Harvard Business School case study. While Hybels and Willow Creek tend not to use apostolic criteria in their material, some scholars have identified their approach as that of an 'apostolic congregation'. In this is embodied a corporate understanding of their being sent to reach the unchurched with the apostolic message of Christianity and a readiness to adapt and contextualize to accomplish this mission (Hunter, 1996, pp. 26–8). Clearly the oversight that Willow Creek exercises is a soft authority deployed through the influence of their resources and the informal relational character of their network. The possibility to develop it into coaching and accountability structures is there, as was the opportunity to avoid it altogether.[10]

More recently the latter days of Hybels' ministry at Willow Creek were caught up in #MeToo accusations of 'sexually inappropriate words and actions'. These led to his standing down as Senior Pastor and the accusations later being found by an independent advisory group as credible in a 17-page report. It was a sobering finding that the megachurch's Board were seen to have been unable to provide effective oversight to keep him accountable. While recognizing his accomplishments the group concluded that 'the negative use of power, influence, and management style caused dysfunction in these organizations' abilities [i.e. Willow Creek Church and the Willow Creek Association] to consistently implement policies, [and] manage personnel', leading staff to feel verbally and emotionally intimidated.[11]

The Hybels case highlights the positive and negative sides of business-style corporate oversight in the American context. The designation of a congregation's leadership as 'the Church Board' is ubiquitous in the United States with its accompanying business overtones, but an emerging pattern among many American megachurches is for their senior functionaries to be dubbed CEOs and COOs, a pattern replicated by Willow Creek as they sought to appoint Hybels' successor. In analysing the published job description, the theologian Scot McKnight highlights its biblical and theological weaknesses, not least in the fact that a theological degree and pastoral formation were not required elements of the person specification, while someone to 'motivate and inspire high-capacity men and women to use their gifts to further the vision' was. 'What of the 95% who aren't high-capacity?' he asks, concluding that what they were searching for was 'an entrepreneurial leader who expands the Willow Creek brand'.[12] It begs the question of how far business models like this are theologically compatible with the office of oversight, and how their uncritical adoption might subtly, or not so subtly, reshape or reorientate such ministry. The challenge is how to retain the clear advantages of vitality, focus, innovation and effectiveness without falling prey to new and devastating temptations.

Holy Trinity, Brompton

Holy Trinity, Brompton, or HTB as the London Anglican Church in the Royal Borough of Kensington and Chelsea is affectionately known, has long figured on the evangelical landscape as the home of the globally significant Alpha Course. As one of the most influential charismatic/

evangelical churches in Britain it meets each week on five local sites and also runs the Marriage Course, an ex-offenders ministry and, more significantly in the context of providing oversight, the St Paul's Theological Centre, the Church Revitalisation Trust and an annual national leadership conference.[13]

Through its various ministries HTB serves wider evangelicalism, especially in the area of evangelism through Alpha and, to a lesser degree, in theological and leadership resources. However, as an Anglican church the linkage between the St Paul's Theological Centre and the St Mellitus Theological College gives it a strong input into the fastest growing provider of initial ministerial education within the communion. As of 2019 St Mellitus delivers contextually based ordination training from its base in Earls Court, and also in Chelmsford, the north-west, the south-west and the East Midlands. Then, through the Church Revitalisation Trust, HTB is growing a trans-diocesan network of churches. The trust's vision is:

- To recruit and train outstanding clergy and leaders of the future in partnership with the model of St Mellitus College and other national theological colleges.
- To see City Centre Resource Churches become regional hubs for Alpha, the Marriage Courses, and social action programmes that will bless and regenerate their communities.
- To recruit and train 100 exceptional church leaders as well as worship leaders, youth pastors, children's workers, operations directors and social action workers.
  (https://crtrust.org/vision-and-mission; accessed 14.11.2019)

HTB itself already has 56 network churches, of which 19 are City Centre Resource Churches (including congregations in Nairobi and Kuala Lumpur), 33 are in London and a further four outside of London (www.htb.org/network).

HTB is a British incarnation of entrepreneurial evangelicalism. Like Willow Creek it has a pan-evangelical influence that is loosely based on its Alpha network and leadership conference. As such it is a soft influence/authority. However, through its intra-denominational commitments to theological education, ordination training and trans-diocesan church revitalization, it has an authority that is less informal and far more intentionally formational in the oversight to which it contributes.

Hillsong

Hillsong traces its roots back to a church planted in the suburbs of Sydney, Australia in 1983 by husband and wife team, Brian and Bobbie Houston. The son of an Assembly of God pastor who had helped to rebrand his Pentecostal denomination as the Australian Christian Church (ACC), Houston chooses for his Australia-based network to be 'closely associated with' ACC rather than belonging to it.[14] Music has been central in establishing and growing the Hillsong brand, with well over a hundred worship albums released with sales of millions worldwide and a steady stream of gold and platinum discs awarded. The original Hills Christian Life Centre ultimately embraced the name Hillsong Church in 2001, adopting the label of the highly successful music ministry and thus fusing the identity of both (Wagner, 2013, p. 52).

The network of churches that are formally linked with Hillsong are located across 23 countries and have a weekly global attendance in excess of 130,000. In addition, Hillsong College in Sydney has graduated over 10,000 students from 65+ countries since it was founded in 1995, and annually the network hosts numerous conferences around the world attended by tens of thousands of participants. The conversionist objective of their corporate mission statement is clear:

> To reach and influence the world by building a large Christ-centred, Bible-based church, changing mindsets and empowering people to lead and impact in every sphere of life. (https://hillsong.com/about/; accessed 14.11.2019)

In an in-depth study of their fusion of music, marketing and branded spiritual experience, the ethnomusicologist Thomas Wagner observes that they are the religious embodiment of secular 'glocal' branding, harnessing both global and local discourse, epitomized by their global brand tagline 'welcome home' (Wagner, 2013, p. 42). With a religious background in an American Pentecostal church, Hillsong appears to be an 'Aussie Rules' example of American evangelical entrepreneurialism. Indeed, Hillsong itself runs a business with its governance policies following the *Principles of Good Corporate Governance and Best Practice Recommendations* of the Australian Stock Exchange (Wagner, 2013, p. 49). As a hybrid organization, Hillsong is also registered as a non-profit organization and benefits like all churches from a high level of volunteer support.

As with all successful businesses, branding is critically important, and Hillsong is perhaps the pre-eminent example of this corporate expression in an ecclesial setting. Brian Houston himself comments that:

Hillsong has got a credibility that I want to look after. I don't like using a marketing term, but if you did use a marketing term it is a 'strong brand'. I don't want to diminish the brand by just giving it away to anyone and everyone. I try to harness that. (Carswell, 2013)

Wagner concludes that the close control that branding brings to an organization provides a form of governance. It streamlines the flow of information, which in turn shapes the content and expression of the corporate culture. Brand buy-in harnesses the freedom of the individual and then interacts and helps shape and reinforce their values. As a 'branded social system' it is particularly adjusted to the context of Western consumerist culture and those who, globally, aspire towards it (Wagner, 2013, pp. 166–8). For those working within the organization, the meticulous oversight that such branding requires is particularly worthy of note. When asked whether Hillsong was a denomination or not, Houston replied, 'mostly no, but partly yes'.[15] In a formal comparison with his former home with the ACC this is probably true. However, the corporate business structure that holds together Hillsong's Australian campuses and their growing international network of churches alongside their other highly successful global ventures is an emerging form of neo-denominationalism. Within it, oversight is delivered through its management structures and the rigorous demands of glocalized branding.

New apostolic movements

With evangelicals looking to secure their understanding in biblical theology, it is no surprise that the category of apostle and apostolic ministry should figure as significant. It is not surprising either that with the office of bishop carrying the baggage of institutionalized denominationalism and the dead weight of tradition, it is passed swiftly over.

A novel development in apostolic understanding is advocated by the popular missional church authors Alan Hirsch, Mike Frost and Mike Breen. Believing that the Church has lost its way, having been led by those with the gifting of pastor/teachers, they propose a 'revolutionary missional ecclesiology' to correct the situation (Hirsch and Catchim, 2012, p. xvi).[16] While not wishing to minimize the gifts of pastors and teachers, key to their understanding is the need to recapture the fully functioning model outlined in Ephesians 4.11 that also includes the missional designations of apostles, prophets and evangelists (or APEST – apostles, prophets, evangelists, shepherds, teachers). In their view, all members of the believing community fit broadly into one of these categories and work collaboratively in balanced teams. Maturity forms the basis for leadership in each of the ministry areas and, as apostles are 'entrepreneurial by nature', their creative inclination and pioneering experience ensures that apostolic organizations are 'inherently adaptive, flexible, self-renewing, resilient, learning and intelligent' (Hirsch and Catchim, 2012, p. 209).[17] Rather than replicating Christendom models of centralized control, like the historic denominations, they believe that apostolic movements display more of the characteristics of a network. Explaining how this model of oversight works, they state that:

> The most authentic forms of apostolic ministry forgo the hierarchical, top-down, transactional forms of leadership and power and draw mostly on what can be called inspirational, or moral, authority. Built on vision, meaning, and purpose, inspirational authority is able to motivate, and sustain networks ... apostolic ministry therefore creates the web of meaning that holds the networked movement together. (Hirsch and Catchim, 2012, p. 112)

Around these ideas a wide-ranging and informal network has gathered, including the Forge training programmes in Australia and the United States, the 3DMovement that is also based in America but has its roots at St Thomas' Crookes in Sheffield in the ministry of Mike Breen and the popular *Lifeshapes* discipleship material. 3DM also provides seminars, webinars, mutual support through coaching, mentoring and 'strategic huddles', The Order of Mission (TOM – an expression of what has been called 'the New Monasticism') and a range of other initiatives.[18]

Once again, the oversight offered through this movement is rather loose and what does exist is relationally based on the network itself. The APEST teaching is widely disseminated and read, though much less widely adopted as a functioning model. However, the exception to this would be The Order of Mission as its more formal nature ultimately includes a permanent lifelong covenantal commitment to TOM's Rule of Life and the accountability that accompanies this.

Of less significance in the UK context, but nonetheless worth noting in passing as part of the entrepreneurial landscape of evangelicalism, is what C. Peter Wagner has called the 'New Apostolic Reformation' (McNair Scott, 2014, pp. 22–8). He believed it to be changing the shape of Protestant Christianity around the world and it led him to found the International Coalition of Apostolic Leaders (ICAL) in 1999. At that point the Coalition agreed to Wagner's definition of an apostle, namely that:

> An apostle is a Christian leader who is gifted, taught, commissioned, and sent by God with the authority to establish the foundational government of the Church within an assigned sphere and/or spheres of ministry by hearing what the Spirit is saying to the churches and by setting things in order accordingly for the advancement of the Kingdom of God. (Wagner, 2006, p. 143)

While Wagner does not define what 'foundational government' looks like, he is quite clear that such apostles possess 'exceptional authority' and that recognition of an individual holding the office of an apostle follows on from the demonstration of their gift. Membership of ICAL was therefore by invitation only.[19] From an extensive study McNair Scott is clear that the model of ministry espoused in the New Apostolic Reformation is hierarchical and that the spiritual authority of an apostle takes precedence over all other ministries in the Church (pp. 182–3). While he concedes that such apostolic ministries will continue to gain a hearing in the UK at conferences and through their publications and broadcasts, he sees the embeddedness of charismatic Christianity in the historic denominations and new church networks, alongside the health of networks like New Wine and Soul Survivor, making their pitch to Britain unlikely to make much progress (p. 215).

While evangelicalism in Britain may be fragmented, as each of the above examples clearly demonstrates, there is a pan-evangelical subculture into which they make their own distinctive contribution. While there are clear differences between them, Bebbington's identification of biblicism, conversionism and activism are clearly evident forces that shape each of them. Similarly, the influence of an American entrepreneurial business culture provides a significant context in which these elements seek to find expression in the life of the Church and its engagement with wider society.

Conclusion: constants in context

As the three case studies above have sought to demonstrate, to understand how translocal ministry is practised, you have to understand their theological context as well as the historic context of their formation, their journey to the present day and, indeed, the influence of the contemporary context itself. The constants in this instance, with due reference to Bevans and Schroeder, are ecclesiological and missiological; that is, the Church of Jesus Christ, its engagement in the *missio Dei*, and the necessary *episkope* of the community of faith and its work.

Notes

1 A full version of the Anglican Methodist Covenant outlining the affirmations and commitments undertaken by the two denominations is available online at www.anglican-methodist.org.uk/full-text-of-the-covenant/ (accessed 18.10.2019).

2 The Church of England General Synod did not immediately endorse such a move as part of its fulfilling of the Anglican–Methodist Covenant in July 2019, and following on from that, the Methodist Church has withdrawn from any immediate search for its own endorsement through Conference in 2020. Effectively the search for a Methodist embrace of episcopacy is dormant.

3 Martyn Percy also identifies this as the Anglican Trilateral (Percy, 2017, p. 59).

4 Perhaps the most significant controversy that sought to establish this unbroken succession was contained within a volume of essays published in 1946 by a group of senior High Churchmen and edited by K. E. Kirk, *The Apostolic Ministry*. It maintained that episcopal ministry within the established 'apostolic succession' was of the *esse* or essence of the very existence of the Church. This position, that effectively 'unchurched' non-episcopal Protestants, was roundly rejected by serious scholars such as C. F. D. Moule, T. F. Torrance, T. W. Manson, J. W. Hunkin and others. Rather than of the *esse* of the Church, it was argued that episcopal ministry itself was *bene esse*, or for the benefit of the Church rather than a requirement for its existence. Later, High Church theologians advocated an understanding of *plene esse* or for the fullness of the Church's life.

5 Otherwise known as the Lima Document.

6 For an insight into the debate that was engendered by the Green Report see Percy, 2017, pp. 33–6, and the blogs of Michael Sadgrove (http://decanalwoolgatherer.blogspot.com/2014/12/equipping-tomorrows-church-leaders.html), Mike Higton (http://mikehigton.org.uk/re-reading-the-green-report-1-suspicion-retrieval-and-repair/), which runs over a further four posts, and Ian Paul (www.psephizo.com/life-ministry/should-bishops-come-from-a-talent-pool/) (all accessed 14.11.2019).

7 Namely, 'preaching, teaching and admonition; of prayer and sacramental ministry; of caring labour for the welfare of the people; and of networking around the wider church and representation of the church in public' (Green, 2014, p. 81).

8 The EA's press briefings contain the statement: 'We join together hundreds of organisations, thousands of churches and tens of thousands of individuals for the sake of the gospel'; www.eauk.org/press-releases/northern-ireland-abortion-regime-consultation-released (accessed 14.11.2019). While membership figures are not reported, in 2015 their press releases stated that 'we work across 79 denominations, 3,500 churches, 750 organisations'.

9 A term coined by John Jackson and adopted by Mickelthwait and Wooldridge (2009, p. 184) as particularly apt.

10 The Willow Creek story is further explored in Hybels and Hybels (1995), Strobel (1993), Hunter (1996), Pritchard (1996) and Dobson (1993). See also the church website, www.willowcreek.org/ and that of the Global Leadership Network, https://globalleadership.org/ (accessed 14.11.2019).

11 The initial reportage of the accusations was made by the *Chicago Tribune* and a full account of the conclusion of the investigation is reported by *Christianity*

Today, www.christianitytoday.com/news/2019/february/willow-creek-bill-hybels-investigation-iag-report.html (accessed 14.11.2019).

12 Scot McKnight is Professor of New Testament at Northern Baptist Theological Seminary in Lombard, Illinois; www.patheos.com/blogs/jesuscreed/2019/09/16/willow-creek-whats-a-pastor/ (accessed 14.11.2019).

13 For HTB, see www.htb.org/; for the Alpha Course, see https://alpha.org.uk/; for the Marriage Course, see www.htb.org/marriage; for the St Paul's Theological Centre, see https://sptc.htb.org/; for the Church Revitalisation Trust, see https://crtrust.org/ and for the national leadership conference, see www.leadershipconference.org.uk/ (all accessed 14.11.2019).

14 Where not otherwise stated, the information relating to Hillsong has been gleaned from their website, https://hillsong.com; for their UK presence, https://hillsong.com/uk/; and for the live web-based TV channel, https://hillsongchannel.com/ (all accessed 14.11.2019).

15 This followed a 2018 decision to register as such with the Australian authorities for the practical reasons of accrediting their own pastors and for being registered to conduct weddings; https://hillsong.com/collected/blog/2018/10/has-hillsong-really-become-its-own-denomination/ (accessed 14.11.2019).

16 Frost and Hirsch are prolific authors, as is Mike Breen and the 3DM movement, who are particularly active online. For Frost and Hirsch, it was in their early books *The Shape of Things To Come* (2003) and *The Forgotten Ways* (2006) that their ideas began to emerge.

17 Such an understanding would therefore see church planters as apostles. It is not a coincidence that in the British Fresh Expressions movement the decision was taken to identify such individuals as Pioneer Ministers, thereby avoiding any potential confusion with the apostolic nature of Anglican episcopacy (see also McNair Scott, 2014, p. 41).

18 See the following websites: for a fuller outline of the work of St Thomas' Crookes, https://stthomascrookes.org/; Forge, http://forge.org.au/ or www.forgeamerica.com/; 3DM, www.3dmovements.com/; TOM, www.missionorder.org/ (all accessed 14.11.2019).

19 For ICAL, see www.icaleaders.com/.

References

Avis, Paul, 2013, *The Identity of Anglicanism: Essentials of Anglican Ecclesiology*, London: Bloomsbury.

Avis, Paul, 2015, *Becoming a Bishop*, London: T & T Clark.

Baker, Jonathan and Neil Richardson, 2017, *Mission and Ministry in Covenant*; www.churchofengland.org/sites/default/files/2017-10/mission-and-ministry-in-covenant.pdf (accessed 18.10.2019).

Bauckham, Richard and Benjamin Drewery (eds), 1988, *Scripture, Tradition and Reason: A Study in the Criteria of Christian Doctrine*, Edinburgh: T & T Clark.

Bebbington, David, 1989, *Evangelicalism in Modern Britain: A history from the 1730s to the 1980s*, London: Unwin Hyman.

Bevans, Stephen B. and Roger P. Schroeder, 2006, *Constants in Context: A Theology of Mission for Today*, Maryknoll, NY: Orbis Books.

Cameron, Sheila (Chairman), 1990, *Episcopal Ministry: The Report of the Archbishops' Group on the Episcopate*, London: Church House Publishing.

Carswell, Andrew, 2013, 'Hillsong's Message and Music has a Resonance Worldwide that Eclipses that of the Church's Aussie Birthplace', in *CourierMail*, 13 July 2013; www.couriermail.com.au/news/queensland/hillsong8217s-message-and-music-has-a-resonance-worldwide-that-eclipses-that-of-the-church8217s-aussie-birthplace/news-story/f825ce802317f937fa8bf5d99d54d4b9 (accessed 30.03.2020).

Davis, Douglas J. and Matthew Guest, 2007, *Bishops, Wives and Children: Spiritual Capital Across the Generations*, Farnham: Ashgate.

Dobson, Ed, 1993, *Starting a Seeker Sensitive Service*, Grand Rapids, MI: Zondervan.

Faith and Order Commission of the Church of England, 2015, *Senior Church Leadership: A Resource For Reflection*; www.churchofengland.org/sites/default/files/2017-10/senior_church_leadership_faoc.pdf (accessed 01.11.2019).

Finke, Roger and Rodney Stark, 2014, *The Churching of America, 1776–2005: Winners and Losers in Our Religious Economy*, New Brunswick, NJ: Rutgers University Press.

Frost, Michael, 2006, *The Forgotten Ways: Reactivating the Missional Church*, Grand Rapids, MI: Brazos Press.

Frost, Michael and Alan Hirsch, 2003, *The Shape of Things to Come: Innovation and Mission for the 21st Century Church*, Peabody, MA: Hendrickson.

Green, Stephen, 2014, *The Green Report: Talent Management for Future Leaders and Leadership Development for Bishops and Deans: A New Approach*; www.thinkinganglicans.org.uk/uploads/TalentManagement.pdf (accessed 04.11.2019).

Grundy, Malcolm, 2011, *Leadership and Oversight: New Models for Episcopal Ministry*, London: Mowbray.

Grundy, Malcolm, 2014, *'Episkope' as a Model for Oversight and Leadership in the Church of England Examined in the Dioceses of Yorkshire*, The University of Leeds: York St John University, Faculty of Education and Theology; http://etheses.whiterose.ac.uk/6565/1/PhDMLGrundy2014.pdf (accessed 30.10.2019).

Hanson, R. P. C., 2010, 'The Nature of the Anglican Episcopate', in Arthur Michael Ramsey, *Lambeth Essays on Ministry: Essays Written for the Lambeth Conference 1968*, Eugene, OR: Wipf & Stock.

Hirsch, Alan and Tim Catchim, 2012, *The Permanent Revolution: Apostolic Imagination and Practice for the 21st Century Church*, San Francisco, CA: Jossey-Bass.

House of Bishops Occasional Paper, 2000, *Bishops in Communion: Collegiality in the Service of the Koinonia of the Church*, London: Church House Publishing.

Hunter, George C., 1996, *Church for the Unchurched*, Nashville, TN: Abingdon Press.

Hybels, Lynne and Bill, 1995, *Rediscovering Church: The Story and Vision of Willow Creek Community Church*, Grand Rapids, MI: Zondervan.

Jackson, Thomas (ed.), 1978, *The Works of John Wesley, Vol. 8*, Grand Rapids, MI: Baker Book House.

Kirk, K. E. (ed.), 1946, *The Apostolic Ministry: Essays on the History and the Doctrine of Episcopacy*, New York: Morehouse-Gorham.

McNair Scott, Benjamin G., 2014, *Apostles Today – Making Sense of Contemporary Charismatic Apostolates: A Historical and Theological Appraisal*, Eugene, OR: Pickwick Publications.

Mellows, Anthony (Chairman), 2001, *Resourcing Bishops: The First Report of the Archbishops' Review Group on Bishops' Needs and Resources*, London: Church House Publishing.

Mellows, Anthony (Chairman), 2002, *Resourcing Archbishops: The Second Report of the Archbishops' Review Group on Bishops' Needs and Resources*, London: Church House Publishing.

Methodist Conference, 1998, *Episcopacy*, www.methodist.org.uk/media/2007/fo-statement-episcopacy-1998.pdf/ (accessed 21.05.2020).

Methodist Conference, 2000, *Episkopé and Episcopacy*, www.methodist.org.uk/media/2010/fo-statement-episkope-and-episcopacy-2000.pdf/ (accessed 21.05.2020).

Methodist Conference, 2005a, *The Nature of Oversight: Leadership, Management and Governance in the Methodist Church in Great Britain*; www.methodist.org.uk/about-us/the-methodist-conference/conference-reports/conference-reports-2005/ (accessed 17.10.2019).

Methodist Conference, 2005b, *What Sort of Bishops? Models of Episcopacy and British Methodism*; www.methodist.org.uk/about-us/the-methodist-conference/conference-reports/conference-reports-2005/ (accessed 17.10.2019).

Methodist Conference, 2006, *Responses to the 'What Sort of Bishops?' Report*; www.methodist.org.uk/about-us/the-methodist-conference/conference-reports/conference-reports-2006/ (accessed 17.10.2019).

Micklethwait, John and Adrian Wooldridge, 2009, *God is Back: How the Global Rise of Faith is Changing the World*, London: Allen Lane.

Murray, Stuart, 2004, *Post-Christendom: Church and Mission in a Strange New World*, Carlisle: Paternoster Press.

Outler, Albert, 1991, 'The Wesleyan Quadrilateral – in John Wesley', in Thomas Langford (ed.), *Doctrine and Theology in the United Methodist Church*, Nashville, TN: Abingdon Press.

Percy, Martyn, 2013, *Anglicanism: Confidence, Commitment and Communion*, Farnham: Ashgate.

Percy, Martyn, 2017, *The Future Shapes of Anglicanism: Currents, Contours, Charts*, London: Routledge.

Pickard, Stephen, 2009, *Theological Foundations for Collaborative Ministry*, Farnham: Ashgate.

Pritchard, G. A., 1996, *Willow Creek Seeker Services: Evaluating a New Way of Doing Church*, Grand Rapids, MI: Baker Books.

Rack, Henry, 1989, *Reasonable Enthusiast: John Wesley and the Rise of Methodism*, London: Epworth Press.

Stewart, Alistair C., 2014, *The Original Bishops: Office and Order in the First Christian Communities*, Grand Rapids, MI: Baker Academic.

Strobel, Lee, 1993, *Inside the Mind of Unchurched Harry and Mary*, Grand Rapids, MI: Zondervan.

Telford, John (ed.), 1960, *The Letters of John Wesley, Vol I–VIII, 1780–1787*, London: Epworth Press.

Tustin, David, 2013, *A Bishop's Ministry: Reflections and Resources for Church Leadership*, Rothersthorpe: Paragon Publishing.

Wagner, C. Peter, 2006, *Apostles Today: Biblical Government for Biblical Power*, Ventura, CA: Regal Books.

Wagner, Thomas J., 2013, *Hearing the Hillsong Sound: Music, Marketing, Meaning and Branded Spiritual Experience at a Transnational Megachurch*, Unpublished D.Phil Thesis, Royal Holloway University of London; www.academia.edu/9191865/Hearing_the_Hillsong_Sound_Music_Marketing_Meaning_and_Branded_Spiritual_Experience_at_a_Transnational_Megachurch (accessed 14.11.2019).

Wesley, John, 1827, *The Works of the Rev. John Wesley, in Ten Volumes. Volume X. Containing Tracts and Letters on Various Subjects*, New York: J. & J. Harper.

Williams, Rowan and Benedicta Ward, 2012, *Bede's Ecclesiastical History*, London: Bloomsbury.

World Council of Churches, 1982, *Baptism, Eucharist and Ministry*; www.oikoumene.org/en/resources/documents/commissions/faith-and-order/i-unity-the-church-and-its-mission/baptism-eucharist-and-ministry-faith-and-order-paper-no-111-the-lima-text/@@download/file/FO1982_111_en.pdf (accessed 17.12.2019).

3

Contemporary Models of Translocal Ministry: Ecumenical Landscapes

PAUL GOODLIFF

This book is deliberately ecumenical in spirit, and this reflects the widespread conviction among the historic churches that oversight of the Church must be ecumenical in character and practice. In this chapter we will explore the shape of the ecumenical landscape in Britain today, reflect on the differing responses to ecumenism, describe the kinds of ecumenical tasks and collaboration most familiar to those called to regional oversight and find the place of regional oversight within that landscape. This will enable us to map the contemporary models of translocal ministry within this ecumenical landscape.

For most Christian denominations in Britain, ecumenism has become a major aspect of their understanding of their life and witness. At the most local level, and at its minimalist expression, ecumenism is experienced through the activities in the Week of Prayer for Christian Unity, culminating in a shared service among the churches of a town or village, and perhaps in shared ecumenical Lent Groups. More recently the initiative of the Archbishop of Canterbury, Justin Welby, to develop a worldwide season of prayer from Ascension to Pentecost, 'Thy Kingdom Come', has developed a thoroughly ecumenical character. There are exclusive expressions of church that carry a self-understanding that they alone are Christian, and that to participate in ecumenism is to indulge in a rather suspect activity, but they are not very common. Certainly, at the level of Church Leaders' groups, ecumenical engagement will be required and expected if you are a Baptist Regional Minister, Methodist District Chair, Church of England Bishop, United Reformed Church synod moderator or Roman Catholic Bishop.

More formal structures will include Churches Together groups, County Ecumenical Committees, and national ecumenical instruments such as Churches Together in England and Churches Together in Britain and

Ireland, as well as each denomination's ecumenical committees and departments.

There are some who cynically see all this ecumenical activity as just so much shifting of the deck chairs on the fatally doomed *Titanic*: a vain attempt at down-sizing in the face of a declining membership. There are advantages, to be sure, in co-operating together using declining resources, but if the driver to greater ecumenical unity is mere financial expediency, then it will prove shallow and short on commitment. What is required is a deeper theological understanding of why ecumenism matters. That will include a conviction that the truest expression of church is an ecumenical one – anything that falls short of the breadth and sheer variety in the Church that is the body of Christ is deficient in scope and vision. Anything that suggests 'I do not need you' not only contradicts St Paul's firm assertion that we belong to one another and need one another at every level (1 Cor. 12.14–26), but also diminishes the gifts we have to receive from expressions of church different from our own. Quite apart from this desire for the fullest range of expressions of church, the prayer of Jesus in John 17 that his disciples would be one so that the world might believe is fundamental. How can we possibly claim to follow this Jesus, who prays that prayer as he prepares for his death, and walk away from our brothers and sisters?

The current national ecumenical instruments grew out of the earlier British Council of Churches, which consisted largely of the Protestant denominations and some Pentecostals and Orthodox churches. Churches Together in England and its other national equivalents in Scotland and Wales, together with Churches Together in Britain and Ireland (the body that represents all four nations on the international stage), included the Roman Catholic Church in the ecumenical pilgrimage for the first time when it was formed in 1990.[1] Since then the number of member churches of Churches Together in England has grown to 50, with the newer members joining largely in the second decade of the twenty-first century from Pentecostal (especially Black Pentecostal) churches and the Orthodox. This represents the formal ecumenism that is supported by churches with a national presence and a formal structure, rather than local congregations.

There is, however, another, newer movement for Christian unity alongside the older, formal ecumenism, and it is represented by organizations such as HOPE or the 'Gather' movement and has its origins in evangelical and charismatic churches in towns and cities collaborating for mission and social transformation (Sutton, 2017). Supporting both of those is the Evangelical Alliance, a unity movement for the sector of the Church in Britain that was least likely to engage in formal ecumenism, and which is open to membership from churches, national and local, and individuals. That increasingly national churches in membership with the Evangelical Alliance will also be in membership with Churches Together in England reflects the changing approach to formal ecumenism by evangelicals and charismatics willing to engage with a broader range of churches to make common cause.

Responses to ecumenism

1 Resistance

These churches see the ecumenical movement as a detraction from the gospel, a hindrance to witness and an unacceptable compromise of the 'true gospel'. Hard-line evangelicals, a few Pentecostals and some members of the historic churches would wish to undo the achievements of the ecumenical movement. For those churches that continue to resist ecumenical engagement, ecumenism is seen as liberal, politicized and with an over-emphasis on a social gospel. Others view their church as 'the' Church and see any dialogue with others as a denial of this basic theological tenet. It is worth remembering how, until the sea-change towards ecumenism voiced in Vatican II, some Catholics would have espoused this view too.

2 Indifference

Practically speaking, many local churches, while not wishing to overtly criticize the ecumenical movement, just do not get involved. It is an irrelevance. Local church life is just too busy, or they are such a dominant force in the religious life of a society that ecumenical engagement is seen as a luxury. In Britain, indifference would be true of some of the new church streams, and pragmatically close to the attitude of some Free Churches.

Often ecumenical involvement is limited to the Week of Prayer for Christian Unity services and ministers attending ecumenical ministers' meetings when nothing else gets in the diary. Affirmation is so weak as to be barely registered.

3 Affirmation with distance

The official stance of the historic traditions is affirmation now, although with differing levels of commitment and enthusiasm. Baptists at a national level, for instance, officially affirm ecumenism, and are members of the World Council of Churches, the Conference of European Churches and Churches Together in England, while local churches are often members of Churches Together groups. However, it does not necessarily figure centrally in their life. So the appointment of new Regional Ministers rarely involves ecumenical partners in any meaningful way, although the appointment of the two most recent General Secretaries included an ecumenical partner. By comparison, it is not unusual for the Church of England to seek some contribution from their ecumenical partners when a diocesan appointment is sought.

The Roman Catholic Church and the Orthodox Churches, in different ways, affirm ecumenism, especially for Rome after Vatican II, but their engagement is limited by theological understandings of communion. Protestant churches tend to see full communion as a goal to be reached by sharing in the eucharist, whereas Orthodox and Catholic theology sees shared eucharistic fellowship as the fruit of convergence. However, the presence of the Catholic Church as a special observer at all WCC Assemblies and Regional Councils, and the full membership of Orthodoxy in the WCC, are affirmative stances and there are many within both traditions who see ecumenism as a vital and unavoidable aspect of the life of the Church. In particular, the encyclical *Ut Unum Sint*, signed by John Paul II on Ascension Day 1995, follows Vatican II in committing the Roman Catholic Church to ecumenism. It holds that dialogue is the key mechanism on a path to unity characterized by repentance from past errors, common prayer, reciprocal visitation, study of the faith (of what is held in common and what is different) and cooperation in mission and the serving of needy humanity. When considering the steps taken in Vatican II and *Ut Unum Sint* away from an older approach that forbade dialogue, it is possible to see the extraordinary extent to which Catholic ecumenism has transformed the lived experience of ordinary clergy and the faithful. Indeed, in recognizing that 'certain features of the Christian mystery have at times been more effectively emphasised' in communities other than the Roman Catholic Church (para. 14), other church leaders and their theologians are invited into dialogue about the exercise of this 'necessary' ministry in a spirit of 'real but imperfect communion' (Wainwright, 2002, p. 1185).

4 Enthusiasm

There are some in many traditions for whom ecumenism is the most significant dimension of ecclesiology. Here ecumenism is not just an optional extra for enthusiasts of 'that sort of thing', but an unavoidable corollary of the gospel, Scripture and dogmatic theology. Such people often get involved in local or national ecumenical structures and can be a welcome irritant for the rest who do not share their passion or conviction.

In the United Kingdom the church that reflects this commitment above all else is the United Reformed Church, the product of the most successful church union scheme in Britain to date, joining the Presbyterian Church of England and the majority of churches in the Congregational Church in England and Wales in 1992. It was joined later by the Association of the Churches of Christ in 1981 and the Congregational Union of Scotland in 2000.

As each new generation takes its place in leadership of the Church, so the challenge of ecumenical cooperation and understanding must be engaged afresh. Perhaps it is because ecumenical vision is the gift of the Spirit, one of the charisms of the Church, and from the days of St Paul until now, it must be fostered afresh in the witness, life and work of the building of God's kingdom. Perhaps there is also a dimension to human nature that always seeks to build its own empire, or that finds accepting difference and welcoming the other far harder than standing aloof.

Pastoral issues in Local Ecumenical Partnerships

Local Ecumenical Partnerships (LEPs) are now widespread in England, and comprise combinations of Anglicans, United Reformed Church, Baptists, Methodists and Roman Catholics. For instance, the Church of Christ the Cornerstone in central Milton Keynes embraces all five denominations, while Grange Park Church, Northampton, is an Anglican-Baptist only LEP. Many of the earlier LEPs were founded in the New Towns developed after the Second World War as a response to slum clearance and overspill. Stevenage, the first New Town (1947), provided pastoral care and mission in a combination of old historic parishes and churches, such as Bunyan Baptist in the Old Town (where I served as minister from 1992 to 1999), predating the New Town by some half a century, Holy Trinity Church, in whose parish Bunyan Baptist was situated, and the neighbouring parish of St Nicholas, and across the road from Bunyan, the Catholic Church of the Transfiguration. There were some new sole de-nomination churches developed with the New Town – the Parish Church of Stevenage, St Andrew and St George, Bedwell was one such, as was St Peter's Broadwater, but there were also Catholic and Longmeadow Free Evangelical Churches in this category – but in the new neighbourhoods the typical church was an Ecumenical Partnership: All Saints Church, Pin Green is Roman Catholic, Anglican and Methodist; Church of Christ the King, Symonds Green Roman Catholic, United Reformed Church and Anglican, and in Chells, St Hugh and St John was a Church of England and Methodist congregation and perhaps the most successful of all of these. The newest was planted in a current expansion phase in the Great Ashby area to the north of the town. This was a church plant from St Nicholas, Church of England, a parish of evangelical churchmanship, and Bunyan Baptist, with whom there had been long-standing cooperation. Great Ashby Community Church meets in a community centre, as opposed to the earlier generation of LEPs, which had their own purpose-built facilities, albeit with community usage.

The presence of churches with such differing ecclesiologies as congregational Baptists and episcopal Anglicans, with similarly varied baptismal policies, 'co-habiting' in the same local congregation raised significant pastoral questions:

- How are children to be regarded within the fellowship, especially in relation to the eucharist?
- How does the authority of the church meeting relate to the authority of the bishop?
- How are new clergy appointed, and what is the interplay between local call and denominational appointment?
- How do we recognize the growing numbers of men and women in LEPs who do not wish to be categorized as either Baptist or Anglican, but wish to be considered simply as members of such-and-such ecumenical church?

There are, of course, general ecumenical protocols to be followed, but new situations arise often, especially in a post-denominational age. The most recent framework for local ecumenical engagement agreed by the Enabling Group of Churches Together in England, *A Flexible Framework for Local Unity in Mission*,[2] seeks to offer a range of approaches ranging from working agreements (a set of agreed guidelines to enable a group of churches to work together in a particular project), through partnership agreements (which cover more extensive sharing of resources) and constitutional agreements, where a more formal and legal structure is required.

An example from Milton Keynes

In Milton Keynes these questions are raised in at least two forums: the local LEP and the shared oversight group, the Presidents' Meeting, consisting of the Anglican Bishop of Buckinghamshire, Baptist Senior Regional Minister (Central Baptist Association), Methodist Thames North-West District Chair, URC East Midlands synod moderator and the Roman Catholic Bishop of Northampton. This group also includes the Milton Keynes Mission Partnership's senior officer, designated the Ecumenical Moderator until 2012 and now the Director of Ecumenical Mission, who acts as its secretary. In this group, precedence is not afforded to any one tradition, all have equal responsibilities towards the Mission Partnership (the old Milton Keynes Council of Churches), and all equally share the funding of the Director. The chair is a revolving one-year appointment between the five denominational leaders. Issues such as the place of children at communion are debated by this group and their decision recommended to the Assembly of the churches for action. In this way shared oversight is given practical expression.

The Presidents Group uses consensus as its *modus operandi* and relies heavily on the quality of the relationships of the individual church leaders occupying the various roles of *episkope*, within the limits of canon law and denominational practice.

In particular, the responsibilities that cannot be shared by the Anglican bishop (such as confirmations), and the limits of authority exercised by the Baptist Regional Minister in the context of congregational government, place limitations on the degree of ecumenical overlap.

One of the interesting outcomes of those situations where the LEP is joint Anglican and Baptist is a readiness to value aspects of both traditions often weaker in single denomination churches. So the place of congregational decision-making is stronger than it might otherwise be in an Anglican parish, with a regular church meeting held, while the influence of the Regional Minister is stronger than in stand-alone Baptist churches, being institutionalized and structured in a way that ensures influence, as opposed to the voluntarist option that would otherwise be the case.

Episkope

At the level of wider oversight in ecumenical settings, two groups emerge as having significance in offering appropriate *episkope*. County Ecumenical Committees supply the more technical and legal oversight, often with a body in which the properties of shared churches are vested.

In the Diocese of St Albans, for instance, the LEPs that share property, such as Grove Hill Church, Hemel Hempstead, occupy buildings owned by Hertfordshire Shared Churches Ltd. Representatives of the denominations involved act as Directors and Trustees, including senior church leaders, such as an Anglican Bishop and a Baptist Regional Minister. Their task is not merely that of supervising property but also of monitoring the health of the congregations using the buildings.

Less 'hands-on', but perhaps more influential, are the Church Leaders' groups involved. Generally organized around the Anglican diocesan structures, or where a diocese is not co-terminous with a county, at county level, ignoring some unitary authorities as far too recent an innovation, these groups always include Anglican bishops, Catholic bishops, Methodist District Chairs, URC Synod Moderators and Baptist Regional Ministers; they usually also include Salvation Army Divisional Commanders. A few include Orthodox Metropolitans, Pentecostal leaders and new church apostles, but these are the exceptions.

It is in these peer group settings that ecumenical thinking takes place, new and strategic opportunities are discussed and, more generally, peer support is offered to those who share in the oversight of the churches, ecumenical or otherwise. These groups are not formal expressions of 'shared *episkope*', but to a limited extent they are practically so, and in the case of Milton Keynes Mission Partnership, actually so. Whether the Milton Keynes experiment is a blueprint for wider expressions of shared *episkope* remains to be seen, although it has rich potential to act as a model for elsewhere.

Convergence

One of the processes at work in ecumenical cooperation is an awareness of the degree to which some processes seem remarkably similar, even when they arise from different ecclesiological roots. Take the appointment of clergy, for instance. In Baptist churches, the responsibility for a call to a pastorate lies with the local congregational meeting. Candidates are commended by a National Settlement Team comprising Regional Ministers who carry settlement responsibilities, which attempts to match potential candidates for the pastorate of any given church to its expectations and churchmanship, but the decision to call lies not with the Regional Minister who exercises *episkope*, but the local church.

In an Anglican parish, adverts for a job are published in the Church press, or a parish calls for candidates from its archdeacon. It is the patron, together with the churchwardens, who offers the living, but often with wide consultation in the parish, and occasionally ecumenically. The process is different from that in a Baptist church, but remarkably similar in some respects, such as breadth of consultation and requests for nominations.

On the rights of access to a parish or Church Meeting, again similarities appear. A bishop does not possess absolute rights of access to a parish any more than a Regional Minister has rights of access to a Church Meeting, yet both have powers of dismissal and discipline, and both work best when oversight is welcomed by the clergy and parish, and offered in humility and with consultation.

The reality on the ground is of far more similarities than differences between Anglican parish life and a local Baptist congregation, which is not to minimize the outstanding dogmatic differences in areas of apostolicity, baptism, eucharist and ministry. If church leaders find much in common, then so do church congregations of similar theological outlook, with an evangelical parish probably having more in common from day to day with the local charismatic Baptist church than it does with 'St Hilda's', the liberal Anglo-Catholic parish across the town, which affirms same-sex partnerships and participates in multi-faith worship, both of which would be unthinkable in All Saints or Avenue Baptist Church!

The following diagram is intended to provide those exercising oversight with the necessary information to negotiate their way around the ecumenical landscape, and to situate their own responsibilities within it. It will range from the international instrument to the local congregation.

A national church denomination, such as the Church of England or the Baptist Union of Great Britain, will typically belong to its confessional group, a regional ecumenical instrument and the WCC. Conversely, individual churches or parishes will belong to their denominational structures – often with one or more intermediate structures, such as an Anglican diocese or a Methodist district at the larger scale, and a deanery or forum at a smaller – and to ecumenical bodies in their vicinity, such as a local Churches Together group. In addition, this local church may be in a Local Ecumenical Partnership, either as a group of congregations or as an individual multi-denominational congregation. Thus, the body that a translocal minister serves looks in both directions, to the larger national or international scene and to the local church. An awareness of both is necessary.

CONTEMPORARY MODELS OF TRANSLOCAL MINISTRY

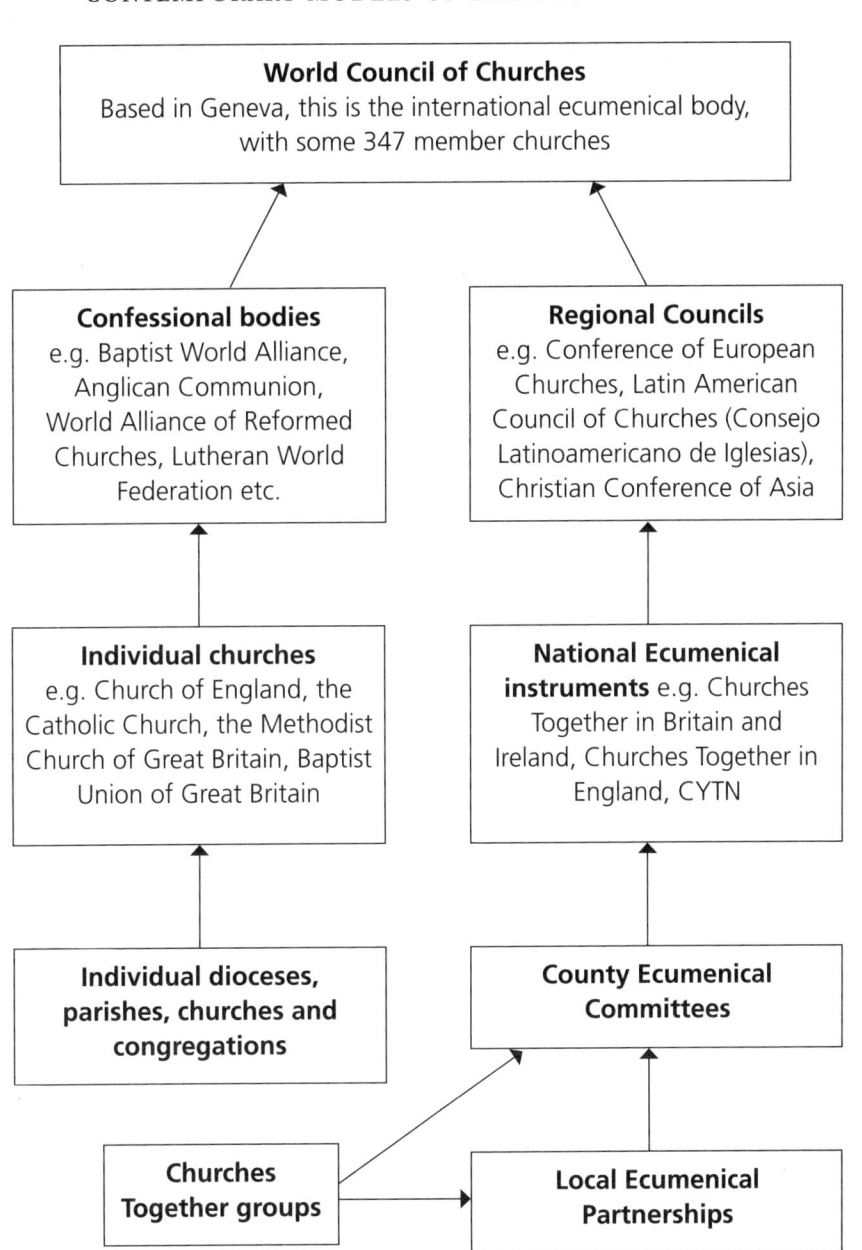

World Council of Churches
Based in Geneva, this is the international ecumenical body, with some 347 member churches

Confessional bodies
e.g. Baptist World Alliance, Anglican Communion, World Alliance of Reformed Churches, Lutheran World Federation etc.

Regional Councils
e.g. Conference of European Churches, Latin American Council of Churches (Consejo Latinoamericano de Iglesias), Christian Conference of Asia

Individual churches
e.g. Church of England, the Catholic Church, the Methodist Church of Great Britain, Baptist Union of Great Britain

National Ecumenical instruments e.g. Churches Together in Britain and Ireland, Churches Together in England, CYTN

Individual dioceses, parishes, churches and congregations

County Ecumenical Committees

Churches Together groups

Local Ecumenical Partnerships

Landscapes of oversight

We now explore the landscape of translocal ministry across its broad horizons. The nature of translocal ministry is shaped by three major factors: the function of that ministry, its personal or collegial character and the tradition in which it is exercised; this is further shaped by the ecumenical dimension that colours it. Here I will map the kinds of translocal ministry exercised in Britain today through function and tradition. It is the latter that contributors from various major traditions in the British church scene will describe from their own experience and understanding, and so the details of the ways translocal ministry is exercised will be left to the practitioners themselves. Here I shall seek to find patterns in the landscape, notice continuities and discontinuities and give the explorer of translocal ministry a map to assist the journey.

The varieties of translocal ministry are many. It is not just the kind of roles that comprise *episkope*, or translocal oversight, that are present, although these are the focus of this book. The term 'translocal' in its broadest sense means beyond the local. There ministry is exercised with responsibilities for the care of a parish or congregation, or the pastoral leadership of a local church. Translocal ministry, however, characterizes many forms of Christian ministry and service in the multi-faceted church in Britain today. I think, for instance, of a colleague in Baptist ministry, who, after leaving the local pastorate for a translocal post in sports chaplaincy, was appointed to two posts consecutively that could properly be termed translocal in parachurch organizations. Neither of these translocal posts comprised regional Baptist oversight of a group of churches – the role Baptists once termed the General Superintendency, and now call Regional Ministers – but they were clearly translocal in nature.

If 'translocal' were to be applied to any role that does not function in that most widespread of varieties of Christian ministry – the local pastor, minister or priest in charge of a church or parish, the role in which the majority of those called to exercise regional oversight will have 'cut their teeth' – then we might include those who are tutors in theological seminaries, those who travel widely with a parachurch organization or those who give national leadership to church, denomination or mission agency. So my story features local pastoral ministry, regional oversight (Baptist Superintendent) and then national leadership in denominational and then ecumenical contexts. Oversight comes in various guises and with a range of foci: some regional, some national; some wholly focused on such oversight, with others where it is an important feature, but not the main role in ministry.

Factors that distinguish translocal roles include the geographical scope (region, diocese or synod, for instance, or national and international in extent); function (regional/diocesan oversight, or another more specific role with, for instance, a parachurch organization); and focus.

Inevitably translocal ministry involves working in teams of various kinds. It may be that there are teams of men and women whose roles are similar, while others will work in teams of specialists. Even where oversight is focused on an individual bishop, for instance, they will be working in teams both within the diocese, where they may be the team leader, and at a wider national level, where the relationship is of peers under the leadership of another.

A second major factor is the nature of collegiality within the role. It is almost a given that every translocal role is in relationship with the whole church in some way, but whether that role is understood primarily in personal terms or collegial ones, and the way those two dimensions relate, adds further colour to the landscape. So one might say that within episcopal ecclesial structures, the authority of the bishop is a personal one. They hold the office personally, and the authority is primarily personal. However, in most cases, the office of diocesan bishop is accompanied by suffragan bishops, to whom some authority is delegated, and together with the archdeacons and other diocesan officers something of a collegial structure quickly emerges to offer the full scope of oversight of the diocese. The bishops themselves form a body in General Synod, The House of Bishops, that offers collegial *episkope* to the whole Church of England, with the Archbishops of Canterbury and York taking a lead both individually within their provinces and together in Synod:

> In the local church the bishop focuses and nurtures the unity of his people; in his sharing in the collegiality of bishops the local church is bound together with other local churches; and, through the succession of bishops the local community is related to the Church through the ages. Thus the bishop in his own person in the diocese; and in his collegial relations in the wider church; and through his place in the succession of bishops in their communities in faithfulness to the Gospel, is a sign and focus of the unity of the Church. (Archbishops' Group on the Episcopate, 1990, p. 160)

Most forms of oversight within the historic churches, both the Catholic and the churches of the Reformation, embrace a collegial character to a greater or lesser degree: the Synod moderators of the United Reformed Church, the District Chairs of the Methodist Church, Baptist Union of Great Britain Regional Minister/Team Leaders, the Catholic Bishops' Conference of England and Wales and its counterpart in Scotland, all share their national roles of oversight in a collegial fashion. There is even more collegiality where international oversight is concerned. The Lambeth Conference of 1988 resolved that:

> encouragement be given to a developing collegial role for the Primates' Meeting under the presidency of the Archbishop of Canterbury, so that the Primates' Meeting is able to exercise an enhanced responsibility in offering guidance on doctrinal, moral and pastoral matters.[3]

Associated with the question of collegiality is the nature of authority. Does authority reside in the person, or the college; can that authority be delegated, and what is the nature of the submission to that authority? Among those who exercise this oversight there is often a fantasy that others find it easier to exercise their role of oversight because their policies or their implementation can be insisted upon. This is nothing new. When those who exercise regional *episkope* in England meet in so-called Church Leaders' groups, it is assumed by those serving the more congregationally governed churches that episcopal governance is easier to insist upon. From an earlier generation of Baptist Superintendents, Henry Bonser, writing in 1949 as he retired, remembered:

> An Anglican bishop once asked me wherein a Baptist Superintendent differed from a bishop. When I replied, 'We have no authority,' he made the facetious admission, 'Between ourselves, neither have we.' I refrained from the obvious retort that we *claimed* none. (Bonser, 1949, pp. 172–9)[4]

I can recollect similar conversations half a century later. In fact, all such oversight depends largely on relationships of mutual trust and respect, and an Anglican bishop, despite oaths of obedience, can do almost as little with a recalcitrant priest as a Baptist Regional Minister with an awkward minister.

In addition to these large-scale structural patterns of functionality, collegiality and authority, there are small-scale, personal distinctives that shape the manner in which oversight is offered in the Church and in the context of the expectations and practices of each tradition. In some regards this will be simply the function that every translocal role of *episkope* demands, developed to a high degree. All are called to defend the faith, but some do so from a strength in apologetics. While all exercising oversight are called to guard the deposit of faith, some do so from the perspective of academic scholarship. 'Scholar bishops' such as Stephen Sykes, Rowan Williams or Tom Wright often find the demands of the administration of their office does not play to their best strengths, and all have returned to the academy, perhaps prematurely, seeking a return to the focus on scholarship before retirement. All three came to the episcopate following an outstanding academic career. This tradition is perhaps stronger among Anglicans than elsewhere.[5]

Others might be best described as missionary bishops, or overseers, either because of the pioneering character of their work (historically the great missionary bishops of the nineteenth century spring to mind, such as Bishop James Hannington, the first Bishop of Equatorial East Africa, martyred within a year of holding that office, aged 35), or because of the emphasis on the mission of the Church (in that regard one thinks of Bishop Graham Cray or the Baptist Regional Minister mission enablers).

Others have strengths in addressing wide issues of public policy, a focus most often seen among Anglicans such as the former Bishop of Oxford, Richard Harries, but also represented among those who hold national translocal roles among the Free Churches that are concerned with public policy – the Baptist Union's Faith and Society Team Leader or the United Reformed Church's Church and Society team.

Reading the obituaries of bishops soon reveals that it is the quality of the man that is remembered, not the office he held, and I believe the same will be true a generation hence, once we enter the period when women bishops' obituaries are also written. Those who are remembered with affection, or revered as examples to follow, are those who are wise counsellors, caring pastors and hard workers. These are the personal qualities that accompany the particular character of the varied role of oversight that an individual develops, be it scholarship, evangelism or political influence.

Notes

1 The document that established the new model, *Next Steps for Churches Together in Pilgrimage* (sometimes called 'The Marigold Booklet'), can be found at www.cte.org.uk/Publisher/File.aspx?ID=138030 (21.05.20).

2 The documents, the most recent of which is May 2019, can be found at www.cte.org.uk/Groups/257506/Home/Resources/Local_Ecumenism/A_New_Framework/A_New_Framework.aspx?redirected=1 (21.05.20).

3 For a fuller account, see www.anglicancommunion.org/resources/document-library/lambeth-conference/1988/resolution-18-the-anglican-communion-identity-and-authority?author=Lambeth+Conference&subject=Unity (accessed 21.05.20).

4 Bonser was General Superintendent for the North Eastern Area from 1923 to 1949.

5 Among the 2013 group of Baptist Regional Ministry Team Leaders, none had

come from the academy, nor had any completed a doctorate at that stage, although two were pursuing doctoral programmes, now successfully completed.

References

Archbishops' Group on the Episcopate, 1990, *Episcopal Ministry*, London: Church House Publishing.
Bonser, Henry, 1949, 'Recollections of a General Superintendent', in *Baptist Quarterly* 13.4 (October).
Fiddes, Paul, 1983, *A Leading Question: The Structure and Authority of Leadership in the Local Church*, Didcot: Baptist Union Publications.
Sutton, Roger, 2017 (ed.), *A Gathering Momentum*, Watford: Instant Apostle.
Wainwright, Geoffrey, 2002, 'Ut Unum Sint', in Lossky et al., *Dictionary of the Ecumenical Movement*, Geneva: WCC, pp. 1184–6.

PART 2

Experience

4

Anglican Episcopacy

The Ministry of Bishops in the Church of England

PAUL AVIS

If we were to stop people in the street and ask the question, 'What's the first thing that comes into your mind when I say the words "Church of England"?', what sort of answers would we get? I have not tried the experiment myself but many years of parish ministry have given me a shrewd idea of the answers our question might receive. The front runners would probably be 'the church in the High Street', 'the parish church', 'church bells', 'lovely weddings', 'our vicar', even 'the Archbishop of Canterbury' or the Queen, who is often said erroneously to be the 'head' of the Church of England. In cathedral cities some might volunteer the answer 'our cathedral', but I doubt very much whether many members of the public would say 'the bishop' or 'our bishop'.

Bishops are possibly the least visible element of the Church of England as an institution. What proportion of the population of any diocese could name their bishop? I suspect that the percentage is minute, except in the dioceses of the Archbishops of Canterbury and York. What percentage of people in any given diocese even know that there is such a thing as a bishop or what a bishop is for?

Yet according to the Canons of the Church of England, which are part of the law of the land, a bishop is bishop of all people within their diocese: 'the chief pastor of all that are within his (*sic*) diocese, as well laity as clergy and their father in God' (Canon C 18.1). Though rather unfortunately expressed, since in 1 Peter 5.4 Jesus Christ is called the 'chief shepherd', this is not a canonical claim to unique authority, to rule the population and to interfere in its life. It is couched in pastoral terms. The days are long past when, as for Richard Hooker in the late sixteenth century, all members of the nation were also members of the Church of England (though it was not quite true even then). Today, as numerous opinion polls remind us, Anglican churchgoers constitute only a tiny proportion of the population, though the active pastoral constituency of those touched by the Church's ministry, especially through the 'occasional offices' or pastoral services, is far larger. Of course, there are many Christians of other denominations, indeed of other faiths, as well as the vast swathes of the population that have only minimal or no contact with the Church and so remain 'unchurched'. So we have to say that 'all that are within his diocese' means all who acknowledge the bishop's ministry, all who are willing to receive the bishop's care, all who do not reject it. However, the old idea of a Christian commonwealth as an organic unity in which church and state were distinguishable in thought but not in life, still contains a kernel of truth. The diocese, like the parish, is a geographical area, not a gathered community. You can opt out of the bishop's care, but you do not need to opt in. Just as the good parish priest bears a pastoral concern for all within the parish and seeks as far as possible to offer Christian ministry to all who are willing to receive it, so the good bishop bears the care of the whole diocese on their heart.

In order to carry out the mission entrusted to the Church, for the sake of all people, bishops, along with all clergy and committed laity, need to be visible; they need to be known and to have a public identity, and that is not easy to achieve. They can be so busy doing the Lord's work that they do not have time to be seen much in public. Unless they are identifiable, recognizable and approachable, the work of bishops will be fruitless. 'Making the Church findable' is the first step. Bishops need to put themselves about, to project themselves on the public stage as an identifiable messenger of Jesus Christ, a living signpost to salvation.

Historical perspective

The ministry of a bishop in the English Church has varied and evolved through almost two thousand years. British bishops attended councils of the Church in the early fourth century (Arles, AD 314). Before the arrival in 597 of St Augustine of Canterbury, on an evangelistic mission ordered by Pope Gregory the Great, who believed that the English were still pagans, there were already bishops in these islands. They had come from the Celtic fringes of the land mass and they retreated back there as the Roman form of Christianity, with the support of kings, spread throughout the land. The Celtic bishops, such as St Cuthbert (c.634–87), were largely peripatetic. Cuthbert received vital support from the King of Northumbria, just as Augustine had the backing of Æthelberht of Kent, and Paulinus of Edwin of Northumbria. After the Norman Conquest, William the Conqueror made his trusted lieutenants bishops to help hold down the subject population. Notably, the bishops of Durham became prince bishops, secure in their castles and able to raise an army to repel the invading Scots.

Medieval bishops were landed magnates with a pivotal role in securing the territorial integrity and social and political stability of the nation, the Christian commonwealth. They were required to attend the king at court for part of the year. As Kaye (2018) demonstrates, the partnership of church and state, bishop and monarch, was not invented by Henry VIII but was typical of all medieval Europe, from Constantine the Great onward.

The civil role of bishops continued in the early decades of the Reformation; Henry VIII, Edward VI and Mary Tudor relied on bishops for political and diplomatic services as their predecessors had done. However, as Foster (2017) points out, Elizabeth I turned to civil lawyers and other civilian officers to fulfil this role. Throughout medieval times, bishops and abbots sat in the House of Lords, the abbots ceasing this function at the dissolution of the monasteries in 1536–41. Church of England bishops continued to hold considerable sway until the 1830s, having the palaces and retainers to enable them to do so. At this point, parliamentary reforms rationalized the ancient, creaking and sometimes corrupt institutions of the kingdom and repealed punitive legislation against Roman Catholics and Dissenters. The number of bishops increased in the late nineteenth and early twentieth centuries, following huge population growth in English cities. Suffragan bishops, appointed to assist diocesan bishops, were first introduced by Henry VIII following an ancient model, and were multiplied until quite recently.

Thus there is substantial historical precedent for several aspects of the role of Church of England bishops today: the diocese as the key unit of the church; the cathedral as the seat of the bishop's teaching and governing ministry (Avis, 2019); the bishop's responsibility in principle for all people within the diocese; a role in the unelected Upper House of Parliament; a special link with the sovereign, from whom they receive the right and responsibility to exercise their ministry within the realm – 'the Spiritualities' of their office. But notwithstanding the establishment of the Church of England by law, bishops now operate in a highly pluralist society and in what is a voluntarist culture. They have little executive authority – even within their dioceses they do not hold the purse strings and must work for results through discussion, example and reasoned persuasion.

The biblical and theological basis of episcopacy in the Church of England

What is absolutely primary in a bishop's ministry is shared with all clergy and indeed with all baptized Christians according to their specific calling within the royal, prophetic priesthood of the Church (1 Pet. 2.4-10), whether they be lay person, deacon, presbyter or bishop. Through baptism, and received by faith, all believers share in the Holy Spirit (1 Cor. 12.13). This is the Spirit of Jesus Christ's threefold messianic anointing as prophet, priest and king. This anointing qualifies and equips the Christian to proclaim the word of God (prophetic), to offer spiritual sacrifices (priestly) and to play their part in the work of the kingdom (regal). This threefold identity roughly matches the mandate given by Christ to his apostles in Matthew 28.16-20 to make disciples, to baptize and to teach, though the order is different. It also corresponds to the widely recognized triple task (or *munera*) of ministry: to preach the gospel to the unconverted and teach the faith to disciples; to sanctify the faithful through the sacraments; and to guide and govern the people of God (Mark 16.15-16; Luke 24.45-49; Acts 2.42). Bishops are, like all clergy, primarily ministers of word and sacrament and pastors of the flock (Avis, 2005).

However, in episcopally ordered churches, bishops have an extended responsibility of oversight. The Church of England's Canons (Canon C 18.4) describe the bishop as 'the principal minister' within the diocese and the one who celebrates 'the rites of ordination and confirmation' and who oversees the churches and chapels and the church services of parishes within the diocese, institutes to benefices and licenses clergy for ministry of a certain sort in a certain place. All this the bishop does as the outworking of their responsibility for oversight. To oversight also belongs the bishop's responsibility 'to teach and uphold sound and wholesome doctrine, and to banish and drive away all erroneous and strange opinions' and to promote unity, love and peace in the Church (Canon C 18.1).

So should a bishop in the Church of England be regarded simply as a priest with enlarged responsibilities in a two-order ministry – which was a respectable medieval view, held for example by St Thomas Aquinas? That tradition partly explains why the ordinal attached to the Book of Common Prayer (1662) referred to the 'Consecration', rather than the 'Ordination' of a bishop. Or should the episcopate be regarded as a third order of ministry alongside the diaconate and the presbyterate? In the Roman Catholic Church, it was only with Vatican II (1962–5) that the episcopate became formally recognized as a third order (*Lumen Gentium*,

21). But there is some truth in the medieval view because a bishop remains a priest or presbyter, just as both bishops and presbyters remain deacons. The Church of England holds, with all of catholic Christendom, that the 'character' of an order, once bestowed, cannot be lost, but is lifelong (Canon C 1.2). The *Common Worship* ordinal rather hedges its bets regarding the question, 'Two orders of ordained ministry or three?' It does not come down on one side or the other: the service for the making of a bishop is entitled 'The Ordination and Consecration of a Bishop'. The practice of the Church of England shows, as we shall see, that the episcopate is understood as a third order, but one that stands in continuity with the diaconate and the presbyterate. The Anglican understanding of holy order is sequential but not hierarchical: there are three full and equal ordained ministries. They are diverse callings within the one ministry of the Church of Christ. Of course, it is all too easy for priests to think of themselves as somehow superior to deacons and for bishops to assume that they are superior in some way to priests, but that would be contrary to the economy of the household of God. I recall David Jenkins, Bishop of Durham from 1984 to 1994 and at the time the best-known bishop in the Church of England, making a comparatively rare appearance in the General Synod and giving one of his tour de force speeches, in the course of which he commented, 'Some bishops seem to think they are important.' It was an uncomfortable moment. Each full and equal order has its specific calling, along with the responsibilities and tasks that belong to it.

In the teaching of the Roman Catholic Church, Christ's apostles are regarded as the first bishops, just as Peter is seen as the first pope (*Lumen Gentium*, 18). But where does the Church of England place bishops in relation to the apostles? Clearly, they are not witnesses of Christ's resurrection, as the apostles were, but there may be other threads of continuity, especially in teaching the apostolic faith and binding together the apostolic fellowship (Acts 2.42). The confirmation service in the Book of Common Prayer (1662) alludes to the example of the apostles in the book of Acts laying hands on the newly baptized that they might receive the Holy Spirit. It refers to 'these thy servants, upon whom (after the example of the holy apostles) we have now laid our hands, to certifie them (by this sign) of thy favour and gracious goodness towards them'. It continues: 'Let thy Fatherly hand, we beseech thee, ever be over them; let thy Holy Spirit ever be with them.' This minimal appeal to apostolic precedent is regrettably absent from the *Common Worship Initiation Services*, but given that the Book of Common Prayer (1662) is one of the 'historic formularies' of the Church of England and is to be looked to for guidance in Christian truth (Canon C 15.1), the implied link between the ministry of the apostles and that of bishops has a measure of authority.

The classic *Anglican Ordinal* (1550, 1662) that derives from Thomas Cranmer (Cummings, 2011, p. 622) states: 'It is evident unto all men diligently reading holy Scripture and ancient Authors, that from the Apostles (*sic*) time there have been these Orders of Ministers in Christ's Church; Bishops, Priests, and Deacons.' Though this claim is repeated in the Canons (Canon C 1.1), the matter is not nearly as obvious to modern scholars of the New Testament and the early Church as it was to the Reformers. Accordingly, the 'Introduction by the House of Bishops' to the *Common Worship* Ordination Services puts the emphasis on the Church's formal intention to uphold a ministry in continuity with that of the apostles, and nothing is said explicitly about the pattern of ministry in the apostolic Church:

> This [threefold] ordering of the Church's ministry has been shaped under the guidance of the Holy Spirit through the processes of human history, and the Church of England has maintained the threefold order of bishop, priest and deacon. Within that threefold order, bishops are ordained in historic succession (that is, in intended continuity from the apostles themselves). This is a sign of the Church's care for continuity in the whole of its life and mission, and reinforces its determination to manifest the abiding characteristics of the Church of the apostles. This is not to deny that other Christian traditions have an authentic concern for apostolicity or that they intend to express apostolic continuity in other ways, but some such sign of apostolic continuity is required for the full, visible unity of the Church.

In the Church of England today, and in the Anglican Communion more widely, there is little concern to validate episcopacy historically, least of all by *ius divinum* or divine right. The apostolicity of the Church does not pivot on episcopacy or 'apostolic succession' in a narrow sense: it is conceived to rest on a broader basis. In this statement of the House of Bishops the focus is mainly on the role of the episcopate in maintaining or cementing the unity and continuity of the Church in time and space.

The bishop in synod

The oft-quoted mantra that the Church of England is 'episcopally led and synodically governed' trips off the tongue all too readily. But it is misleading in two ways. First, bishops are not the only ones who lead. Lay people are not excluded from leadership, but in fact offer a lead at every level of the Church's life, from churchwardens in the parish through deanery and diocesan synod lay (co-)chairs, to the elected lay members of the General Synod, who have their own 'house' with its lay chair, the Archbishops' Council and other national bodies. Second, bishops also govern; they play their part in synodical government. The General Synod includes all the diocesan bishops and several suffragan bishops elected by their peers. They constitute the House of Bishops alongside the House of Clergy and the House of Laity. So bishops properly have a role in governance, as well as in leadership. Diocesan bishops also preside in their diocesan synod and, together with any suffragan or assistant bishops, comprise the House of Bishops there, alongside the other two houses. Thus, the phrase 'the bishop in synod' is more appropriate to describe the polity of the Church of England than the oft-quoted mantra mentioned above.

The whole body of the Church must ultimately carry responsibility for its life and mission. This is the key ecclesiological principle of the conciliar tradition of the whole Christian Church. Through councils and synods at various levels, the Church takes counsel with itself as it gathers around the open Bible and prays for the guidance of the Holy Spirit. In conciliarity the Church acts in a representative and constitutional way and seeks the consent of the faithful, through an open process of reception, for any decisions that it has reached. In episcopally ordered churches, the bishops have a pivotal role in the conciliar process. For the Church of England, this involves their participation in, and presiding over, their own diocesan synod and participating in the General Synod when it meets, usually twice a year. For all bishops of the Anglican Communion, it also means taking part in the ten-yearly Lambeth Conference at the invitation of the Archbishop of Canterbury and in the Archbishop's diocese and cathedral of Canterbury. While the Lambeth Conference cannot decide or legislate anything for the self-governing member churches, or provinces, of the Anglican Communion, historically it has passed resolutions that express its mind, and has issued teaching documents for the guidance of Anglicans. Because it is composed of bishops, who are ordained to have a special but not exclusive care for the faith and order of the Church, the Lambeth Conference has considerable moral and pastoral authority when it conducts its business in a responsible and careful manner. In my view, the Lambeth Conference is an estimable expression of the conciliar dimension of the Christian Church.

In the General Synod, matters may be brought forward for the synod's attention by a private member's motion or by resolution of a diocesan synod. But by virtue of their ordination, bishops, both individually and collectively, have a special but not exclusive responsibility for faith and order. This aspect of their oversight embraces doctrine, worship/liturgy and ministry. Thus under the Standing Orders of the General Synod, matters that come under those three headings may only be debated in terms agreed by the House of Bishops. It is as though the bishops come to the other two houses to consult with them and to seek their consent. In matters of importance, each of the three houses effectively has a veto; bishops do not 'call the shots' in the Church of England. If the bishops' proposals prove unacceptable to a majority of clergy and laity in the synod, the bishops must take the matter back for further reflection; they must think again. The bishops alone do not decide issues of doctrine, worship or ministry; only the General Synod, following the lead of the bishops, can decide and then speak for the Church of England.

Episcopacy and the ecumenical quest

Anglicans generally tend to have an ambivalent attitude to bishops, almost a love–hate relationship. They love the ideal of episcopacy, but sometimes strongly deprecate particular examples of it! Anglicans are wedded to episcopacy as an institution of the Church, but they are certainly not uncritical admirers of individual bishops. Within the Anglican tradition over time, there have been various views about the nature of episcopacy, ranging from high to low. However, the Anglican Communion holds, in accordance with the Lambeth Quadrilateral (1888, 1920), that the historic episcopate is necessary to the unity and continuity of the Church (Avis, 2010, pp. 116–40). But as the Quadrilateral itself states, the form of episcopacy may be 'locally adapted' according to the particular needs, in its context, of the church concerned.

Anglicans have never claimed, in their official teaching or in their ecumenical dialogues, that episcopacy is of the essence of the Church, so that without it there could be no Church. The many ecumenical agreements to which Anglicans are party, such as the Anglican–Methodist Covenant in the UK, show that Anglicans can formally recognize the ecclesial authenticity or reality of the ministries of word, sacrament and oversight within partner churches that are not ordered in the 'historic' or other forms of episcopate. Indeed, the two churches in dialogue, having established that each holds the faith of the Church through the ages on the basis of Scripture and the creeds, have been able to recognize the presence of the one Church of Jesus Christ in each other's churches. This recognition is the pivotal step that enables the two churches that are in dialogue to go forward into a relationship of full visible and sacramental communion, with future ordinations taking place within the economy of the historic episcopate.

In 1956, Archbishop Geoffrey Fisher, acknowledging that the conversations with the Free Churches, triggered by the 'Appeal to All Christian People' of the Lambeth Conference 1920, had become stuck, encouraged those Free Churches to 'take episcopacy into their system' and to 'try it out on their own ground' and then to come back to the Church of England so that two (now) episcopally ordered churches could then consider jointly and equally how to enter into communion (Carpenter, 1991, pp. 310–14). The proposals that have recently emerged under the Anglican–Methodist Covenant, which pivot on the idea of a President-bishop of the Methodist Conference, are a refinement of the approach that Geoffrey Fisher outlined nearly 75 years ago. The Joint Implementation Commission that was set up under the Covenant was encouraged to make that proposal by the fact that the Methodist Conference had stated many times, over many years, that it was willing in principle for the Methodist Church of Great Britain to accept episcopacy. The logic of the Covenant, as of all other approaches to ecclesial communion on the part of Anglicans in recent decades, completely avoids any hint of the (re)ordination of those not episcopally ordained. The key to the strategy, grounded on mutual recognition of ecclesial authenticity, is the possible incorporation of the existing ministries of a Church without bishops into the historic episcopate, within their own communion, by their own act, and according to their own ecclesiology and polity. Within this approach, the historic episcopate is regarded as an ancient and salutary form of the Church, just as the canon of Scripture, the ecumenical creeds and the sacraments of baptism and the eucharist are also ancient and salutary forms of it. To see the historic episcopate as an ancient and salutary form within the polity of the Church chimes in with the prevailing Anglican perception of episcopacy. In the Church of England, bishops are not idolized or obeyed uncritically or treated with undue deference, but they are honoured and respected and looked to for guidance and support as under-shepherds of Christ's flock.

References

Avis, Paul, 2005, *A Ministry Shaped by Mission*, London: T & T Clark.
Avis, Paul, 2010, *Reshaping Ecumenical Theology*, London: T & T Clark.
Avis, Paul, 2019, 'Towards an Ecclesiology of the Cathedral', *Ecclesiology* 15.3 (2019), pp. 342–54.
Carpenter, Edward, 1991, *Archbishop Fisher: His Life and Times*, Norwich: Canterbury Press.
Church of England, 1998, *Common Worship Initiation Services*, London: Church House Publishing.

Church of England, 2017, *Canons of the Church of England*; www.churchofengland.org/more/policy-and-thinking/canons-church-england (accessed 08.07.2019).

Cummings, Brian (ed.), 2011, *The Book of Common Prayer: The Texts of 1549, 1559, and 1662*, Oxford: Oxford University Press.

Foster, Andrew, 2017, 'Bishops, Church, and State, c. 1530–1646', in Anthony Milton (ed.), *The Oxford History of Anglicanism, Volume 1: Reformation and Identity, c. 1520–1662*, Oxford: Oxford University Press.

Joint Implementation Commission, 2008, *Embracing the Covenant: Quinquennial Report*, Peterborough: Methodist Publishing House; www.anglican-methodist.org.uk/embracing-the-covenant-0813.pdf (accessed 09.07.2019).

Kaye, Bruce, 2018, *The Rise and Fall of the English Christendom: Theocracy, Christology, Order and Power*, London: Routledge.

Pope Paul VI, 1964, *Lumen Gentium, The Dogmatic Constitution on the Church: solemnly promulgated by His Holiness Pope Paul VI on November 21, 1964*; www.vatican.va/archive/hist_councils/ii_vatican_council/documents/vat-ii_const_19641121_lumen-gentium_en.html (accessed 08.07.2019).

Taylor, John B. and Barry Rogerson, 2001, *An Anglican–Methodist Covenant: Common Statement of the Formal Conversations between the Methodist Church of Great Britain and the Church of England*, Peterborough: Methodist Publishing House; London: Church House Publishing; www.anglican-methodist.org.uk/common_statement0506.pdf (accessed 09.07.2019).

Further Reading

Avis, Paul, 2006, *Beyond the Reformation: Authority, Primacy and Unity in the Conciliar Tradition*, London: T&T Clark.

Avis, Paul, 2007, *The Identity of Anglicanism: Essentials of Anglican Ecclesiology*, London: T&T Clark.

Avis, Paul, 2013, *The Anglican Understanding of the Church: An Introduction*, 2nd edition, London: SPCK.

Avis, Paul, 2015, *Becoming a Bishop: A Theological Handbook of Episcopal Ministry*, London: Bloomsbury.

Avis, Paul, 2016, *The Vocation of Anglicanism*, London: Bloomsbury.

Avis, Paul, 2019, 'The Conciliar Tradition and the Anglican Communion', in Paul Avis, Angela Berlis, Nikolaus Knoepffler and Martin O'Malley (eds), *Incarnating Authority: A Critical Account of Authority in the Church*, München: Herbert Utz Verlag.

Avis, Paul, 2019, 'Lambeth 2020: Conference or Council', *Theology*, Volume 122 (1), pp. 3–13.

Davie, Martin, 2008, *A Guide to the Church of England*, London: Continuum.

Podmore, Colin, 2005, *Aspects of Anglicanism*, London: Church House Publishing.

Church of England Bishops as Pastor and Evangelist

STEPHEN COTTRELL

Let me start with a story. Earlier this year I did that thing that many bishops do; I put up a marquee in the garden and invited shedloads of people round for lunch day after day. One group were the retired clergy of the diocese. It was a way of saying thank you. Without them the Church of England could easily fall apart. Some of them arrived early. Very early. Too early. I looked out of my window at about ten o'clock and found several wandering round the garden. One passed on greetings from someone who had known me when I was a teenager. I vaguely remembered the person he was referring to. He said that they had expressed surprise when they heard I had become a bishop. 'Oh, did they!' I replied. 'Yes', he continued. 'They said you must have changed a lot.'

And yes, I suppose, I have changed a lot. But not in the way that phrase is usually used. I think I have become more myself. I think the Holy Spirit is changing me into the person I am meant to be. And for me, being a priest and now a bishop is part of that.

This is the first thing I want to say about episcopal ministry from an Anglican perspective: the ministry I have been called to is not something I put on in the morning and take off at night; it is a sacramental identity, part of what it means for me to be baptized, to be a follower of Jesus. But this is also the first thing I would want to say about the Christian faith: we, with our 'unveiled faces, seeing the glory of the Lord as though reflected in a mirror, are being transformed into the same image' (2 Cor. 3.18). Therefore, the main task of the bishop is to oversee the Church in such a way that it remains focused on the apostolic work that is the transforming power of the gospel itself. This is why the Church exists. It is not an institution that needs managing, but the community of men and women who have been impacted by Christ and who are now his presence in and for the world. Because it is such a large community, it requires organization. But this will always be subordinate to the first task and first love, which is the gospel itself and the way it draws people into community with God and with each other and is the sign, and at its best even the foretaste, of God's kingdom. However, if the organization and management of the Church breaks down, everything else breaks down as well. This is the reason, for instance, that safeguarding is so vitally important. It is also a good example of how the pastoral and the apostolic inform each other. The pastoral care of the Church requires the Church to be a safe place for everyone. Failings in this area will have devastating effects in the lives of vulnerable individuals. It will also do untold harm to the reputation of the Church, and rightly so. But getting it right is not only a good thing in itself but is a proclamation of the gospel, demonstrating that all are welcome – even offenders being carefully monitored and chaperoned.

The bishop is the one who has oversight of this Church and every aspect of its life and mission. The ministry of every bishop is, therefore, pastoral and apostolic. The bishop is called to be chief pastor and chief evangelist.

The pastoral ministry involves both the organization and management of the Church and the concern and care of its ministers, people and communities.

The apostolic ministry concerns both the safeguarding of the continuity of the historic and revealed Christian faith, and the communication of that faith in fresh and diverse ways through evangelism and mission. The Anglican ordinal puts it this way:

> Bishops are ordained to be shepherds of Christ's flock and guardians of the faith of the apostles, proclaiming the gospel of God's kingdom and leading his people in mission. (*Common Worship, Ordination Services*, p. 55)

Let us begin with the apostolic. The bishop is the one who ensures the unity and continuation of God's mission through the Church. The bishop ensures that the life and ministry of the Church in each place and time is the same as in every place and time. The bishop embodies and carries this apostolic vocation. But the ministry itself is something that belongs to the whole apostolic Church. The bishop therefore does not do all the ministry alone but builds up the body of the Church so that it can faithfully fulfil its vocation. This is particularly obvious when a bishop ordains new ministers, who in turn go out to teach and proclaim what God has done in Christ, or when, in the Anglican tradition, at the licensing of a new parish priest, the bishop says, 'Receive the cure of souls which is yours and mine.' The bishop is the one who holds together the unity and the continuity of the Church. The bishop is sending others out. That is what the word apostle means – to be sent. The apostolic Church is not merely the Church built upon the foundation of the apostles, but the Church that is sent out like the apostles.

When we do this we find ourselves compelled to translate the never-changing gospel into the constantly changing languages of a constantly moving culture. Our mission – or to be more accurate, our share in the mission of the apostolic God – always reveals new challenges. The culture in which we are set asks new questions of the gospel: this in turn requires new ways of communicating that gospel. We not only find new ways of communicating old truths, sometimes the gospel itself is expanded by the encounter and we find new truths for ourselves. Although the arguments over women bishops are not concluded in the Anglican Church and certainly not in the worldwide Church, in the Church of England it has been our experience that encounter with the questions being asked of us by those who saw in the gospel God's equal regard for women and men led us to find something new. The subsequent ordination of men and women as bishops has been a source of huge blessing. The bishop who is an evangelist will therefore also be a teacher and a theologian. And to be a good teacher and theologian means you must also be a good student and a good disciple.

In the New Testament we see the early Church growing for three interconnected reasons:

1. The credibility and intellectual integrity of the faith that was being shared;
2. The ability of faith to clothe itself in the various cultures it encountered;
3. The evidence in people's lives for the veracity and transforming energy of the gospel.

In other words, the work of evangelism (the making known of the gospel of Jesus Christ) was woven tightly together with apologetics (the reasoning, arguing and commending of faith) and spirituality (the lived experience of Christian life).

Open to new encounters, hungry and thirsty for what is right, this is the sort of holistic approach to evangelism that we should be nurturing in our Church and for our world. Incidentally, its emphasis on apologetics and catechesis as much as proclamation, make it a pastoral approach to evangelism that is well suited to the Anglican story and ethos. Bishops have a particular responsibility to teach, embody and encourage this ministry.

I think it was Billy Connolly who said there is no such thing as bad weather only the wrong clothes. It is the bishop who must see life this way; not just moaning about the weather but finding the right clothes for each new context. Therefore, one of the first responsibilities of a bishop is to be a messenger and an evangelist, the one who endlessly and constantly tells the story of what God has done in Christ. In my own episcopal ministry it is these opportunities that bring the greatest challenges and the greatest joy. Whether it is taking a school assembly, showing the children my mitre and explaining that I wear a flame on my head to remind the whole Church of our apostolic vocation and our Spirit-led mission, or speaking in the House of Lords on human trafficking, the bishop is the Christian voice for a region, always looking for opportunities to tell the Christian story and present the Christian world view as good news for individuals and good news for society. As we have noted, this is a theological task, understanding the gospel and interpreting it into the languages of the different cultures the Church serves, but also a creative task employing one's best gifts of wit and wisdom to winsomely present the story of Christ.

I do not much like the soundbite culture we live in, but if you pushed me into a corner and demanded one from me, I think I would say that for our culture at this particular time, it is that in Christ you can become yourself. You can be set free from the snares and temptations of a world that tells you that you are not good enough, not good-looking enough, not thin enough, not clever enough, not young enough, and find a new identity and become completely yourself as you are meant to be. The gospel message is that this is discovered in that communion with God which the death and resurrection of Jesus Christ makes possible. As teacher and evangelist this is the first job of the bishop.

Much of my ministry is spent working out how to tell this story, or actually doing it in many different settings. I try to see every opportunity to speak as an opportunity to say something about Christ and the Christian world view in such a way that those who listen will be intrigued, challenged and even delighted by the message of the gospel. The bishop is therefore not the Managing Director of Church of England plc but storyteller, poet and theologian. This is also why being a bishop is so dangerous. If we draw back from such an uncomfortable proclamation, we end up holding back the Spirit's sure advance into all truth.

Meanwhile, too many people still treat us with the wrong sort of deference and respect, and, believing our own publicity, we sometimes collude. The only way to save ourselves from this is through the disciplines of prayer that undergird and sustain every Christian minister. I know that as a bishop the most important thing I do each day is to pray. Each day begins with the Office. I also know that this life of prayer is constantly being destabilized by my own weaknesses and the assaults of those dark forces that only want to drive me away from God and therefore away from my truest and best self.

This aspect of the Christian life must probably be emphasized above all others and must be evident in the bishop's own life and ministry. Inseparable from the call to evangelize is the call to prayer, which is the call to enjoy the company of God. Evangelism happens when the truth and compelling beauty of Christ is evident in the life of the one who proclaims. The apostolic Church is also the holy and catholic Church, called into community with God and community with each other. Effective evangelism always flows from the wellsprings of love, affirmation and forgiveness that we receive through the relationship with God that we have in Jesus Christ. We give from the overflow of what we receive. As we become a people of prayer the veracity and transforming energy of the gospel is evident in our lives. The bishop must live this out.

Attempting to describe to his clergy what sort of ministers we need to be, and how we might see what this gospel says to the people we serve, that celebrated teacher of the faith, Gregory the Great, drew on a strong, but often neglected biblical theme, of God's minister as sentinel. This word is not actually used of a bishop in the Anglican ordinal – though it is of a priest. Gregory said this:

> A sentinel always selects a high vantage point in order to be able to observe things better. In the same way, whoever is appointed as a sentinel for a people should live on the heights so that he can help his people by having a broad perspective. (Atwell, 1995, p. 183)[1]

This seems to me to be hugely significant for a bishop's ministry. What are we looking at? Where do we go? To whom do we speak? What is our perspective? What demands attention? And what is it we choose to ignore? Are we just going to be a Church for those gathered in; or, once again, a Church for all the world? There is also a strong prophetic element to this vocation. We are called to bear witness to what the world could and should be, not just minister to what is. In my own ministry as a bishop this has led me to stand alongside Irish Travellers in Dale Farm near Basildon whose site was being cleared by the local council; to support those who protested against the illegal deportation of asylum seekers; and to celebrate the eucharist outside the gates of Faslane as part of a united witness against the proliferation and expense of nuclear weapons. These actions made me enemies as well as friends. I am not saying I have always got it right. But in every case my action was about bearing witness to what the world could be. It was the work of a sentinel, seeing and interpreting through the lens of the gospel.

These aspects of episcopal ministry are gathered up for me and embodied in the act of blessing. This is another one of those things that in the Anglican and Catholic traditions of episcopacy are reserved for the bishop, if the bishop is in the building. So, for instance, at Choral Evensong in the cathedral I may just sit in my chair for most of the service, while other members of the body play their part in reading and interceding, in singing and expounding, but the bishop alone declares God's absolution and gives the blessing at the end. It is a significant and an emblematic act. It is also a very beautiful thing to do, requiring generosity and discernment. Judgement and sensitivity are required about what to bless and, I suppose, about what not to bless. And when blessing is given, the whole Church, represented by the bishop, is asking that God's goodness and God's abundance rest upon and flow into that person, or even that thing. I happily bless all sorts of people and all sorts of things: the people of God at the end of worship; people in the street; those on the edge of death and those charging into life; a new toilet in a village church; a school extension; a social housing estate; a child's buggy, but in each case I represent the blessing of the Church and I bless in the name of God. Through the act of blessing I demonstrate God's involvement with and blessing upon the world in all its glorious complexity and challenge.

In Marilynne Robinson's book, *Gilead*, the hero, the Reverend John Ames, says this: 'I became a minister not for any of the usual reasons, but because it gave me the opportunity to confer blessing.' He says that is one of the advantages of being a minister – 'It's a thing people expect of you.' Not that you have to be a minister to confer blessing, you are simply much more likely to find yourself in that position (Robinson, 2004, p. 275).

As my colleague Roger Morris, the Bishop of Colchester, has commented: 'What a beautiful way of understanding our role. We exist in order to confer blessing.'[2]

Of course, we often make mistakes, we bless the wrong things, or withhold blessing from the right things. Right now in the Church of England, much of our internal discussion centres on whether same-sex unions should be blessed or not. We are divided on what the answer to this question should be.

Similarly, we fail in many other ways to present the gospel winsomely or coherently. In the same homily quoted above, Gregory goes on to reflect painfully on his failings as a minister, not least the very public demonstration of failure when our actions do not match our words:

My preaching is mediocre, and my life does not cohere with the values I preach so inadequately. I do not deny that I am guilty, for I recognise in myself lethargy and negligence.

It is this honesty, humility and aspiration that church leaders need more than anything. For to be a sentinel – a contemplative watchman for the Lord – is, to quote Sister Isabel Mary SLG, 'hard, combative and boring' (Eyre, 1992, p. 58); it is not to detach yourself from the world but to stand on the heights and survey the world in all its joys and horrors, interpreting the world to the Church and the Church to the world warning of danger when everyone is feeling safe, and proclaiming the victory of Christ when everything looks and feels defeated. This is why a bishop is a bishop for the world, just as much as for the Church. We are the identifiable presence of Christ in the public square. If we only look and sound like managers, the Church is in big trouble. But if we speak from the wellsprings of what we have received; if we dare to be sentinels standing on the heights and surveying the world, then we will have something to say that will speak to the heart of the world. Bishops like Desmond Tutu have achieved this. But many do not.

We cannot all be Desmond Tutu, but Gregory's wisdom does not permit him to wallow in his own shortcomings, and nor must we. After all, if this were the case, every bishop would run screaming from the cathedral agreeing that some terrible mistake had been made as soon as the Archbishop uttered these words at the consecration service:

> Remember always with thanksgiving that God has entrusted to your care Christ's beloved bride, his own flock, bought by the shedding of his blood in the cross. (*Common Worship, Ordination Services*, p. 63)

No one is equal to the task of episcopal ministry. Not in our own strength or with our own resources. That is why the declaration continues, 'pray for the grace and power of God ... pray you may be more and more conformed to the image of Christ.'

Gregory further reflects in his sermon, 'Perhaps my very awareness of my feelings will gain me pardon from a sympathetic judge.' That judge is Christ himself, the one to whom we shall render account for our stewardship of the Church.

This leads me to my second and final point: the bishop as pastor. As chief pastor the bishop is concerned for the right ordering of the Church and for its discipline.

Good leadership also requires good administration. I believe doing this efficiently is itself a mark of good pastoral care. This encompasses all the many aspects of the Church's life, which need to be cared for and developed. However, most of these, from book-keeping to canon law, will be managed by those with particular expertise. The bishop may have some of these skills, but the overarching gift must be the gift of presiding and conducting. The bishop must be the person who conducts the great orchestra of the Church in such a way that no one instrument dominates, that all are heard and properly employed, and that there is harmony and balance. Along with 'sentinel', another key biblical word that undergirds this ministry is 'steward'.

The place where the bishop is most obviously the one who stewards and conducts is at the eucharist. Whenever the bishop is present the bishop must preside, because the bishop is the sign and safeguard of the Church's unity. This is very visibly embodied when the bishop stands at the altar, supported by the clergy and surrounded by the whole Church. And the eucharist itself is the place where we discover our profound unity and belonging with each other, and where impairments in that unity are healed: 'though we are many we are one body, because we all share in the one bread.' In my own episcopal ministry my favourite service of the year is the Eucharist for the Blessing of the Oils on Maundy Thursday, where deacons, priests and bishops also reaffirm the commitments they made at their ordination. As I gather with the clergy of the diocese, I see them as my congregation, the people to whom I have a special responsibility to lead and serve. And yet we stand as equals around the table. We have our different roles and responsibilities, but we are one by sharing the one bread.

So, finally, the bishop is the vicar for the vicars. The bishop is the one who must love and care and understand the people they serve, and who knows them self well enough to build a team where the gifts and abilities they do not possess are lived out in the body of the Church. This vision of ministry belonging to the whole people of God must be the guiding principle and motivation for episcopal ministry. Let me quote Gregory one last time:

> What kind of sentinel [and we might add what kind of pastor, what kind of evangelist] am I? I do not stand on the pinnacle of achievement; I languish in the pit of my frailty. And yet although I am unworthy, the creator and redeemer of us all has given me the grace to see life whole and an ability to speak effectively of it.

That is a wonderful image for episcopal ministry: to be given the grace to see life whole and an ability to speak effectively of it.

What is it like being a bishop in the Church of England? Well, 90 per cent of it is joy. It is joy to confirm those who have come to faith and hear the stories of how God is at work in their lives; it is joy to find doors of opportunity open into so many parts of life that would remain closed to most other ministers; it is joy to preside at cathedral ordinations and lay hands upon those who will further the agency of the kingdom.

But there is also horror. Failures in safeguarding; financial challenges; dealing with those who misbehave; and just the sheer unrelenting busyness of keeping the show on the road all take their toll. There are many days when I feel unequal to the task and want to run away. I cannot climb that mountain of emails, still less meet the huge expectations and projections that people pile upon me. Sometimes I find I have to say to myself that it is a good thing that these are the Bishop of Chelmsford's problems, not mine. But although it is right and healthy to keep some emotional distance between myself and the episcopal office I hold, there is certain inevitability in the Christian life that if you wish to share the joys of ministry you must also bear the sorrows. So I do take my work home with me. Many of the insuperable challenges I face live inside my head. I have not grown the thick skin others told me was necessary for the task. I still hurt and, strangely, I am not really sure I want it to be different. Wounded healers are usually the more effective ministers.

So let me finish with another story. One of the many King Louis of France – I cannot remember which one – used to sign himself Louis of Poissey. There were many other grand titles he could have used, and when asked why he used this one he said that Poissey was the place where he was baptized: he considered it his greatest honour.

I love being a bishop, but it is not what defines me. That is my baptism, and, since water is thicker than blood, I am confident that the Christian story of barriers broken down, of unity with each other and with God made possible, is worth living for and the only hope for the world. At the moment I do this as a bishop in God's Church, that high and holy calling to lead and pastor the Church and tell the Christian story. But one chapter of life leads to another.

Notes

1 Gregory the Great, *A Servant of the Servants of God*, Homilies on Ezekiel 1, 11, 4—6. In Atwell's version the word 'sentinel' is rendered as 'watchman'.

2 Roger Morris, sermon for Chrism Eucharist, preached at Chelmsford Cathedral, Maundy Thursday, 18 April 2019.

References

Atwell, Robert, 1995, *Spiritual Classics from the Early Church*, London: Church House Publishing.
Church of England, 2007, *Common Worship, Ordination Services, The Ordination and Consecration of a Bishop*, London: Church House Publishing.
Eyre, Richard, 1992, *Faith in God*, London: Darton, Longman & Todd.
Robinson, Marilynne, 2004, *Gilead*, London: Virago.

Church of England Bishops as Religious and Civic Leaders

JAMES JONES

It is not exactly a secret, but it happens behind closed doors. It is never broadcast. It is an ancient ceremony that lies at the heart of our unwritten constitution. The closed doors are to be found deep in the portals of Buckingham Palace. The ritual involves the Queen. The other principal participant is dressed in black and white. Kneeling on the footstool before the sovereign with only two others present (the Home Secretary and the Clerk of the Closet), with praying hands enfolded by the monarch's own ungloved hands, the supplicant does homage to Her Majesty and declares in no uncertain terms 'that no other foreign prelate or potentate has any jurisdiction within this realm'. This is the oath of homage performed by every newly appointed diocesan bishop in the Church of England. It is enunciated line by line by the Home Secretary, repeated by the bishop and takes about 60 seconds in all. Here is the full text.

> I, James
> Lately Bishop Suffragan of Hull
> Having been elected Bishop of Liverpool
> and such election having been duly confirmed
> Do hereby declare
> That your Majesty is the only Supreme Governor
> of this your Realm
> In Spiritual and Ecclesiastical things
> As well as in Temporal
> And that no foreign prelate or potentate
> Has any jurisdiction within this Realm
> And I acknowledge that I hold the said Bishopric
> As well the Spiritualities and Temporalities thereof
> Only of Your Majesty
> And for the same temporalities

I do my homage presently to Your Majesty
So help me God
God Save Queen Elizabeth

Laying aside the origin and history of the oath, which dates back to the sixteenth century, the significance is plain both ecclesiastically and politically. Henry VIII clearly had the Pope in his sights as he sought marital freedom to secure a male heir, and Elizabeth I obviously worried about the threat to national security posed by Philip II of Spain, one of the Pope's European lackeys.

In the Coronation Oath, in addition to the sovereign eschewing political and religious interference, the unique and privileged settlement of the Church of England 'established by Law' is assented to (Maer and Gay, 2008, p. 8):

Archbishop: Will you to the utmost of your power maintain the Laws of God and the true profession of the Gospel?

Will you to the utmost of your power maintain in the United Kingdom the Protestant Reformed Religion established by law?

Will you maintain and preserve inviolably the settlement of the Church of England, and the doctrine, worship, discipline, and government thereof, as by law established in England?

And will you preserve unto the Bishops and Clergy of England, and to the Churches there committed to their charge, all such rights and privileges, as by law do or shall appertain to them or any of them?

Sovereign: All this I promise to do.

It is a truism to say that our unwritten constitution is always in a state of transition as society evolves. Indeed, it could be argued that its unwritten nature is a virtue as it allows for nuance and shades of meaning to evolve and change without too many clashes that come from challenging principles and ideas written in stone.

What many people, and indeed many lawyers, do not appreciate is that ecclesiastical law is the law of the land and that Canon 7 of the Church of England, which is headed 'of the Royal Supremacy', states that 'the Queen's excellent Majesty acting according to the laws of the realm, is the highest power under God in this kingdom, and has supreme authority over all persons in all cases, as well ecclesiastical as civil.' In this way the monarch is identified and affirmed as the one who unifies the spiritual and temporal aspects of national life within the constitutional framework. Of course, it raises the question of how this can be so in an age when the spiritual life of the nation is more pluralistic than it was in the sixteenth century, and it presents a challenge for the next Coronation Service, which must blend the Christian essence of the service with a more diverse nation and commonwealth.

For me, the acknowledgement in the oath of homage that 'I hold the said bishopric as well the spiritualities and temporalities thereof only of your Majesty' is fundamentally important and merits deeper examination.

Without going into too much technical detail, 'the spiritualities and temporalities' of 'the bishopric' cover all the material, spiritual, pastoral and juridical responsibilities of the bishop in their diocese. And for this we need to know that there is not a square inch of England that is not covered by one of its 42 dioceses or one of its parishes.

The parish system of the Church of England gives expression to a particular understanding of God and his world. The kingdom of God is not just the Church. It is the world. Whether people believe in him or not, God is sovereign and rules over the world. The pastoral care that priests exercise extends to all who live in the parish and not just to the gathered congregation.

The same principle applies to the ministry of a bishop. Although bishops have oversight both juridical and pastoral of the churches in their diocese, their pastoral care is not limited to church members but extends to all people of all faiths and none within the diocesan boundary. Thus, bishops exercise a civic leadership and engage in affairs that affect the welfare of the region. It is their rootedness in the realities of local communities that gives them their authority when members of the House of Lords. In the Upper Chamber they speak as 'Lords Spiritual' not just on ethical and religious issues but on the full range of topics, from education to the environment. All this flows from their theological understanding of the 'spiritualities and temporalities' for which they did homage to the sovereign.

This can prove irksome to some, especially when the bishops emerge as critical of a particular stance because of its impact on those for whom the bishop is responsible pastorally. Their critics might tell the bishops to stick to God and to stop meddling in politics. They might even quote Jesus saying, 'My kingdom is not from this world' (John 18.36). If that quote were true it would fly in the face of everything else Jesus did and taught, not least in the Lord's Prayer, which pleads for God's will to be done not only in heaven but also on earth. In fact, the quote is taken from the trial and the exchange between Pontius Pilate and Jesus. It is about sovereignty and jurisdiction. Pilate thinks he has the power of life and death over Jesus. Jesus defies him, 'You would have no power over me unless it had been given you from above' (John 19.11). In the clash between the two, Jesus emphatically asserts an alternative perspective in which the source of his authority is higher than Pilate's. It is from above. This does not mean that Jesus denies the validity of Pilate's own jurisdiction. Far from it; in effect he lays the foundation for a Christian understanding of the state, which is later developed by St Paul in his letter to the Romans (13.1–4).

> Let every person be subject to the governing authorities; for there is no authority except from God, and those authorities that exist have been instituted by God. Therefore whoever resists authority resists what God has appointed, and those who resist will incur judgement. For rulers are not a terror to good conduct, but to bad. Do you wish to have no fear of the authority? Then do what is good, and you will receive its approval; for it is God's servant for your good. But if you do what is wrong, you should be afraid, for the authority does not bear the sword in vain! It is the servant of God to execute wrath on the wrongdoer.

It is remarkable that these letters were written when Nero was Emperor of Rome. In spite of his brutal persecution of Christians, which would lead to Paul's own imprisonment and execution, Nero and his state officials are seen not just as public servants but 'God's servants'.

This high view of the divine ordinance of the state does raise fundamental questions about what you do when the state behaves in an immoral and oppressive way. However, putting that to one side, for now it is sufficient to acknowledge that this does underline how Christians have viewed those in authority and recognized the providence and purpose of God in the sovereignty of the monarch in Parliament. In particular, it has informed my own understanding of the role of bishops and their relationship with the sovereign, with Parliament and with the state.

If that is a more formal theological and institutional understanding, I have also personally found the issue of justice a key and compelling one in my own experience. One of the first phrases to come 'out of the mouths of babes and sucklings' is 'That's not fair!' Whether this is nature or nurture, it shows that at an early age there is a capacity to frame a moral proposition.

It makes me believe that together with the instincts for survival, sex and food there is also a moral instinct whereby we intuit right and wrong. I believe this instinct is universal although it may well be undeveloped in various cultures at different times. Human progress is measured by the approximation of humanity to those absolute values of which justice is among the principal ones. Although you do not have to be a believer in God to subscribe to such absolute principles, people of faith see God as the locus of these values. It seems to me that the calling of the Church is to help people trace back from their moral intuition to the divine source and especially to the figure of Jesus Christ, who personified these values of justice and mercy. Justice is one of the pillars of the Christian faith, and it lies at the heart of mission and with those charged with its episcopal leadership and engagement with wider society.

If justification by faith and doing justice represent the two sides of the coin of Christian mission, each expressed by the evangelical and liberal traditions of Christianity, then it was going to Hull as its Suffragan Bishop in 1994 that enabled me to begin to make connections between the two. I remember at my interview with Dr John Habgood, Archbishop of York, being asked about the differences between the two traditions. The evangelical tradition from which I came was very good at definitions, I said, but that once you had read one book about a theological idea you had read them all; whereas the Liberal tradition it seemed to me was about the imagination and exploration beyond the boundaries. The Archbishop said he thought the liberals could do with more definition; I replied that I thought evangelicals could do with more imagination.

My own imagination was to be stretched within months of arriving in Hull. On Easter Sunday 1995, through the extraordinary ministry of a church community worker and at her invitation, I took the service in the church on the Longhill Estate, one of the most challenging in Europe. A young girl called Stacey had written two prayers, which she read at the end of the service. Six weeks later she was murdered when someone set her house on fire. The family asked me to take her funeral. Without breaking pastoral confidences, all that I had learnt thus far about faith and ministry turned to dust in my hands as I tried to minister to the family and to the community. But the whole experience left its mark on me and shaped my ministry in Hull and Liverpool. What was evident was that when it came to fairness, Stacey did not share the same opportunities and privileges as my own children. In terms of justice it was intuitively manifest that the world in which Stacey was born and died was anything but fair.

In both Hull and Liverpool I threw myself into the regeneration of the cities which, like most northern cities, suffered from urban diabetes. The blood pumps around the heart of the city with its prestigious buildings but fails to reach the extremities of the outer estates, which atrophy and die. I came to see that the key to regeneration is to unblock those arteries and get the blood and the money circulating around the whole body. To do this you need to engage and empower local people, but there is so much that militates against their involvement.

The language itself reveals the problem. Those who live in communities use organic language like planting, seeds and branching out. But those who control the purse strings use not organic but mechanical language like triggers, levers, buttons, start-ups and outputs. I was asked to chair the New Deal for Community programme in Liverpool and soon discovered with the people that you cannot prescribe mechanical solutions to organic problems.

In both Hull and Liverpool the words of Jesus that resonated with me were those he wept with as he looked over the city: 'If only you knew the things that made for peace.' What blights areas of challenge is low self-esteem and low aspiration. But if justice is about levelling the playing field, especially for children and young people, how do you even out esteem and aspiration? Justice requires both intervention and immersion. They are the two dynamics of the incarnation, and both require imagination. We have to put ourselves in the shoes of the other and try to see the world through their eyes.

John McIntyre, in *Faith, Theology and the Imagination* (1987), says that imagination was the prelude to the incarnation. It is only because God could imagine what it was like to be traumatized by sin and evil that he sent his child Jesus into the world. This is both the inspiration and the pattern for Christian engagement. It is why I value the Church of England's understanding of the kingdom of God and of its mission in its parish coverage. We believe the kingdom of God is the world and not just the Church. When a person rings up a vicar for help, she's not asked if she comes to church, but where she lives. If she lives in that corner of God's kingdom covered by their parish, the vicar is there for her. It's called the cure of souls.

This national presence in every parish is the unique contribution of the Church of England to the mission of God. But the centralizing of funding and of decision-making about mission may well put at risk this universal presence. Making congregations pay for their own clergy and controlling mission initiatives could well eventually withdraw funding from areas of challenge unable to sustain a Christian presence.

Historically it has been the Church that has remained faithful to communities abandoned by the banks, shops, pub, schools and surgeries. Where people have suffered from consolidated poverty, low self-esteem and low aspiration, it has been the Christian community of laity and clergy who have valued them. Their intervention and immersion in a neighbourhood has voiced God's presence. By their deeds they have spoken of God's requirements of all who would follow him 'to do justice, to love mercy and to walk humbly with God' (Micah 6.8).

In talking about justice there is a real need to understand what exactly we mean when we use this majestic idea. Throughout the Bible we find episodes where people act unjustly. For example, in the Old Testament David steals Bathsheba the wife of Uriah the Hittite and conspires to kill him, and is censured by Nathan the prophet for the injustice of his adultery and murder. In the New Testament, Jesus tells a parable about the injustice of an unjust judge who will not grant justice to a widow. In all the cases of injustice it is about damaged relationships needing to be restored. Justice is relational.

Lactantius, a fourth-century Christian apologist from North Africa, offers a definition: 'The whole point of justice consists in our providing for others through humanity what we provide for our own families through affection' (Bowen and Garnsey, 2003, 6.12.31). This is to set the bar at a very high level, not least because 'families' in this context would have meant the extended family and tribe. But in my ministry, both in Hull and Liverpool, I have seen Christians of every denomination seek to serve their local communities with that degree of commitment. They live out daily the imperative of Jesus, 'Seek first the kingdom of God and his justice.' It is when we are seen righting wrongs that the Christian faith becomes credible and real to ordinary people, not least because in each person there is this moral instinct and innate hunger for fairness.

These theological and ecclesiological sketches expound the basis upon which I entered into and contributed to public life in Liverpool and beyond and through, for example, chairing the Hillsborough Independent Panel.

When a community allegedly finds itself failed by the police, the press, politicians, Parliament and even the judiciary, to whom do they turn? The Church of England, for all its own failings and shortcomings, has through its pastoral care and social justice programmes a reputation for seeking the welfare of the people. That was the context in Liverpool when I was approached to chair the Panel (Jones, 2017, pp. 3–10).

I remember with the announcement of the setting up of the Panel by the Home Secretary in 2010 that questions were asked regarding why it was being led by a bishop and not a judge. Independent Panels are *ad hoc* and *sui generis*. In other words, there is no formula. I believe that it was what the Panel found on the pathology of the 96 victims that more than anything else led the Attorney General to appeal to the High Court to quash the original verdicts and order fresh inquests. The day after the longest inquests in British legal history returned their determination of 'unlawful killing', the Home Secretary, Theresa May, announced in the House of Commons that she was asking me to work with the Hillsborough families to write a report for Parliament based on their experiences so that their 'perspective should not be lost'. Reflecting on the methodology of the

Hillsborough Independent Panel, a number of things occur to me regarding the role of a bishop as its chair.

The Panel interrogated documents, not people. Its terms of reference were shaped by the families' long-standing concerns and questions but were not defined by these because the Panel had to maintain its independence and had to be free to go wherever the documents led us. We had three objectives: to secure maximum possible disclosure of all documents from nearly 100 stakeholders, to research and analyse them and to write a report that added to public understanding of the disaster and its aftermath. In effect, through the documentary interrogation we sought to establish whether there was a case for anyone to answer.

Halfway through our work we began to form a picture and scratched our heads wondering how it had come to this. The way the families of the 96 and the survivors had been treated amounted to the patronizing disposition of unaccountable power.

Our terms of reference called on the Panel to engage with the families. The Panel members were all expert in their own fields of data access and protection, police procedures, medical knowledge, coronial courts, academic research, media practice. We were served by a secretariat of extremely dedicated civil servants headed by Ken Sutton, whose outstanding initiative and leadership set the course for our work. Regular consultations with the families and survivors drew them into the process, and although we were candid from the start about not disclosing any details of our progress until the end, we heard some say, 'This is the first time we've been listened to … the first time anyone has taken us seriously.' Where Enquiries can often leave victims feeling alienated because of barristers, costs and timescale, a Panel can affirm their centrality to the process.

Although it was never specified in my appointment, I found myself continually drawing on my own pastoral experience both with the families and survivors and also with the Panel as we encountered deferred grief, soured relationships, sublimated guilt, mental distress and anguish and anger aggravated by two decades of frustration. When outsiders wondered why there were three groups of families and a large number who wanted no contact at all, I offered the observation that many marriages do not survive grief, so why should friendships?

My own work with the families continued after the Panel concluded its work as I chaired a forum that enabled them to meet with the Crown Prosecution Service, the Independent Police Complaints Commission and the Police Investigator to understand the process whereby the Crown Prosecution Service would decide whether to bring charges. These meetings took place in the spirit of Article 2 of the Human Rights Convention, which recognizes the right to life and the legitimate interests of the family of a loved one, allegedly killed by the state, to be included in the process of investigation.

A further arena in which bishops gain experience of, and expertise in, the law is the House of Lords in its role as a legislative chamber where Bills are debated and amended. The hours and days spent in committee stage open one's mind to the complications of drafting and applying legislation. It is where the Upper Chamber excels. Members bring the experience and expertise of their profession to bear upon legislation, which makes it a much more effective revising chamber than the House of Commons with its more partisan nature.

As well as contributing to the legislature, the bishops also exercise a pastoral and liturgical role in the House of Lords. In the decade I spent as a member, there were many occasions when peers would confide in you as a parishioner would do their priest. And a surprisingly large number would come to Prayers in the Chamber that begins each day. When the Law Lords sat in the House and gave their judgements, prayers were brought forward. The Order Paper was ominously headed 'Judgement Day' and right underneath it printed the name of the duty bishop! I recollect that when the Supreme Court was established, I and another bishop wrote to the President suggesting the tradition of prayers should be continued. The offer was declined! I recall the response referred to the Annual Judges Service at Westminster Abbey and to the fact that there were now other faiths in the land.

This raises the question as to how long the Church of England can maintain its special relationship with the state expressed in that phrase 'by law established'. Significantly, the challenge comes more from atheists and secularists than it does from other faith leaders, who appreciate the role the Church of England plays both locally and nationally in bringing together the different faith communities and enabling their leaders to share the platform in public life. I had direct experience of this both in Liverpool and in my role of Bishop to Prisons. When it came to the appointment of the present Chaplain General there were moves within the Ministry of Justice to open the post up to people of other denominations and faiths. What is little known is that the 1952 Prison Act specifies only three posts for a prison: a governor, a medical officer and a Church of England priest. I argued that given the responsibility for recruiting, training and deploying Anglican clergy there was in effect 'an occupational requirement' for the Chaplain General to be an Anglican. But what was most significant is that the support for this position came from the leaders of other faith communities. They recognized that it was the leadership of the Church of England Chaplain General that had paved the way for ministers of other faiths to minister in prison on an equal basis. In many prisons now the leader of the chaplaincy team is often of a different denomination or faith.

As mentioned in a previous chapter, the unique role of the Church of England as convenor and enabler of all faiths is articulated in the words of its own Supreme Governor when in her Jubilee Year in 2012 she spoke at a reception at Lambeth Palace hosted by Archbishop Rowan Williams and attended by the faith leaders of the UK:

> ... we should remind ourselves of the significant position of the Church of England in our nation's life. The concept of our established Church is occasionally misunderstood and, I believe, commonly under-appreciated. Its role is not to defend Anglicanism to the exclusion of other religions. Instead, the Church has a duty to protect the free practice of all faiths in this country.
>
> It certainly provides an identity and spiritual dimension for its own many adherents. But also, gently and assuredly, the Church of England has created an environment for other faith communities and indeed people of no faith to live freely. Woven into the fabric of this country, the Church has helped to build a better society – more and more in active co-operation for the common good with those of other faiths.[1]

The Queen was reinforcing the point made by the Prince of Wales, who sees his future role as 'Defender of the Faith' as the protector of the rights of all people to practise their faith freely. The interventions of the Queen and the Prince of Wales are part of that evolution of the constitution of Great Britain. I have no doubt that we will see further developments when it comes to the next Coronation.

It is interesting to reflect that the more I entered into the work of the Hillsborough Independent Panel the more it resonated for me with so much of what Jesus taught about justice, not least in the parable of the unjust judge in Luke 18.1–8:

> Then Jesus told them a parable about their need to pray always and not to lose heart. He said, 'In a certain city there was a judge who neither feared God nor had respect for people. In that city there was a widow who kept coming to him and saying, "Grant me justice against my opponent." For a while he refused; but later he said to himself, "Though I have no fear of God and no respect for anyone, yet because this widow keeps bothering me, I will grant her justice, so that she may not wear me out by continually coming."' And the Lord said, 'Listen to what the unjust judge says. And will not God grant justice to his chosen

ones who cry to him day and night? Will he delay long in helping them? I tell you, he will quickly grant justice to them. And yet, when the Son of Man comes, will he find faith on earth?'

At the twenty-seventh and last Hillsborough Memorial Service at Anfield I spoke about the parable and how I had read it every day for three months prior to publishing our report.

When I got to that point of the story and pointed out that although the widow's plea for justice was rejected by the unjust judge, *she would not give up*, the widow's dignified defiance connected with the 27-year struggle of the families for justice and accountability and the whole stadium of over 20,000 people burst into applause.

On my way home that night I could not help reflecting that here were thousands of ordinary people cheering the words of Jesus that resonated with their own deepest longings. In that moment I also felt frustration at all the talk of living in a 'post-Christian culture'! No. Here were people cheering a Jesus who championed their own innate sense of fairness and justice. The only reason society might be deemed post-Christian by the Church is because the Church becomes sub-Christian when it fails to address the dreams and dreads of the human family in the light of God's requirement for justice and mercy by preferring its own internal agenda.

This chapter is drawn from the content of two lectures: A Journey Around Justice. The Ebor Lecture 2016, delivered at York St John University on 23 November 2016, and Jurisdiction within this Realm, The Harry Street Lecture 2016, delivered on 10 November 2016 at the University of Manchester School of Law.

Note

1 www.royal.uk/queens-speech-lambeth-palace-15-february-2012 (accessed 26 June 2019).

References

Bowen, Anthony and Peter Garnsey (trans.), 2003, *Lactantius*, Liverpool: Liverpool University Press.
Jones, James, 2017, 'Hillsborough and the Church of England', *Theology* 120.1.

Maer, Lucinda and Oonagh Gay, 2008, *The Coronation Oath*, Standard Note: SN/PC/00435. London: House of Commons Library.

McIntyre, John, 1987, *Faith, Theology and the Imagination*, Edinburgh: The Handsel Press.

Translocal Ministries in the Church of England as Institutional Leadership

JULIAN HUBBARD

In an age that mistrusts organized religion and its institutions, the kind of translocal ministries that characterize the Church of England need some explanation if not justification, both within and beyond the Church. In short, no church can avoid having institutional elements in its life and its ministries. They are inevitable and necessary, but admittedly a risk in a body whose true citizenship (*politeia*) is in heaven (Phil. 3.20) and whose end lies in the kingdom rather than earthly power. Nonetheless, institutions remain vital for churches as a way of staying true to themselves and their purposes across time and places.

As a Church with long history and wide scope, the Church of England comprises a range of translocal ministries, institutions and organizations. The structure has grown by long accretion and contingent historic requirements. It presents a complex, overlapping picture, of which this chapter is a sketch and not a full portrait. Further detail on the history, law and structures of the Church of England is found in Chandler (2006), Davie (2008), Hill (2018) and Podmore (2005).

Preceding chapters focus particularly on bishops. This chapter describes how this translocal oversight is extended to others, through the roles, structures and institutions of the diocese and national Church.

What does translocal mean in the Church of England?

The word translocal translates into three words: episcopal (belonging to the bishop), diocesan (belonging to the diocese for which a bishop is responsible) and national. The two historic fundamental units of the Church are the diocese and the parish. The historic institutional significance of the parish should not be underestimated (Snell, 2006, p. 14). These are not merely units of administrative convenience: they reflect what the Church of England believes about itself as part of the catholic church and as shaped by the Reformation.

In terms of institutional identity, the Church of England is an episcopal, national, territorially based local Church, established by law, practising priestly ordination, governed by canon law in the Western Catholic tradition and established by the law of the land, reformed in its liturgy and church government with full lay participation, holding to the authority of Scripture, reason and tradition, open to the fresh interpretation of the gospel in the present day.

Put more simply, it is axiomatic that the Church of England ensures a presence in all communities across England. It is inextricably linked to the nation and committed to the common good. It is part of the wider Church across the world. Its translocal ministries sustain the Church of England in that identity.

Translocal ministries in a diocese

A diocese is the geographical area and family of churches where the bishop is principal minister in worship, mission, governance and pastoral care. All ministry is shared and commissioned by the bishop as guardian of the gospel and in succession to the apostles. So all translocal ministers are appointed or licensed by the bishop. This reflects one gospel, one baptism and one body, symbolizing the call to serve together in obedience to Christ.

The diocese is governed through the diocesan synod, which the bishop chairs jointly with an elected lay chair, effectively the diocese's leading lay member with a translocal leadership role. The synodical system is represented at national (General Synod), diocesan and deanery levels and has three houses or parts, namely bishops, clergy and laity. It is the main translocal representative body in the diocese and reflects a Reformation principle of the joint responsibility of clergy and laity for governing the Church.

The translocal ministry of archdeacon

The most senior translocal ministers in the diocese after the bishop are the archdeacon and the dean. Historically, the archdeacon's role was in church courts and jurisdiction over diocesan property. It is now concerned with organization of parishes and local ministries, care of churches and parsonages, care of clergy and matters of discipline and law across the geographical area of the archdeaconry. The archdeacon participates in diocesan strategic leadership, being widely engaged throughout the archdeaconry, visiting churches, clergy and churchwardens, facilitating and advising on plans and problems. Formal and legal responsibilities are therefore balanced by commitment to the Church's progress in mission and evangelism. Archdeacons must be priests, so preaching, leading worship and pastoral care are integral to their office.

They also have an official role in legally prescribed procedures for complaints and clergy discipline. This has created difficulties since it tests the working relationship between clergy and archdeacons in their disciplinary rather than a collegial or pastoral role. It highlights the need for archdeacons to be acutely aware of role. It reflects interestingly on translocal ministry in practice: distance can be a help in enabling all sides to fulfil their responsibilities.

Archdeacons work collegially, but some matters are for them to decide and judge personally in their role. So integrity, transparency and diligence are at a premium. While not principally a mission role, it is key to health and growth in local churches, with a large measure of what St Paul the apostle described as 'the care of all the churches' (2 Cor. 11.28, KJV).

The dean of a cathedral

The dean of the cathedral in a diocese has, besides overall responsibility for the cathedral, a translocal ministry both in the diocese and in the local area and community, including its institutions and organizations. Cathedrals are centres for worship, diocesan learning events and celebrations, where local meets translocal and a diocese's unity in Christ and its catholicity are experienced and realized. The dean symbolizes these alongside the bishop.

Cathedrals hold cultural and historic significance for a city and county, with high potential as places of welcome and meeting. Their regional economic and social value can be significant. So the dean's translocal ministry has several senses: with people from a range of localities at a focal point; people of all faiths and none, whose commitments are in a different 'place'; people with needs, seeking faith, quiet or pastoral care or wanting to move to a different place in their lives. Cathedrals as locations and spaces have great spiritual potential, which draws people in a fascinating instance of translocality.

The diocesan chancellor and registrar

A diocese works within the system of church or canon law, as well as civil law. Each diocese therefore has a chancellor, a judge within the diocese, and a registrar providing legal advice to the diocese, its clergy and other officers. The chancellor and registrar are not formally ministers but their work is bound up with mission and pastoral concerns. So both are required to be members of the Church and in some cases are ordained.

Like archdeacons, they are increasingly involved in establishing new forms of ministry and church, such as Fresh Expressions and new congregations. Their legal work frequently concerns territory and place, and their involvement can appear to slow down or frustrate new projects. Experience and greater familiarity on both sides are helping to ease this. However, if a project is to be part of the wider Church, properly accountable with public presence like other local churches, it needs a sound and durable basis.

The structures of diocesan translocal oversight and governance

Diocesan synodical structures bring local churches together; and similarly, episcopal structures draw in clergy and leading lay members to extend the oversight exercised by the bishop. This includes the archdeacon and the dean, and also vicars, incumbents or rectors with oversight of churches and other clergy. Among these, area or rural deans are appointed by the bishop to be *primus inter pares* among the clergy and to chair the deanery synod.

Deaneries originated as medieval administrative subdivisions of a diocese, which also grouped clergy for mutual support and learning in a chapter (it met to read a chapter of Scripture). The current role of area deans draws them into strategic planning in the diocese alongside traditional roles of pastoral care and leadership. In some cases, proactive area deans engage in work for change and renewal across the deanery through deanery plans.

In addition to these five historic roles, a range of other diocesan ministries and forms of service have developed. The framework of dioceses was reset in the nineteenth century's 'great diocesan revival', described by Burns (1999) as an era of major church expansion and diocesan improvement. Diocesan staff now cover a range of professional expertise meeting legal requirements over finance, property, human resources and data and safeguarding compliance, and supporting translocally mission, ministry, evangelism, community development, inter-faith work, social responsibility and faith development in local churches. Substantial diocesan work in education and church schools also often creates translocal networks across its area.

Translocal ministries in the national church

The concept of a national Church is problematic. The term can mean the Church that historically provides for the nation its civil religion and some of the symbols of its cultural identity. Within the Church of England, it also means the dioceses collectively and its national bodies and institutions. All three meanings contribute to its national translocal ministries.

The House of Bishops is the national body for episcopal oversight, comprising all diocesan bishops and some suffragan (assistant) bishops. It exercises collective oversight of worship, doctrine and ministry in the Church of England. It is also one of the three houses of the General Synod, where it shares in oversight of governance, finance and strategy for the Church of England. A formula expresses this arrangement: the Church episcopally led and synodically governed, with bishops present in Synod.

The two Archbishops exercise institutional rather than organizational leadership: there is no organizational hierarchy that gives them overall management of the Church of England. They ordain new bishops as a sign of their authority as Archbishops. *Ex officio* they preside and chair in Synod and other bodies. They exercise pastoral care towards bishops and support them through advice, guidance and discipline, if required. Paradoxically, the lack of management responsibility means more freedom as translocal leaders. When invited, they visit, encourage and inspire dioceses and communities not as the organization's CEO but apostolic missioners, evangelists and teachers, and Christians with their fellow believers.

National church institutions

There are five national church bodies. The Pensions Board oversees the assets and payment of church pension funds. The Church Commissioners oversee financial and property assets and liaison with government. There are secretariats for both Archbishops at Lambeth Palace and Bishopthorpe.

The Archbishops' Council oversees the executive work of national staff in areas largely corresponding to the work of diocesan staff. This supports the translocal ministries of bishops and others and provides guidance for dioceses to help the Church of England maintain a common standard or a common mind across dioceses where needed.

Current challenges in translocal ministry

Those entering translocal ministries now face significant challenges in their role. It is widely perceived that institutional translocal ministries are part of a dying covenant and a decaying organized Church destined to give way to a breakdown of structures and renewal, releasing energy for mission. This is partly pragmatic, about the cost and resources required to sustain current structures. There are also more profound reasons for this shift in perception, and good grounds to question it as a programme.

Changes in church and wider culture

It is common to recognize low levels of trust in society around established institutions. Whatever the cause, the effects are evident in social attitude surveys. These attitudes extend to organized religion. The Church of England has seen rapidly reducing levels of confidence and affiliation in the population (Lee, 2014). Generic mistrust is enhanced by changes in religious attitudes favouring personal autonomy and choice rather than adherence to denominational doctrine and practice. A significant minority still relates with institutional belief (Stolz et al., 2016, p. 54), but atomization seems a settled feature in English society.

The Church of England has followed other organizations in developing communications to address this popular mood through greater informality and transparency. Operating in a critical environment has influenced the public style of translocal leadership. However, changes in English religiosity pose deeper challenges for a Church that is institutionally linked to the nation.

Identity, history and the present

There is a widespread view that societies presently exist in a post-Christendom context in which national churches have lost legitimacy and should redefine themselves around their own perception of their mission, not around the features of historic establishment. There is an opposing view, which sees the structure of establishment, both high and low, as a framework and discipline for a Church that, in the remark often attributed to William Temple, is the only institution that exists primarily for the benefit of those who are not its members.

The conflict between these views unearths major theological issues about the Church that are unresolved. A feature of life for Church of England translocal ministers is that they rarely find themselves operating from a clear systematic basis. They need to 'work out salvation in fear and trembling', and in engagement with received institutions embodying what the Church of England is in itself and is for in the life of the nation. Part of their necessary equipment is an understanding of institutions, how they function and change, and how to exercise institutional leadership.

Faithful improvisation

The term 'faithful improvisation' has been popularized through debate around church leadership ignited by the recent initiative to improve organizational and management capacity among bishops and deans (Alexander and Higton, 2016). The focus has been on the agency of leaders. It should be extended to the institutions they lead, to the song not just the singer. The reality for translocal ministers is that what they inherit, including the still present and significant debris of Christendom, is a given with which they must engage. It is like working intelligently and skilfully with an existing building from several architectural periods rather than constructing on a greenfield site.

The contribution of institutionalism theory

In this debate, organizational categories have predominated and reflection on institutions is underdeveloped. Theory from the 'new institutionalism' (Peters, 2019 and Lowndes and Roberts, 2013) might have been invented to help bodies like the Church of England understand what is happening to, in and around them.

Current theory broadens the definition of institutions from formal, legally constituted bodies like schools, government or churches, to include less formal and tangible elements such as rules, norms, practices and narratives. These express for communities, groups or organizations their meaning, culture and history, 'who we are and what we do'. They provide channels and familiar pathways, and act as a powerful constraint on decisions and actions. They have a degree of stability and 'stickiness', and resist sudden change; equally, as the cumulative product of decisions and actions, they are dynamic and subject to evolutionary or occasionally revolutionary change. So while the language of institutions may suggest conservatism and reaction, in fact it implies constant change and reframing.

Comparative features of organizations and institutions

The distinction between organization and institution is problematic in terms of theory (Scott, 2014, p. 182). For example, an organization can be described as an institution, such as a school. In other cases, institutions exist within an organization in the form of rules or practices. In brief, an organization is defined as a group gathered for a particular purpose and organized according to roles, resource allocation and time-framed objectives. An institution is custom, tradition or practice of long standing that gains authority, sometimes taking concrete form as law or the organization established to sustain an institution.

A Church includes both organizations and institutions. Translocal leaders need the skills that belong to each, and the fundamental relational skills to lead the Church in its primary category as a community. An organizational leader is concerned with the efficient performance of the task, the effective use of scarce resources and the fulfilment of objectives. This leader relates to others as fellow members of a workforce or, in the case of other organizations, as potential partners, competitors or features of the operating environment.

Institutional leadership

An institutional leader is concerned with the identity and integrity of an organization or community over time, its alignment with its founding purposes and the change needed to stay true to them. This leader is a guardian, example and representative (or apologist) for the institution. Institutional leadership has political, social and cultural elements, whereas organizational leadership aligns more with the economic, managerial and entrepreneurial.

It is mistaken to depreciate one of these forms of leadership or place them in rank order. They are complementary but can conflict. For example, one of the distinctive features of institutional leadership is the authority given to what is inherited and not to effectiveness only. Thinking institutionally has a moral element: it entails respect for custom and practice, and attentiveness to its meaning for others and the future

(Heclo, 2007, p. 4). Faithful improvisation observes the cardinal rule of jazz improvisation, which is to listen.

Institutional leadership is also political. It sees members of the Church as citizens of the divine society and not a workforce. In this case, the role of institutional leader is to protect the character of the community as a judging body and not merely a source of labour to get the job done. The political culture of churches is often weak: the temptation of organizational leadership is to exploit this, and the institutional leader needs to resist. In a Church where complexity, diversity and localism are increasing, and the capacity of central organizations to control is reducing, a purely organizational approach will have diminishing returns.

The hidden cost of organization

It is a feature of applying organizational methods to churches that they tend to alienate and exclude non-members. The hardening of roles, boundaries and accountabilities is counter-productive, even when the Church is being organized precisely for the purpose of mission (Thung, 1976). An institutional approach to leadership mitigates this, which is crucial for the Church of England, an institution that exists for the people of England rather than its congregations. Institutional leadership maintains public presence and responsibility, outward relationships and open borders.

Institutional failure and renewal

Mistrust of institutions is at times richly deserved. Institutions can instantiate prejudice, abuse and injustice. 'Who we are and what we do around here' may reflect unexamined, ignorant or simply dishonest attitudes to difference, the exercise of power or disregard for the vulnerable, which translate into policy and practice. It is hardly necessary to quote examples in the Church around racism, disability, gender, sexuality and sexual abuse. The role of institutional leaders here is complex: they simultaneously represent and stand over against the institution, as part of both the problem and the solution. Public judgement is rightly severe in the cases of child sexual abuse, where the gap between espoused and inhabited values became glaringly obvious. The problem is not merely organizational or structural but cultural and institutional.

Despite the current tendency to talk the Church of England down and to make it small by focusing on decline and an organizational response, it remains a large and complex institution with a significant set of institutions within it. As Dulles' classic survey of models of the Church shows, the institution may not be primary, but it is an inalienable, albeit problematic model (Dulles, 2019, p. 38). Inhabiting a bureaucratized, liberal democratic society requires the Church to face the responsibilities of its institutional existence, while keeping true to what Jesus gave and taught us, and what we have learnt since. Good institutional leadership is crucial in this context, and a key aspect of translocal ministry in the Church of England.

References

Alexander, Loveday and Michael Higton, 2016, *Faithful Improvisation: Theological Reflections on Church Leadership*, London: Church House Publishing.
Burns, Arthur, 1999, *The Diocesan Revival in the Church of England c.1800–1870*, Oxford: Oxford University Press.
Chandler, Andrew, 2006, *The Church of England in the Twentieth Century*, Woodbridge: Boydell Press.
Davie, Martin, 2008, *A Guide to the Church of England*, London: Bloomsbury.
Dulles, Avery, 2019, *Models of the Church*, New York: Doubleday.
Heclo, Hugh, 2007, *On Thinking Institutionally*, Boulder, CO: Paradigm.
Hill, Mark, 2018, *Ecclesiastical Law* (4th edition), Oxford: Oxford University Press.
Lee, Lucy, 2014, '12. Religion: Losing Faith', in *British Social Attitudes 28*, www.bsa.natcen.ac.uk/media/38958/bsa28_12religion.pdf (accessed 19.11.2019).
Lowndes, Victoria and Mark Roberts, 2013, *Why Institutions Matter*, Basingstoke: Palgrave Macmillan.
Peters, B. Guy, 2019, *Institutional Theory in Political Science: The New Institutionalism* (4th edition), Cheltenham: Edward Elgar Press.
Podmore, Colin, 2005, *Aspects of Anglican Identity*, London: Church House Publishing.
Scott, W. Richard, 2014, *Institutions and Organisations* (4th edition), Thousand Oaks, CA: Sage.
Snell, K. D. M., 2006, *Parish and Belonging: Community, Identity and Welfare in England and Wales 1700–1950*, Cambridge: Cambridge University Press.
Stolz, Jorg, Judith Könemann, Mallory Schneuwly Purdie, Thomas Englberger and Michael Krüggeler, 2016, *(Un)believing in Modern Society: Religion, Spirituality, and Religious–Secular Competition*, Abingdon: Routledge.
Thung, Mady, 1976, *The Precarious Organisation*, The Hague: Mouton.

5

The Roman Catholic Church

Theological Dynamics for Understanding the Roman Catholic Episcopate in Britain

JACOB PHILLIPS

Introduction

As for each of the Christian denominations discussed in this book, the history, understanding and contemporary practice of Roman Catholic translocal ministry in the UK are unique and particular. In terms of origins, the official history cites the arrival of St Augustine of Canterbury on the shores of Kent in 597, sent by Pope St Gregory the Great to evangelize the Isles of Britain. After 597, episcopal structures of some form were in place under the ecclesiastical governance of the See of Rome. Augustine was the first Archbishop of Canterbury, and the governmental structure he began grew and held sway until his eventual successors underwent the full break with Rome during the sixteenth century. From 1688 there were no Catholic dioceses in Britain, meaning it was classed as 'mission territory'. Translocal ministry in this period took the form of four 'Apostolic vicariates', where leaders act on the direct authority of Rome as envoys, not as bishops of dioceses or archdioceses. Such is the case in modern-day Syria or Turkey, for example. The Apostolic vicariates ended in 1850 after the Catholic Emancipation act, when Pope Pius IX re-established the Catholic hierarchy with the Papal Bull *Universalis Ecclesiae* (Universal Church) promulgated in 1851. Pope Leo XIII then re-established the episcopate in Scotland in 1878, and so the broad picture of Catholic translocal ministry in Britain is twofold: with the Bishops' Conference of Scotland having the two archdioceses of Glasgow and St Andrews and Edinburgh, and six dioceses. England and Wales now have five metropolitan archdioceses: Westminster, Southwark, Cardiff, Birmingham and Liverpool, and 17 dioceses.

This snapshot indicates the peculiar historical trajectory behind today's structures of Catholic Church governance. The contemporary situation accentuates this distinctiveness further. This chapter focuses on two contemporary circumstances: that British society is religiously plural in the first place; and that it evinces a marked secularity in the second. On the first point, there are not only different religious faiths here but a vibrant plurality of Christian traditions, as witnessed by this volume. This makes life very different for a UK bishop compared to one in, say, Italy, or Poland. On the second point, Britain is also undergoing a significant decline in religious practice, particularly among the more 'indigenous' and formerly Christian members of the population. Translocal leaders thus minister to regions with growing numbers of people opting out of church life or knowing nothing of the Church at all. Bishops are often therefore faced with the challenge of explaining their existence and its rationale against the background of a relatively unsympathetic British media and, occasionally, an equally misunderstanding popular mindset.

This intertwining of secularity and religiosity makes the work of any Christian translocal minister in Britain unique, and for Catholics this uniqueness is rendered more acute by the peculiar trajectory of Catholicism having once been the established Church, before living through a period of rupture from political authority, and now in good standing with the civic order, yet constitutionally separate from it. It is rare for a Catholic episcopate to operate alongside an established Protestant Church with its own diocesan structures, especially considering that many members of the Church of England understand their community to be in continuity with pre-Reformation English Christendom. To understand the Catholic episcopate, then, it is necessary to unpick its theological underpinnings in order to explore some key dynamics at play in this historically complex situation.

In what follows, we shall outline salient aspects of a paradigmatic presentation of episcopacy provided by the early Apostolic Father St Ignatius of Antioch, and then explore these aspects through the writings of the former Bishop of Munich and Freisling, Joseph Ratzinger (later Pope Benedict XVI). Ignatius' writings often provoke certain concerns that could also apply to our contemporary situation. The first concerns are intra-ecclesial – misgivings about the immense importance that Ignatius apportions to bishops. Exploring this issue in some theological depth brings out certain core elements to the Catholic episcopate, particularly regarding its relationship with the ultimate seat of translocal (universal) leadership in the See of Rome. Exploring this vexed issue promises to help in understanding today's Catholic episcopate, particularly in relation to civil authority and other Christian traditions. The second concerns are extra-ecclesial – arising from the strongly institutional tenor of Ignatius' work. This institutional focus raises questions about the orientation taken by bishops to the world 'outside' the Church, especially in a situation of widespread secularity where the institution only has jurisdiction over a small minority, however grand its claims might be. On both fronts Ratzinger's writings provide resources for articulating helpful theological responses, so that contemporary Catholic translocal ministry can be brought into clear relief.

The Antiochene Paradigm

St Ignatius of Antioch provides a well-developed theology of the episcopate early in the Church's history.[1] While he does not spell out the key doctrine of apostolic succession, he does offer a remarkably full iteration of the office of bishop, which remains authoritative today. Indeed, he is cited far more than any other Apostolic Father in the Catechism of the Catholic Church (Clarke, 2016, p. 240, n. 43). At first glance, Ignatius' writings seem the least likely place to look for understanding today's episcopate. His approach has long been classed as 'monarchical', suggesting close analogues with earthly, political power, for the word comes from the Greek 'arche', meaning origin or power, and 'mon-', meaning one, as in 'one of power' or ruler. By giving those charged with spiritual or supposedly divine authority a name closely related to the exercise of political authority, this monarchical approach seems guilty of just the sort of 'institutional deification' that makes people suspicious of strongly hierarchical ecclesiologies (Clarke, 2016, p. 230, n. 17). These suspicions surround the dangers of giving fallible human creatures an unwarranted authority, assuming people subject to weaknesses like greed and ambition can have a divine or pseudo-divine standing.[2]

Ignatius writes: 'the hierarchy [i.e. Church governmental structure] is the earthly copy of the government which exists in heaven' (Lawson, 1961, p. 121). This is reminiscent of the contention in Hebrews 8 that the earthly temple of Jewish worship is a copy or shadow of the heavenly sanctuary. There is thus, for Ignatius, a clear continuity between heavenly and earthly realities, and the Church is the focus and mirror of heavenly realities on earth. He takes this continuity to astonishing levels. Specific offices within earthly ecclesial structures are analogues or types of divine life itself. For the Greek Fathers, the word *episkopos* was of course immediately recognizable as meaning 'overseer'. The omniscient God is of course the ultimate *episkopos*, and so, for Ignatius, an earthly *episkopos* stands in an analogous position to none other than the all-seeing Father himself, who 'watches over all who love him' (Ps. 145.20). This is a typological approach of the sort common in premodern scriptural interpretation, but here being applied to concrete ecclesial realities. The Father is the *typos* (type, model or pattern) for each individual bishop. Confusingly, Ignatius also closely associates the office of bishop with the person of Christ, whom he describes similarly as 'the episkopos (bishop) of all' (Schoedel, 1985, p. 108). In this vein, one commentator links Ignatius' mention of the man Onesimus as the Ephesian's 'bishop in the flesh', as implying there is 'another Bishop who is not in the flesh' (Clarke, 2016, p. 237).

Interrelating the types of both Father and Son in the office of bishop becomes less confusing by considering that Ignatius operates with a complex scheme of interrelationality and interdependence – a perichoretic indwelling, if you will – between believers and the ecclesial hierarchy, and between humanity and God. He considers that the bishop must submit to God, as Christ submitted to the will of the Father, just as members of the Church must submit to their bishop, who stands as *typos* of the Father in their respective imitation of Christ. In this way, the bishop himself imitates Christ in his submission to the all-seeing *episkopos* of the Father, and then operates as a type of the Father in his flock's submission to his ecclesial oversight. Ignatius makes frequent use of the New Testament term *hupotasso*, meaning submission or obedience to another, but he puts it in the middle-passive participle, so it exhibits a dual reference, to both the bishop and to those obedient to him (Clarke, 2016, p. 223). Calling to mind Christ's words as he grapples with submitting to the Father's will ('let this cup pass from me', Matt. 26.39), we encounter a eucharistic dimension. Imitating Christ's submission, the bishop is passed the chalice of Christ's blood, giving him the authority to pass this on to his flock, whose own submission grants their communion with Christ's sacrificial offering. With this background, we can glimpse the theology behind the authoritarian-sounding statements for which Ignatius is well known, such as 'the Lord did nothing without the Father ... so you must not do anything without the bishop'.[3]

Another important scriptural locus for interpreting Ignatius is found in the Johannine farewell discourses. Here, Jesus pleads with the Father for the disciples to be graced with participation in the mutual indwelling of the Father and the Son, 'that they may be one, as we are one' (John 17.22). For a Greek-speaking audience, a title like *mon-archos* would have an immediate theological application, because unity, or oneness, with the bishop enables one to share in God's Trinitarian unity or oneness, the oneness between Father and Son. *Mon-archos* thus means unity with the origin, beginning, or source (*arche*) of divine life. This

Trinitarian oneness was fully articulated at Nicaea in 325, with the statement that Christ and the Spirit share the same divine nature (*ousia*) as the Father, being *homousious*, 'of one substance' with him. This is where one should look to discern the significance of church unity and doctrinal homogeneity for Ignatius and the subsequent Catholic tradition. Aidan Nichols states: '[a] bishop's job is to preserve his community within the greater unity of the whole Church' (Nichols, 2005, p. 247), and this unity extends even to the ultimate unity of the Godhead itself, which is the exemplar and ground of ecclesial unity under authority, in Greek *exousia*, a 'coming forth' from God's nature.

Ignatius' monarchialism provokes strong reactions, and this might well be the case for this volume's ecumenical readership. For simplicity, we can group common reservations around the challenges of navigating two particular issues with ecclesiastical power. The first of these is intra-ecclesial. On this front, many readers involved in Christian ministry might consider Ignatius' words about a homogenous indwelling of the *episkopi* and God at best optimistic or at worst, severely naive. Commentators feel uneasy about divine typology applying to historical subjects, insofar as any earthly power, or power at least wielded 'on' earth, could be appropriated for some form of denominational triumphalism.[4] Such reservations invariably turn to the status awarded to one particular bishop, the bishop of Rome. Seeking to understand this status brings us to one of the most divisive touchstones in Christianity, which is particularly relevant here given the troubled British history.

The second set of reservations are extra-ecclesial, pointing to the tension between a Church of 'institutional deification' and the world outside it. In a society where church membership is on a marked downward trend, and a secular mindset, while not fully definitive, is still widespread and influential, one of the sticking-points for many in viewing Catholicism is the strong sense of church authority, especially when that authority speaks out on deeply counter-cultural issues, like maintaining ordination as for males only, resisting the British government's legal redefinition of marriage in 2013, and the neuralgic debates around abortion. On issues like these, episcopal authority is often represented as a juridical form of governance looming menacingly in the background. There is thus tension between a society predicated to some degree on personal and individual autonomy, with a seemingly ancient and outdated model of obedience and submission to a corporate teaching authority. If power corrupts and absolute power corrupts absolutely, Ignatian episcopal monarchialism seems rather worrying.

More recent reflections

1 Intra-ecclesial dynamics

Taking up the gauntlet thrown by Ignatius, let us now gather resources to enable us to tackle the issues outlined above. Joseph Ratzinger's work offers certain distinctions which show that episcopal power is in fact limited. Studying this limitation necessitates a discussion of the papacy, which is particularly important given the peculiarities of the British situation. The first step is to outline Ratzinger's position that, during Ignatius' time, *episkopi* were not necessarily translocal in the sense of having an office that pertains in all places, but often only had jurisdiction in a particular region. Ratzinger points out that the biblical expression 'twelve apostles' includes two distinct terms. The first, 'the twelve', was 'simply an eschatological symbol of the restoration of God's people', a connection with 'the final restoration of the twelve tribes' of Israel (Ratzinger, 1965, p. 40). With the emergence of the second term 'apostles', however, Ratzinger argues that the twelve are 'no longer limited to the Jewish people', for an apostle is 'sent forth to all the corners of the world' (DeClue, 2008, p. 645). Universal translocality is intrinsically linked with apostleship. Ratzinger gives St Paul as an example, claiming he never had oversight ('was never the bishop') of 'any particular place' (Ratzinger, 2005, p. 188). He then argues that after the apostolic age the office of bishop was initially distinct from apostolic office, meaning it was a local office. It is perhaps the last of the original apostles dying out that caused their missionary mandate (Matt. 28.18–20) to be handed over to their successors. From that point, we read, bishops 'have concern [...] for the Church as a whole spread throughout the world' (DeClue, 2008, p. 652). This is the origin of the apostolic succession, the passing on of Christ's teaching to specific individuals, the overseers who now both manage local affairs and participate in the translocal apostolic mandate. Those who receive this mandate thus make up the college of bishops, or collegium, which 'has taken the place of the collegium of the apostles'. The collegium points to the profound interconnection of the bearers of these offices with each other. Someone could only rightly be called an apostle if the message proclaimed was the same truth proclaimed by the other apostles, and so an 'apostle had his function by belonging to others who together with him formed the apostolic community'. Interdependence is thus a key aspect of episcopal office, for it defines how, today, 'each bishop has his office only by belonging to the collegium' (DeClue, 2008, p. 655, n. 40). As put by *Lumen Gentium*, 'one is constituted a member of the Episcopal body in virtue of [...] hierarchical communion with the head and members of the body' (§22).

Bringing the vexed issue of the papacy into view, Ratzinger notes that the collegium is not the only instance of an office of succession in the early Church. He claims that there is another distinct office imparted from Jesus Christ to St Peter. The two offices of 'the twelve' and 'the apostles' intermingle in the disciples, but with Peter a third office is bestowed: 'the rock'. Like 'the twelve' this is linked to the symbolism of Israel (cf. 2 Sam. 22.3; Ps. 18.2). In Catholic tradition, Peter is essentially a leader of the twelve, based not only on the classical, but contentious, reading of Matthew 16.18, but also in episodes like that in Acts 1.15-26, where his decision-making seems authoritative over his other apostolic brethren. St John Chrysostom comments that this passage 'shows the degree of his authority' (Adams, 1989, p. 37). Ratzinger also draws attention to the fact that particular eminence was given by early Christians to those sees with an apostolic origin, of which three were considered Petrine: Antioch, Alexandria and Rome, with Rome as pre-eminent, being the site of Peter's martyrdom. As early as Eusebius' *Ecclesiastical History*, according to Ratzinger, the ecclesial authority of Rome has a normative role, in measuring 'the standard of the authentic apostolic tradition as a whole' (Ratzinger, 1996, p. 69).

The issue of Petrine succession, and its normative priority, is at the core of intra-ecclesial reservations concerning monarchical approaches to the episcopate. This is because it restrains the apparently limitless power of bishops, yet it does so by giving authority to one particular bishop in a way that proves unacceptable to other Christian traditions. It thereby demarcates a key identity marker of the Catholic episcopate, particularly in the British context. This also applies, arguably, to other faiths. This is because Petrine pre-eminence seems to be an instance of precisely the sort of audacious thinking about the proximity of humanity and God that is at the root of the scandal of the incarnation.

To survey the rationale behind Petrine primacy, let us first consider Heim's point that, '[j]ust as Peter belongs to the company of the apostles and at the same time assumes a special role within it, so too the successor of Peter is in the *communio* of the college of bishops' (Heim, 2007, p. 451). That is, the Petrine office resides in the global episcopal collegium, not outside it. Similarly, Ratzinger states that the episcopate and the 'primacy' 'are intrinsically linked', that 'there cannot be one without the other' (Heim, p. 451). Heribert Schauf gives the image of 'an ellipse with two foci, primacy and episcopate' to characterize this complex relationship (Rahner and Ratzinger, 1962, p. 43). In this sense, we read, 'the Lord himself established [the rock] both "beside" and "together" with the office of the "twelve" [the collegium]' (Ratzinger, 1965, p. 51). Petrine authority is therefore actually limited. Ratzinger argues that the division it represents from much of Christendom results from the 'confusion and mixture of three distinct functions enjoyed by the pope' (DeClue, 2008, p. 666). These functions are (i) bishop of the diocese of Rome; (ii) Patriarch of the Latin Church; (iii) 'holder of the office of the Rock' established by Jesus (Ratzinger, 1962, p. 761). It is only the third of these that is of 'divine right' and provides primacy over other bishops, it is only this that succeeds from Peter himself. As bishop and patriarch, the Pope 'stands not over, but next to' his peers (Ratzinger, 1962, p. 761). The 'supreme apostolic authority over the whole Church' (DeClue, 2008, pp. 668–9) is not something to be wielded willy-nilly by meddling in local affairs but pertains in its fullness only in particular statements that will fulfil certain conditions. These are statements that are made *ex cathedra* (with the full authority of the office of the rock) and that apply to matters of faith and morals. What the Pope says about, say, political matters (not faith and morals), in a setting that does not invoke his supreme office (like a newspaper interview, or synodal position paper), is the voice of a bishop and patriarch, and not normatively authoritative in an ultimate sense.[5]

Nonetheless, papal proclamation fulfilling the two conditions just outlined limits the collegium of bishops. Petrine primacy requires that bishops must be in alignment with the Pope on issues of faith and morals promulgated *ex cathedra*. That is, only in communion with Rome is the 'oneness' of the *mon-archos* as universally translocal overseer guaranteed. Communion with Rome provides universality or, better, catholicity. Ratzinger writes: '[o]nly communion with Rome gives [the bishops] Catholicity and that fullness of apostolicity without which they would not be true bishops' (Heim, 2007, p. 451). The imitation of the divine life of Ignatius' typological approach is not therefore without theological rationale, even if this rationale will of course not sit easily with members of other traditions. But its description should help our understanding of Catholic episcopacy in the religiously plural British context, and also its unsettled history. This issue has long been mentioned in relation to tensions between Catholic bishops and civil authority, insofar as it seems to render papal authority supreme over the state. But this should not be the case except in highly exceptional circumstances (if civil authority enforces some practice antithetical to a Catholic teaching on faith and morals proclaimed *ex cathedra*). This point was therefore not fully understood by people like John Locke, or William Blackstone, who complained that Catholics had 'principles' of their religion that 'extend to a subversion of the civil government'. If they wanted to be 'upon the footing of good subjects', he said, they must 'renounce the supremacy of the pope'.[6]

2 Extra-ecclesial dynamics

The second set of reservations raise the question of how episcopal office can and should relate to the world outside the Church, in and for which it operates and functions. This is particularly pressing today, due to the place given to personal autonomy and individual decision-making in the contemporary mindset. Ignatius' language of submission and suchlike is unlikely to carry much traction with twenty-first-century readers for whom 'submission' sounds dangerously close to oppression, or even totalitarianism. There is also here a real danger of exclusivism by investing translocal leaders with immense authority based on a supposedly heightened proximity to God, against the background of widespread secularism. This threatens to make the business of being a bishop something that works only against the world, and focused on opposition to, and correction of, the populace within a diocesan jurisdiction.

In assessing whether the office of bishop in contemporary Britain is inevitably exclusivist, Ratzinger again provides valuable resources. Exclusivism tends to heteronomous authority, to a jealous guarding of ecclesial power thought to trump any misgivings centred in personal judgement and autonomy. Ratzinger tackles this problem by demonstrating that the dichotomy between individual autonomy on the one hand and collective (church) heteronomy on the other, is actually not the most accurate way to approach matters. For Ignatius, both the bishop and the flock stand under the same command for 'submission'. Similarly, Ratzinger argues that not only members of the flock, but indeed all humanity, stand ultimately under God's authority. Now, of course, few in a deeply secularized society might explicitly recognize or acknowledge that authority in a confessionally religious sense, but the crucial point is that Ratzinger maintains that humanity is always orientated towards truth, committed atheist and Christian alike. Ratzinger considers that truth converges on human experience through the conscience, which he defines as an innate orientation to truth embedded in human subjectivity, yet something that can only encounter the fullness of truth in the revelation of Jesus Christ (John 14.6).

Ratzinger uses this insight to explore important aspects of being a bishop. He does so by seeking not to lapse into either making individual human conscience an ultimate authority over church teaching, nor make church authority a heteronomous imposition from some merely external institution. When church teaching is at variance from the great swathes of the populace, the issue is not a dichotomy between individual judgements and institutional authority but between two different forms of conscience: the individual conscience, and the collective, ecclesial conscience. This distinction arose in Ratzinger's writing when Catholic Church teaching on artificial contraception was codified in the document *Humanae Vitae* in 1968. The problematic reception of this document led to a newspaper statement by the West German Bishops Conference, which agreed with the official teaching but stated that, regarding those who disagree, 'a responsible decision made in conscience must be respected by all' (Twomey, 2007, pp. 20–1). This deeply concerned Ratzinger insofar as it seemed to push the respect for individual conscience, well established in Catholic doctrine, to the point of implying that individual judgements of conscience supersede church teaching. But Ratzinger does not respond by simply imposing church authority on people. Rather, he presents such difficulties as essentially a conflict of differing consciences, an individual struggle to accept the teaching, and an ecclesial call to adhere to it. By approaching the issue in this way, Ratzinger gives us two key facets for understanding the role of a bishop in the face of increasing secularization.

The first facet is the bishop's own interiority, and the second, his activities vis-à-vis the world. In the first place, Catholic tradition holds that church teaching succeeds continuously from the apostles and develops through history by the ongoing articulation of Christ's revelation in the lives of the Church's historical subjects. It is thus the sedimentation of human experience, of people unearthing hitherto hidden riches and insights of the revelation first given definitively in the Scriptures, hence the term for tradition: 'deposit of faith' (*depositum fidei*). Uncovering new dimensions of this revelation for novel historical circumstances, or speaking out to enforce aspects of it threatened by new developments in the world, or discerning how best to transmit that teaching today, are therefore things bishops must do through the cultivation of their consciences; that is, through attuning their own orientations to truth to the fullness of truth in Jesus Christ as 'truth as person',[7] and the witness of that truth held to proceed through history in the Church.

Those charged with the authority to speak out, and make pronouncements through synods and conferences, must adopt a marked interior attentiveness, enabling them to hear and respond to the conscience of the Church as best as possible. In this sense, the rootedness of the bishop in prayer is absolutely central. Bishops are called to place their own inclinations to one side, and to seek to encounter the truth as fully and as accurately as possible. Collective decision-making by bishops, then, should not be about campaigning and politicking, but about working together from an interior disposition of readiness to be addressed by God through conscience. As Ratzinger states, 'conscience is the place where faith dwells' and so 'conscience of faith' must be 'formed to be open from within, alert and listening' (Boeve and Mannion, 2010, p. 207). Synod and conference gatherings of bishops are significant, says Ratzinger, as a means by which bishops' consciences can be informed through hearing God's word 'distinctly', not about 'lots of decisions and position papers'. The work of collective decision-making, then, is about making 'consciences clearer and thus more free on the basis of truth'. The discussion between bishops at these events should therefore be envisaged as an 'effort of communal listening', and also speaking, or rather, an 'emergence and verbalisation of the truth that is already present in conscience' (Boeve and Mannion, p. 207). In this sense, bishops are 'servants of Christ and stewards of the mysteries of God' (1 Cor. 4.1; *Lumen Gentium* 21).

The second consequence of Ratzinger's focus on differentiating individual and ecclesial conscience affects bishops' relations with the world, with the people inhabiting their translocal jurisdictions. One need not overlabour the point that individual consciences are often not aligned with church teaching, and that society frequently adopts directions that seem antithetical to Christ's self-revelation. But the job of a bishop in such situations is not to impose Christ's teaching, as such. Rather, a bishop is seen as seeking to cultivate a society in which individual consciences are well formed and given the means to make good moral decisions: forming people to be orientated to the truth, which only finds its proper home in Jesus. This helps to explain the operational realities on which bishops expend much of their time, particularly on Catholic education, which is focused particularly on forming people in their personhood. It also contributes some of the rationale behind working with domestic and international aid agencies, in keeping with Dietrich Bonhoeffer's statement that 'If the hungry do not come to faith, the guilt falls on those who denied them bread' (Bonhoeffer, 2005, p. 163). Ensuring optimum conditions for the proper cultivation of conscience, enabling others to be alert, attentive and responsive to truth, is therefore at the heart of the bishop's calling as 'teacher', bringing to mind the common pre-conciliar term for the episcopate: *ecclesia docens*, or 'teaching Church' (Heenan, 1962, p. 67). This final aspect of the episcopal calling is highly important given the widespread secularity of our contemporary British situation.

Notes

1 For key doctrinal documents on the Catholic episcopate, see *Lumen Gentium* chapter III, *Christus Dominus*, and Libreria Editrice Vaticana, 1999, *Catechism of the Catholic Church*, 2nd edition, London: Geoffrey Chapman, §§874–896. For Ignatius of Antioch on the episcopate, see particularly his letter to the Ephesians and to Polycarp, in William. R. Schoedel, 1985, *The Letters of Ignatius of*

Antioch, Philadelphia, PA: Fortress Press. For a discussion on the episcopate in the full Ignatian corpus, see Kevin M. Clarke, 2016, '"Being Bishoped by" God: The Theology of the Episcopacy According to St. Ignatius of Antioch', *Nova et Vetera* 14.1, pp. 227–43.

2 cf. Terence, L. Nichols, 1997, *That All May Be One: Hierarchy and Participation in the Church*, Collegeville, MN: Liturgical Press, p. 4 and p. 97, which claims 'we [...] see [in Ignatius] the "capturing" of the activity of the Spirit by the bishop, and the equation of the bishop with Christ.'

3 Ignatius, *Magn.* 7.1; Schoedel, 1985, p. 116. The full clause continues 'and the presbyters'; I have left to one side the question of where priests or presbyters fit into this scheme.

4 Cf. Nichols, 1997, p. 4: 'a misunderstanding of hierarchy as domination has (1) resulted in the factioning of the Body of Christ into different denominations, (2) led to a loss of credibility and to decline in modern Catholicism.'

5 These conditions are articulated in the Apostolic Constitution *Ineffabilis Deus* from 1854.

6 William Blackstone, 1765, *Commentaries on the Laws of England*, Bl. Comm. IV, c.4 ss. iii.2, p. 54, www.gutenberg.org/files/30802/30802-h/30802-h.htm (accessed 11.07.2019).

7 For a discussion of Pope Benedict's papal motto ('co-worker in truth'), see Peter Seewald and Pope Benedict XVI, 2016, *Last Testament: In His Own Words*, trans. Jacob Phillips, London: Bloomsbury, p. 241.

References

Adams, Michael (trans.), 1989, *The Navarre Bible: Acts of the Apostles*, Dublin: Four Courts Press.

Blackstone, William, 1765, *Commentaries on the Laws of England*, Online: Project Gutenberg.

Boeve, Lieven and Gerard Mannion (eds), 2010, *The Ratzinger Reader*, London: T & T Clark.

Bonhoeffer, Dietrich, 2005, *Bonhoeffer Works Volume 6: Ethics*, Minneapolis, MN: Fortress Press.

Clarke, Kevin M., 2016, '"Being Bishoped by" God: The Theology of the Episcopacy According to St. Ignatius of Antioch', *Nova et Vetera* 14.1, pp. 227–43.

DeClue, Richard G., 2008, 'Primacy and Collegiality in the Works of Joseph Ratzinger', *Communio: International Catholic Review* 35.4, pp. 642–70.

Heenan, John C., 1962, 'A Glance at the Position of the Roman Catholic Church', in William Glyn Hughes Simon (ed.), *Bishops*, London: The Faith Press, pp. 67–75.

Heim, Maximilian Heinrich, 2007, *Joseph Ratzinger: Life in the Church and Living Theology*, trans. Michael J. Miller, San Francisco, CA: Ignatius Press.

Lawson, John, 1961, *A Theological and Historical Introduction to the Apostolic Fathers*, New York: Macmillan.

Libreria Editrice Vaticana, 1999, *Catechism of the Catholic Church* (2nd edition), London: Geoffrey Chapman.

Nichols OP, Aidan, 2005, *The Thought of Benedict XVI: An Introduction to the Theology of Joseph Ratzinger*, New York: Burns & Oates.

Nichols, Terence L., 1997, *That All May Be One: Hierarchy and Participation in the Church*, Collegeville, MN: Liturgical Press.

Rahner, Karl and Joseph Ratzinger, 1962, *The Episcopate and the Primacy*, trans. Kenneth Barker et al., New York: Herder & Herder.

Ratzinger, Joseph, 1962, 'Primat', in Josef Höfer and Karl Rahner (eds), *Lexicon für Theologie und Kirche*, Vol. 8, 2nd edition, Freiburg: Verlag.

Ratzinger, Joseph, 1965, 'The Pastoral Implications of Episcopal Collegiality', in *Concilium, Vol. 1: The Church and Mankind*, Glen Rock, NJ: Paulist Press.

Ratzinger, Joseph, 1996, *Called to Communion: Understanding the Church Today*, San Francisco, CA: Ignatius Press.

Ratzinger, Joseph Cardinal, 2005, *Pilgrim Fellowship of Faith: The Church as Communion*, trans. Henry Taylor, San Francisco, CA: Ignatius Press.

Schoedel, William R., 1985, *The Letters of Ignatius of Antioch*, Philadelphia, PA: Fortress Press.

Seewald, Peter and Pope Benedict XVI, 2016, *Last Testament: In His Own Words*, trans. Jacob Phillips, London: Bloomsbury.

Twomey, Vincent D., 2007, *Pope Benedict XVI: The Conscience of Our Age: A Theological Portrait*, San Francisco, CA: Ignatius Press.

6

The Methodist Church

A Connexion of Translocal Ministry, Oversight and Episkope

MARTYN ATKINS

Introduction

In a very real sense, all Methodist ministers are translocal and all are expected to exercise levels of oversight required by their role in ministry, to which they are appointed by the Methodist Conference. Thankfully, we can be more specific because the presbyteral[1] roles that exercise levels of oversight throughout the various structures of contemporary Methodism can be identified. Put simply, there are four interrelated 'structures' or 'circles of belonging' with which we are concerned: the Connexion, the Conference, the Circuit and the District. To each of these are appointed presbyters whose roles include specific aspects of oversight. For the purposes of this chapter they are these: in respect of the Connexion, every Methodist presbyter; in terms of the Conference, its officers – the President and Secretary; in the Circuit, its Superintendent minister; and in the District, the Chair of District.

It is vital to note at the outset that oversight in Methodism is undertaken by both ordained and lay people. John Wesley exhorted every Methodist to 'watch over one another in love', and that instruction still stands. All the governance bodies of connexional Methodism – the Conference, the District Synod, the Circuit Meeting and the local Church Council – have a defined membership of whom about half or more are lay people. Ordained presbyters, alongside their common ministry of word, sacrament and pastoral care, have specific responsibilities according to their role. They exercise governance, management and leadership on behalf of the Conference, the very essence of oversight according to a report to the Conference in 2005.[2] It might be said therefore that at every level of its connexional being, Methodism exercises a corporate oversight and *episkope*, which presbyteral ministers represent, enact and lead, but do not create by being ordained.

Some historical information is needed, not because reverence of John Wesley is expected or required, rather because by the time he died in 1791, or very soon afterwards, the key self-understandings and structures that have shaped Methodist oversight and *episkope* down to today were largely in place. Each of these has evolved over time of course, but much survives and shapes the present.

Connexion

Long before it adopted the name 'Church', Methodism understood itself to be a connexion,[3] the word itself taking the eighteenth-century spelling of the more familiar 'connection'. In terms of understanding Methodism, past and present, it is hard to overstate the significance of connexionalism – connoting connectedness, interrelatedness, mutual belonging and responsibility. The 'connexional principle' determines in large measure the spirituality and structures of Methodism, and accordingly the nature and role of the Conference, Circuits and Districts are shaped by it.

Over his long ministry of preaching, writing and travelling, coordinated networks of those 'in connexion' with the Wesleys were established. Known as 'Mr Wesley's preachers' or 'Assistants', some were ordained in episcopally ordered churches, such as Wesley's own Church of England; many more not. However, they were all 'in connexion' with Wesley himself and associated themselves with his teaching, ministry and modus operandi. As such they 'assisted' him in leading the fast-growing local societies of 'the people called Methodists'.

Today, in a much different context of significant decline, official Methodist reports tellingly emphasize the 'gift' of connexionalism in the face of various acknowledged challenges. Among these is a dogged lack of understanding of it among increasingly post-denominational Methodist Christians, accompanied by a pervasive practical congregationalism in many places. Ecumenical relationships too, though welcome and sought, nevertheless cut across Methodist circuit and district boundaries and their accompanying loyalties, impacting on the 'connexionality' of contemporary Methodism. Yet connexionalism remains a crucial aspect of Methodist ecclesiology and identity. It involves a commitment to interrelatedness and interdependence which, Methodist reports assert, is of theological and organizational significance. It gives practical expression to the 'one body' imagery found in the New Testament and the concept of

Koinonia. It shapes the structures and ministry of the Methodist Church and, it is claimed, equips it for mission.

A key issue in the strategically renewed conversations about connexionalism is to what extent the principle necessarily requires the present structures – and indeed, some present practices such as an itinerant ministry – to embody it. Thus, the size and frequency of the Conference; the sustainable number of Circuits, Districts, ministers, and central and devolved staff; and the widely held view that increasing rules, requirements and responsibilities are stretching the Connexion beyond tolerance, are commonly rehearsed themes.

One strand of connexional thinking is particularly relevant here, namely the principle of *subsidiarity*, meaning that 'decisions ought not to be made on any issue in the church at a higher level than they need to be. The more local the problem, the more local the jurisdiction that applies to it' (Beck, 1991, p. 48). Certainly, the *Constitution, Practice and Discipline of the Methodist Church* – its 'book of rules' – seems to bear this out, providing separate sections in which the responsibilities and roles of the Conference, the Districts, the Circuits and the Local Churches are delineated. In practice however, there is a rumbling narrative that Methodism has not yet sufficiently employed subsidiarity, and an unhealthy imbalance between central authority and devolved authority and autonomy persists. Nevertheless, the oversight required of presbyters in their different appointments, whether in a local circuit or the Superintendent of it, whether a Chair of District or an officer of the Conference, is essentially the complex and challenging business of taking a lead in holding healthily together central and devolved aspects of governance, polity, discipline and management.

The Conference and its officers

From 1744, John Wesley began to gather together his senior ministers to confer about the things of God. Alongside the declared core purposes of the Conference – 'what to preach', 'how to preach' and 'what to do', meaning how to regulate doctrine, discipline and practice – was the need to coordinate a quickly expanding Connexion. Just how much genuine conferring went on, at least in Wesley's lifetime, is a moot point. One participant in 1774 noted wryly that 'Mr. Wesley seemed to do all the business himself.' A decade later, in his later seventies, Wesley made provision for the 'Yearly Conference of the People called Methodists' to lead the Connexion after his death rather than appoint a human successor. Thus, a form of personal *episkope* became a form of corporate *episkope* that exists to this day.

Another decision made in the last years of Wesley's life, and reasserted after his death, related to the President of the Conference. 'Pope John', as some quietly referred to him, had presided over the Conference for nearly half a century. From 1792 to the present day the presiding over the Conference by an elected senior presbyteral minister became a one-year-long appointment, and only very rarely has any person served twice. We can only imagine the multiple meanings and emotions captured by one writer marking Mr Wesley's death and the beginning of the new, annual pattern of leading the Conference: 'Never again shall there be such a king in Israel'!

The Conference remains the supreme governing body of the Methodist Church and the supreme source of oversight under God for the whole Connexion. Inevitably, however, a body of over 300 members meeting once a year for a handful of days is required to devolve oversight/*episkope* to other places and people. The 'Methodist Council' does a good deal of the work of the 'Conference between Conferences', with central and devolved staff teams performing much of the spadework. The President of the Conference, necessarily an ordained presbyter, and a lay Vice-President together represent the Conference in a variety of ways, in roles sometimes described as monarchical. However, there is more to the offices than this, especially regarding the President. Though they rarely undertake the work entirely themselves, the President oversees what one recent occupant of that office referred to as 'the night soil of the Church': ministerial discipline cases, resignations, reinstatements, and 'Inquiries' into Circuits and other contexts where situations and relationships have gone seriously awry and other more normal processes of oversight have failed.

In practical terms though, the officer most responsible for the work of the Conference in its many aspects is not the President of the Conference but its Secretary – also required to be an ordained presbyter. Presidents quickly come and go, giving rise to periodic heart searching about whether the role should become one of several years' duration, providing longer term and more consistent leadership to the Conference; a suggestion that has, to date, always been rejected. By contrast, the Secretary of the Conference is an appointment of several years' duration. Consequently, this office, and the staff who support it, are as representative agents of the Conference, the supreme oversight body and primary location of corporate *episkope*, the most concentrated locus of organizational power and authority in the Methodist Connexion.

Ordination and reception into Full Connexion

Methodism, then, presently ordains two orders of ministry – presbyters and (permanent) deacons – and the Conference plays a crucial role in ordination. Accepted and trained candidates for Methodist ministry are normally ordained into the Church of God during the annual Conference, usually in large local churches and loaned cathedrals. Significantly, the act of ordination is always performed by the President of the Conference or, given that several ordination services take place on the same Sunday, one of their predecessors.

As part of the Covenant entered into between the Church of England and the Methodist Church in 2003, Methodism is currently considering the question of a 'President-bishop' (Baker and Richardson, 2017). This is critically important to the Church of England as it provides a way by which the Methodist Church can be recognized as sharing in the historic episcopate, without which all other progress as imagined by the Covenant is rendered impossible. That it is the Conference's ministry of oversight and *episkope*, particularly in relation to ordination, that is proposed as the most appropriate locus for a personal form of connexional episcopal ministry to be established is itself significant.

The notion of a President-bishop is an acknowledged challenge to many Methodists. Though the Conference has asserted several times in recent decades that there is no theological reason why bishops cannot be adopted by British Methodism, to date there is no firm consensus as to what *kind* of bishop or indeed the desirability of any sort of bishop. Then there is the challenge of making what is a corporate *episkope* also a personal *episkope*, inevitably creating a British Methodist model of episcopacy.

Significantly, prior to their ordination, Methodist ordinands, together with ordained ministers from other denominations transferring into the Methodist Church, are 'Received into Full Connexion'. They confirm to the Conference that they believe and preach 'our doctrines', and pledge to faithfully observe and administer 'our discipline' as determined by the Conference. As such they are given the full status and privileges and are subject to all the obligations of a presbyter or deacon in the Methodist Church. It is on this accepted basis that they proceed to ordination later that same day, and these pledges are required to be repeated annually throughout their ministry. Thus, all Methodist ministers are connected to the Conference – the corporate *episkope* of Methodism – just as the earliest Assistants were in connexion with Mr Wesley.

Accordingly, it is the Conference that appoints and deploys all Methodist ministers each year. To be sure, many people and committees are involved in managing what remains an itinerant ministry, albeit a system under some strain. An annual process of 'stationing', in which District Chairs and the Warden of the Methodist Diaconal Order take a leading role, determines which minister on the move is 'matched' with which Circuit, and normally which presbyter is proposed as Superintendent of it. District Chairs are appointed by a different system involving advertisements and requiring either nomination or personal application followed by interview for shortlisted presbyters. Nevertheless, it is the Conference that formally appoints each minister to their 'station', whether to a Circuit, District or connexional role.

Circuits and their superintendents

The 'societies' of earlier Methodism were comprised of 'classes' – small group meetings intended to deepen discipleship through Christian fellowship, study, prayer and mutual accountability. Lay leadership was vital; class meetings were usually led by lay people, and lay 'society stewards' coordinated the life of local societies. In time, a more settled pattern of pastoral ministry of clergy and congregation would come about, but initially and essentially Mr Wesley's Assistants were, like Wesley himself, itinerant travelling preachers who visited, encouraged and occasionally disciplined the proliferating societies of Methodists. Such travelling preachers exercised their ministry over areas comprising several Methodist societies, and these groupings of societies, which were usually identified by geographical areas and primarily configured by preaching arrangements, were known as 'Circuits'. Formally, from 1796, the senior Assistant charged with overseeing the Circuit was appointed as the Superintendent.[4]

Circuits remain to this day the key network structure of the Methodist Connexion. Ministers are appointed by the Conference to Circuits rather than local churches, and most presbyters have 'pastoral charge' of several local churches and exercise their ministry alongside other colleagues. It is in relation to serving a Circuit rather than, primarily, a local church that all Methodist ministers might be said to be 'translocal'.

In recent years, the number of Circuits making up the Methodist Connexion has fallen by around a quarter, with the inevitable consequence that many merged and newly configured Circuits have become geographically larger. Some are now the size of a small county or cover a whole city centre and contain dozens of local churches supported and resourced by many ministerial and lay staff. In consequence, the workload, responsibilities and potential sphere of influence and authority of some Superintendents is growing, resulting in the appearance of 'co-Superintendents' and 'separated Superintendents' – the latter meaning that they have oversight of the whole Circuit but, unusually, do not serve as the pastoral minister to any local churches in it. This development is beginning and will surely continue to pose questions of the relationship between a separated Superintendent and a separated Chair of District.

In terms of governance and local oversight it is, unsurprisingly, the Circuit Meeting rather than the local church that is the more influential and significant, although both are usually populated by many more lay people than those who are ordained. Similarly, in ministerial terms it is the Superintendent who exercises oversight/*episkope* of Methodist churches in a Circuit and all the other ordained and lay employees working in it. The Superintendent leads a Circuit Leadership Team and presides over the Circuit Meeting, which has considerable decision-making powers. Though often undertaken collegially, the Superintendent is responsible for the 'Preaching Plan' and the ordering of the life of the Circuit, which now normally entails both the closure of chapels and the creation and staffing of Fresh Expressions of church and pioneering ministries. Though rarely an issue in practice, such is the authority of a Superintendent in their Circuit in terms of its life and mission that the role of the District Chair is sometimes said to be mainly advisory. However, as we turn to that role, the dynamics and responsibilities are more subtle than that.

Districts and Chairs of District

The 1791 Conference divided the Connexion into 27 Districts, 'for the preservation of our whole economy as the Revd. Mr. Wesley left it.'[5] However, more important than the Districts themselves, which had few roles and little power, was the role of the Chairman (*sic*). Chosen from among the preachers serving in the Circuits of a District, the Chairman was a senior and experienced minister whose role quickly became one of arbitrator in disputes and overseer in terms of discipline on behalf of the Conference. This was not a full-time role, and Chairmen, like Superintendents, continued to be appointed to Circuits and undertook local pastoral ministry in them. Indeed, 'separated Chairs' only began to become normative after Methodist Union in 1932[6] and particularly from the late 1950s. Throughout the nineteenth century, in the various branches of Methodism, Chairmen exercised oversight/*episkope* as *pastor pastorum* on behalf of their respective Conferences. In the Primitive Methodist and Bible Christian traditions, they presided over the District Meetings at which, from the 1820s, the ordination of ministers took place. By the end of the nineteenth century, Wesleyan Methodist 'District Meetings' had become known as Synods.

In recent decades the role and powers of the District and its Chair have slowly increased. Today, the District offers various resources and expertise to the Circuits and their local churches, such as District grants to support mission projects and specialists in relation to safeguarding. It provides training of various sorts for both lay and ordained Methodists. The District normally embodies the connexional character of the Church over a wider geographical area than the Circuit. The role of the District Chair has also developed. Chairs continue to have responsibility for the pastoral care, discipline and stationing of ministers. They also preside over the District Synod, which has both presbyteral and 'representative' sessions, the latter including lay and ordained members.

In recent years, as part of the soul-searching currently going on in a declining denomination, the notion of the Chair as effectively the 'District Missionary'[7] responsible for encouraging evangelism and vitality in all Circuits, originally found in reports about the role in the 1950s and 60s, has undergone something of a revival. Further responsibilities, both those officially designated and those arising by happenstance in fast-changing contexts, have fallen to District Chairs. They are the most common representatives of the Methodist Church in terms of ecumenical commitments and relationships, and also with secular organizations and wider society. Consequently, District Chairs are the most natural colleagues of translocal ministers in the other Christian traditions and denominations outlined in this book.

The role of Chairs of District as a corporate body of officers is significant, and though the 'Chairs Meeting' is strictly without formal governance and decision-making powers, it brings together what many regard as the senior Methodist presbyter in each District. Every Chair is a member of the Conference and there is hardly a significant working party or committee of Methodism that will not have at least one Chair among its membership. Between 1999 and 2018, 14 of the 20 Presidents of the Conference have been serving District Chairs. Their significant role in widely recognized patterns of oversight and *episkope* is unquestioned.

In conclusion, in addition to the common ministry of word, sacrament and pastoral care, all Methodist presbyters are stationed by the Conference, the supreme corporate *episkope* of Methodism, and on its behalf, exercise the various levels of oversight. The nature and extent of that oversight depends on the role to which they are appointed and the responsibilities which that role carries. However, it is primarily through Superintendent ministers, Chairs of District and Conference officers that the exercise of those ministries that contain the generally recognized and accepted elements of oversight and *episkope* throughout the one Church of Christ are exercised through their different roles within the one Connexion.

Notes

1 Until recent decades the term 'minister' was used to describe all ordained clergy in the Methodist Church, as only one 'Order' of ministry was recognized. However, in the later 1980s the Methodist Diaconal Order (MDO) was (re)founded out of the older Wesley Deaconess Order, but with three important developments. First, the MDO was open to both men and women. Second, it was recognized and affirmed as both an Order of Ministry and a Religious Order. Third, it was a 'permanent' Diaconate. As a consequence, for the first time Methodism affirmed two Orders of ministry and identifying them in relation to the other became necessary. Methodism now refers to presbyteral and diaconal ministries and uses 'ministers' to refer to both presbyters and deacons.

2 *The Nature of Oversight: Leadership, Management and Governance in the Methodist Church in Britain*, a report to the 2005 Methodist Conference.

3 All the main branches of Methodism officially referred to themselves as a 'Connexion' until the later nineteenth century.

4 For a fuller account of the history and roles of a Superintendent minister, see *What is a Superintendent?* A report to the Methodist Conference, 2005, www.methodist.org.uk/downloads/co_08_whatisacircuitsuper_0805.doc (accessed 16.07.2019).

5 *Minutes* of the 1791 Conference.

6 From the early nineteenth century a small number of Methodist traditions and connexions arose, most as a secession from the 'parent' Wesleyan Methodist Connexion; for example, Primitive Methodist, United Methodist and Bible Christian Methodist Connexions. In 1932, after many years of conversation, the Wesleyan, Primitive and United Methodists become the Methodist Church of Great Britain, as it is today.

7 1956 report to Conference.

Reference

Baker, Jonathan and Neil Richardson, 2017, *Mission and Ministry in Covenant*, a report of the Faith and Order bodies of the Church of England and the Methodist Church, prepared for the Conference of the Methodist Church in Great Britain and for the Church of England General Synod, www.churchofengland.org/sites/default/files/2017-10/mission-and-ministry-in-covenant.pdf (accessed 16.07.2019).

Beck, Brian E., 1991, 'Some Reflections of Connexionalism (2)', *Epworth Review* 18.3.

7

The Baptist Union of Great Britain

The Theory and Practice of Translocal Oversight in a Baptist Context

DIANNE TIDBALL

Beginning as a regional minister in our union of Baptist Churches is a bit like entering a foreign country without a map yet thinking you know the territory well.

Within the Baptist Union of Great Britain (BUGB), translocal oversight is primarily located in one of the 13 regional associations into which the Union is organized. Each constituent part of the Union is a separate organizational entity with its own charity registration, infrastructure and other component parts. Committed to a congregational ecclesiology, if oversight fits the Baptist model of translocal ministry at all, it would be recognized by most as belonging to the function and office of regional minister. Each of the 13 Associations has at least one regional minister, one has four, with the others somewhere in between.

Baptist ecclesiology and oversight

As with all church traditions there are varieties of perspectives among Baptists about ministry in general and translocal ministry in particular, perhaps best typified by identifying them as rooted in either functional or sacramental views of ordination. Some argue that ordination is a setting apart for a function within the body of Christ that recognizes a person's particular gifts and the filling of the Holy Spirit and permits the development of the calling received from God. Others suggest that those in the office of a minister are particularly anointed for a more sacramental ministry of leading worship, including presiding at communion, preaching, pastoral care and leadership. There is significant variation within these two perspectives, though the emphasis is perhaps more on who or what the minister is, rather than a focus on what the minister does, as being important (Goodliff, 2010, p. 3).

Those who view ministry as a particularly anointed office might also logically take the view that translocal ministry confers a modest authority, allowing leadership to be recognized and oversight to be endorsed in all churches within a regional minister's responsibility. In practice, the more common view sees the function of the regional minister as serving the churches, recognizing their independence and their local responsibility for discerning the leading of God through the Holy Spirit for themselves.

To understand how translocal ministry operates within the Baptist Union, first it is necessary to appreciate the underlying ecclesiology. The Declaration of Principle of the Baptist Union is foundational in this regard and contains the statement:

> That our Lord and Saviour, Jesus Christ, God manifest in the flesh, is the sole and absolute authority in all matters relating to faith and practice, as revealed in the Holy Scriptures, and that each Church has liberty, under the guidance of the Holy Spirit, to interpret and administer His Laws.[1]

A Baptist Regional Minister is always aware that each congregation in their care, as a constituted local Baptist church, has the responsibility of hearing what God is saying under the guidance of the Holy Spirit, and to follow what they believe is God's way for them. The local church may call upon their regional minister to support and encourage them at any given point, and indeed, if they are wise, they will take seriously their responsibility to discern the mind of Christ and not do so in an isolationist and independent way. Rather, with an awareness of their covenantal relationship with other Baptists, they will seek to understand more clearly their way forward in association with others.

Within this context it becomes apparent that the regional minister has little automatic authority to oversee local congregations except in those rare cases where a legal process is to be enforced. All opportunities to offer oversight are therefore the result of good relationships, proven wisdom, leadership skill and the willingness of the local congregation to receive translocal ministry. Most local churches have a good relationship with their regional minister, which is hardly surprising as regional ministers are appointed by a regional association, for the purpose of serving the churches of the association. However, some local Baptist congregations do not participate in the wider life of their association, either because of a separatist disposition or because they look to build relationships elsewhere. The congregational nature of Baptist ecclesiology makes this a real possibility, and may follow because of theological differences, poor relationships, competing loyalties with other networks, or for historical reasons that may, or may not, have been lost in the mists of time. Thankfully such congregations are a small minority.

Regional ministers are usually appointed as those with experience, proven gifts and evidence of being a leader among leaders. It is hoped that, through gaining the respect of the churches whom they are appointed to serve, they will be able to use their wider understanding to support and encourage others. The only real resource a regional minister has in giving guidance to a church is their own wise persuasion and counsel. The congregational nature of a church and its independence in decision-making means that disastrous choices can be contemplated, and unwise propositions debated, and all a regional minister is able to offer is advice or seek to persuade them to adopt another course of action. Of course, they may not even be aware of what is under consideration, even in urgent and extreme situations.

BUGB maintains a national list of accredited ministers whose vocation has been tested and who have successfully undertaken an approved programme of ministerial formation. These individuals are considered to be in a covenantal relationship with others in Baptist ministry.[2] When a person enters Baptist ministry they commit themselves to the behaviours and practices that conform to the guidelines of acceptable lifestyle and they can be subject to disciplinary procedures for misconduct, or what has historically been named among Baptists as 'conduct unbecoming to the ministry'. The role of the regional minister in such cases is not to police the Baptist guidelines. When a minister appears to have failed to live in keeping with this covenant relationship and the threshold to trigger the disciplinary process has been crossed, cases are referred to the National Ministry Team. The role of the regional minister is to provide pastoral support and be an advocate for the minister while others take responsibility for the disciplinary process itself.

Pastor to the pastors

Historically, one of the main functions of the translocal minister has been to care for and support ministers in the pressures and demands of local church ministry. 'Therefore we state bluntly that the fundamental priority of the[ir] ... work must be the support, encouragement and care of ministers.'[3] Having been local church ministers themselves, regional ministers can offer an understanding ear, a person to discuss ideas with and a caring lead when a minister faces significant issues such as ill health, bereavement, family and marriage pressures. Often the regional minister can be an advocate with the church when the minister ought to ask for help but is reluctant to do so.

One of the hardest contexts for a translocal minister is when there is conflict between the local minister and their congregation because of differing expectations of the minister's role. The resulting stress can be overwhelming and the regional minister is often invited into the situation to give a lead in a context that is exacerbated by the congregational nature of the church. Frequently the churches want too much control and the minister wants too little accountability. Finding a life-giving balance in such situations can prove a complex task.

It is a truism in pastoral care that the more that is provided, the more is consequently demanded. It is no different in regional ministry, where those who benefit most significantly from the care and support that is offered often see it as having been inadequate. The entitlement culture, when a minister expects there to be the kind of help that takes problems away, is increasingly common but wholly unrealistic in its expectations. Similarly, churches in difficulty may expect a regional team to be available to help them when this is not always possible or wise, not least because it frequently implies maintaining failing situations, dysfunctional relationships or non-missional practices.

Processes, management and translocal ministry

More recently the Baptist Union has entered a period of transition and structural change, as it is clear that national resources are reduced while regional demands increase. Those providing translocal ministry may not be able to do all that is needed but they need to ensure that essential matters are covered and the requirements of good practice are met. Some of the areas that translocal ministers are asked about are:

- Safeguarding policies, practice and concerns.
- Financial matters involving falling income for a local church, grants for mission and ministry, good practice in managing a church's assets.
- Maintaining the processes of calling, training and development of church leaders, including accredited Baptist ministers and second register ministries, such as youth workers and parish nurses.
- Property matters, lease back for a minister's housing, issues to do with manses and church buildings.

- Constitutional and charitable trust enquiries.
- Legal issues.

All these main concerns, along with an almost endless stream of others, are important, significant and potentially critical for a given congregation or individual. In simpler times, though these issues have always been present in some form, ministry was primarily concerned with preaching the Word, caring for the flock and being respected in the community, and these matters did not figure so highly. Translocal oversight has become more complex and involved in a way that mirrors wider society.

Key within the life of a Baptist regional association is the Regional Minister/Team Leader. Within the BUGB their responsibilities can vary significantly. For example, one oversees a small team working among 50 churches while another oversees a network of over 300. Some Regional Team Leaders have a job description that reflects a more traditional pattern of giving pastoral and missional leadership, while others discover that the reality of their service is that they are the CEO of a multimillion-pound organization.

Missional associations

In day-to-day terms translocal ministry among Baptists operates in a number of different ways:

- Encouraging and inspiring local churches to follow their essential calling to be communities centred on Christ and to fulfil the mission God gives them.
- Offering pastoral care and support to church leaders, including ministers and lay leaders.
- Making available and facilitating ministerial development and professional training.
- Being a prophetic voice as appropriate, calling Baptist people to exercise justice, righteousness and kindness.
- Managing the process by which ministers move to new appointments, often referred to in the BUGB as the 'settlement system'.

Recent years have seen a move to clarify the role and purpose of the regional associations, which in some quarters has led to an emphasis on their being understood as 'missional associations'. As part of the restructuring of the Baptist Union in 2013, the national Mission Department was dissolved with the expectation that the associations would continue to fulfil the role of encouraging and resourcing mission within local churches. Indeed, it would be fair to summarize the denominational reforms of 2002 and 2013 as being highly influenced by the desire that the BUGB be a more effective missional movement among Baptists. The mission task of the Church and the love of Christ for his world is a core denominational conviction that is ingrained in its spiritual and historical DNA, and there is little debate that mission has to be the primary calling of all ministers, including those in translocal roles.

The increasingly popular idea of having 'missional associations' has resulted in an emphasis on each region having a strategic plan for developing local churches in healthy, missional ways. It is my observation that this is a more intentional emphasis on a particular dimension of regional oversight that has always been a significant part of the role of translocal ministers. In looking to understand what that might look like, it has been suggested that being a 'missional association' will include some or all the following elements:

- Prioritizing conversations and reviews of churches by regional ministers that emphasize being outward looking, resisting maintenance as an approach to church vision, and seeking a willingness to embrace change in order to resonate more fully with local cultures and society.
- Regional ministers seeking to be proactive in encouraging local churches to adopt strategic thinking about mission and seeking God for a vision for mission in their area.
- Discerning gifts of missional leadership in those exploring a call to ordained ministry within the BUGB.
- A missional association clarifying its objectives in terms of utilizing its resources to inspire mission effectiveness within local churches.
- Ensuring regular review of mission grants and use of resources to ensure that mission remains a priority not only in what is done but in how the association and its churches are structured and the culture they share.

Apostolic office and translocal ministry among Baptists

Influential voices in the conversation about missional churches and missional associations sometimes place a significant emphasis on 'apostolic leadership'. With the original meaning of 'apostle' being one who is sent, the recovery of this office in the current reflections on translocal ministry is appropriate. In Ephesians 4.11 the apostle Paul commends the fivefold ministry of apostles, prophets, evangelists, pastors and teachers. The purpose of these ministries is to build up the body of Christ and to equip the Church for service. While prophets, evangelists, pastors and teachers have a local and translocal focus, it is the role of apostle that is specifically translocal and requires some consideration as an emphasis for Baptist Regional Ministers. It is widely held in the missional church movement that the apostolic function is one that is 'usually conducted translocally, pioneers new missional works and oversees their development' (Frost and Hirsch, 2003, p. 169).

Clearly, Paul's understanding of apostolic ministry flows out of a dynamic, emerging and informal context of a developing network of churches rather than reflecting the more formal structures of an established institutional expression of church. However, the apostolic role has a renewed significance in the context of a declining Church, an increasingly secular society and in a context where many Baptist churches experience difficulty in finding their place and voice in their own locality. Ensuring that the people of God are sent out to build new communities of love and faith as an expression of God's mission in Christ is a crucial task, and an apostolic one.

Mediation and conflict, translocal ministry and Baptist congregations

When there is tension within a congregation between them and their pastor, the regional minister inevitably carries the pressure of divided loyalties for the well-being of both the church and the minister. Consequently, it is easy to end up upsetting both! When a regional minister enters into the situation they are often accompanied by the expectation of both parties that they will 'sort out' the other side of the dispute because, clearly, they are in the right. A regional minister cannot win. Whichever 'side' is perceived to have won, the other automatically concludes that it is down to bias. 'The regional minister is a minister, and of course they will side with the minister!' Or, alternatively, 'Pastors come and go, but at the end of the day, the church won't ever stop being the responsibility of the regional minister come what may!' Rarely are such contexts simple; there are usually a wide range of factors that have brought things to the difficult, presenting issue.

The role of the regional minister can never be 'to knock a few heads together' and demand they learn to behave in a more loving way. In a congregational ecclesiology, regional ministers do not have this authority or power and maybe that is a good thing. The way forward for the translocal minister is to follow basic principles in mediation and, indeed, many regional ministers have benefitted from formal mediation training.[4]

Often regional ministers are approached when relationships have become too strained for easy resolution or when perspectives are so entrenched that resolution is not possible. In many circumstances the regional minister is put in the position of circumventing as much anger and pain as possible and allowing a parting of ways in the most generous and gracious manner that can be achieved.

Relationship and the Trinity

The Trinitarian God is a God whose very essence is expressed in relationship. The greatest tool the translocal minister has is that of maintaining good relationships. The ecclesiology of Baptists denies the regional minister any formal authority to go to a local church and require certain decisions be made or courses of action taken. However, good relationships can be far more fruitful than a more directive approach.

Jesus' prayer that his disciples might be one (John 17.21) fits ministry in a local church as much as in an ecumenical context. While Baptists believe in the freedom of the local church to discern how God is leading them, they also believe in associating and covenanting together to 'watch over one another' in the gospel. Many networks or clusters of churches exist happily in relationship together without any translocal support. However, when difficult days arrive and they begin to struggle, the translocal minister who has built good relationships and demonstrated wisdom and graciousness will be well received and have opportunities to help. Investing in relationships is difficult to measure but the evidence from more formal reviews of Association life suggests that where translocal ministers meet with ministers, lay leaders and congregations and build substantive relationships, that is appreciated and forms the basis for future fruitful engagement.

New expressions of church, pioneer ministry and church planting

As a congregational model of churchmanship, Baptist ecclesiology identifies the local church as the key component in its understanding of the church. BUGB is, first and foremost, a union of churches, then of associations and colleges. Consequently, there is some tension when an association acts as an initiator of pioneer church planting and other new expressions of church, as received understanding has traditionally maintained that it is the local churches that should initiate such pioneering practice.

It is a fact that most regional teams are stretched by the combination of their routine responsibilities and the exercise of pastoral care. Indeed, it is easy to deploy all available time, and more, in reacting to important matters that maintain current structures and patterns of working to the exclusion of pioneering opportunities and creative missional initiatives. Those translocal ministers who carry a specific mission brief, and those associations that have adopted an explicitly missional approach, must work hard to facilitate new mission in their regions. Finding ways to explore presenting opportunities, to identify sustainable funding patterns and develop models of new expressions of church are all part of the remit of the translocal Baptist minister.

Ecumenical – unity and working together

One further function of the role of Baptist translocal ministers is to relate to others in parallel roles in other denominational traditions. These relationships are important for developing a united Christian voice on issues of justice and for working together in evangelism and church planting in establishing new worshipping communities and new ways of being church.

A significant issue to have arisen for Church Leaders' Groups in recent years is how to avoid being merely cosmetic and only serving the bonhomie of church leaders who attend. It is easy to meet, share developments, eat good food and enjoy hospitality, yet achieve little for the sake of God's kingdom. An ongoing review of the purpose and effectiveness of such meetings is a necessary antidote to this. A second issue that has arisen is that ecumenical relationships need somehow to include the more fluid church movements that are prevalent in urban and suburban areas: ethnic churches, charismatic fellowships and communities that might be loosely defined as contemporary independent networks of Christians. Often these are the groups at the cutting edge of mission and discipleship and that give inspiration and encouragement for missional churches and associations.

Multi-faith engagement and translocal ministry

My own experience is in Leicester, a city where minority ethnic populations are the majority. In such a city it is apparent that the increasing need to relate is not just to ecumenical colleagues but also across the various faith communities. Leicester is a city where faith has a fundamental role in the social framework and cultural developments. Politicians ignore this at their peril. There is much that the Christian Church and the translocal minister can be drawn into in regard to multifaith dialogue and developing inter-faith responses to issues raised by the English Defence League, cuts in welfare benefits, food banks, racism and legislation regarding marriage and sexuality. Standing together on such issues, the voices of the faith communities are more likely to be heard, rather than speaking separately and risking being ignored. For some translocal ministers this is a significant part of their work in representing the churches they serve.

Regional ministers can also be bridge builders by supporting work towards creating harmonious communities and being alongside the leaders of other faith communities in countering attempts to marginalize or eradicate faith and spiritual life from civic structures and political dialogue. This is likely to be an increasing factor in the work of translocal Baptist ministers in the years ahead, particularly in urban settings.

Conclusion

Translocal Baptist ministry is a privilege, a responsibility and, in many ways, an impossibility. To the many facets of translocal ministry identified above could be added significant institutional responsibilities like the national Home Mission Appeal, the responsibilities of a charity trustee and engagement in national and international relationships on behalf of the BUGB nationally.

Interestingly, when our Baptist way of being church is understood, the function of the Baptist Regional Minister is not so different from the function of other translocal ministers in other denominations. Ultimately, it is the desire to see God's kingdom come and to work towards that end is its focus and substance.

Notes

1 This was adopted by the annual Baptist Assembly in 1938 (Payne, 1958, p. 212).

2 While most ministers of churches in the Baptist Union are on this accredited list, congregations are free to appoint an individual of their own choice to such roles, so that being a Baptist minister in a local church does not necessarily also mean that minister is nationally accredited.

3 Baptist Union of Great Britain, 1996, *Transforming Superintendency: The Report of the General Superintendency Review Group*, Baptist Union Council (November 1996), p. 3. NB: Regional ministers came into existence in 2002; prior to that, oversight was provided by 12 nationally appointed General Superintendents, to which this report refers.

4 Rooted in the Mennonite tradition, the Bridge Builders programme has proved to be a particularly helpful one: www.bbministries.org.uk/ (accessed 06.12.2019).

References

Baptist Union of Great Britain, 1996, *Transforming Superintendency: The Report of the General Superintendency Review Group*, Baptist Union Council (November 1996).

Frost, Michael and Alan Hirsch, 2003, *The Shape of Things to Come*, Peabody, MA: Hendrickson.

Goodliff, Paul, 2010, *Ministry, Sacrament and Representation: Ministry and Ordination in Contemporary Baptist Theology, and the rise of Sacramentalism*, Oxford: Regents Park Publications.

Payne, Ernest A., 1958, *The Baptist Union: A Short History*, London: Carey Kingsgate Press.

8

The United Reformed Church

Synod Moderators

ROBERTA ROMINGER

In the beginning ...

The United Reformed Church's synod moderators trace the origin of their role to a decision of the 1919 Assembly of the Congregational Union of England and Wales. The churches had long since entered into county groupings for mutual support and united action. The 1919 proposals brought counties together into provinces, each to appoint a full-time moderator.

It would be fascinating to travel back in time to eavesdrop on the debate at that Assembly. Both proponents and naysayers would be expressing convictions that continue to inform the life of the United Reformed Church (URC) today. Our passion is for the witness of the local worshipping congregation. Anything that intrudes on its freedom under the Spirit to obey Jesus Christ, its only ruler and head, is held in great suspicion. But left to themselves, local churches can get stuck. Sometimes they need help from outside. Unhealthy power dynamics put them at the mercy of domineering members. More positively, they look outward at national and global issues warranting a Christian response and feel helpless on their own to make a difference. They recognize that by banding together they can offer good training for ministers and guard themselves against self-appointed spiritual leaders who can do them harm. By pooling their resources they can enable worthwhile things to happen that otherwise could not be afforded.

The moderators who were appointed to these new provinces took a cautious experiment and turned it into a denominational fixture. They did this by building personal relationships and demonstrating the kind of wisdom and concern that gradually allayed the fears of the sceptical.

They won themselves the authority that comes with genuine servant leadership.

The creation of the United Reformed Church in 1972 brought denomination-wary Congregationalists into fellowship with Presbyterian denominational enthusiasts. Presbyterians approached with gusto the common life where Congregationalists always trod a bit warily. The Presbyterians recognized wider discipline and authority as healthy, bringing with them a central payroll system that transformed the lives of Congregational ministers who had been at the mercy of poor collections or miserly church treasurers. However, the Presbyterians had no tradition of regional ministry and thus contributed yet another brand of suspicion to the URC mix: a moderator must never be allowed to subvert the authority of a council of the Church. A conciliar Church must beware of personal leadership.

It is within this arena of enthusiasm and suspicion that the present-day synod moderators exercise their ministries. Their role emerged out of the urge to transform mere federations of local churches into families where effective pastoral care, encouragement and, if necessary, intervention could be delivered. The first moderators embodied the churches' yearning for mutual relationship and their cautious desire for a common life. As that common life developed, the role of the moderators developed with it, until today the moderator is the lynchpin at the centre of an enormous cluster of practical and spiritual concerns.

Present-day realities

The 1,500 congregations of the URC are organized into 13 synods (one in Scotland, one in Wales and 11 in England), each with a moderator, a clerk, a treasurer and a trust body. In principle, the office of the moderator has been open to women as well as men from the time that women ministers gained the necessary experience to be eligible. In fact, the first woman moderator was appointed in 1990. Currently four of the 13 moderators are women (2019).

Each of the 13 synods has its own distinct culture, not least because the historical wealth each brings to its work results in a wide disparity of resources. Thus, some of the moderators work in well-staffed and well-resourced teams, while others work primarily with volunteers. Some synods have comprehensive committee structures while others run streamlined operations. This lack of uniformity can be bewildering to ecumenical partners, and it makes joint working across the denomination challenging. However, it represents the freedom that the synods and their moderators enjoy in shaping their life according to the needs and possibilities of their context.

The role – officially

The official definition of the moderators' role is contained in the Structure of the United Reformed Church [para. 2. (4)]:

> There shall be a moderator for each synod being a minister appointed from time to time by the General Assembly according to its rules of procedure and responsible to the General Assembly.
> The moderator shall:
>
> - be separated from any local pastoral charge,
> - stimulate and encourage the work of the United Reformed Church within the province or nation,
> - preside over the meetings of the synod and exercise a pastoral office towards the ministers, church related community workers and churches within the province or nation,
> - suggest names of ministers to vacant pastorates, in consultation with interim moderators of local churches,
> - preside, or appoint a deputy to preside, at all ordinations and/or inductions of ministers and all commissionings and/or inductions of church related community workers within the province or nation,
> - fulfil the responsibilities ascribed to the Moderator of Synod under the ministerial disciplinary process and the incapacity procedure.
> - The moderators of the synods shall meet together at regular intervals for the better discharge of their duties.

Alongside this definition stand other key convictions. Ministry in the United Reformed Church belongs to the whole people of God and is rooted in baptism, which:

> makes explicit at a particular time and place and for a particular person what God has accomplished in Christ for the whole creation and for all humankind – the forgiveness of sins, the sanctifying power of the Holy Spirit, and newness of life in the family of God. (Basis of Union, para. 14)

It is every Christian's joy and privilege to respond to God's saving work by offering their life in service. The priesthood of all believers is seen as the entire company of the faithful making this offering together.

We affirm that,

> The Lord Jesus Christ continues his ministry in and through the Church, the whole people of God called and committed to his service and equipped by him for it ... For the equipment of his people for this total ministry the Lord Jesus Christ gives particular gifts for particular ministries and calls some of his servants to exercise them in offices duly recognised within his Church. (paras 19–20)

The Basis of Union mentions elders, ordained ministers of word and sacraments and church related community workers. It does not mention moderators. They are ordained ministers of word and sacraments, appointed and set apart for fixed terms (currently seven years, with the possibility of renewal for a further five) for the exercise of a particular ministry. If their terms do not take them to retirement age, typically they return to service in a local pastorate. In theory their role carries no special status or authority: that status and authority are vested in the councils of the Church. They are ministers who exercise ministry within and on behalf of the churches that together constitute a synod.

The role – as it really functions

Having bent over backwards to deny the moderators any special status or authority, the Church then proceeds to place impossible expectations on them. Their core work is the pastoral care of ministers and churches. A recent review of the role of the synod moderator urged that the Church remove any burdens or obstacles that prevented the moderators from giving their primary attention to this responsibility. Ministers work under enormous pressure in today's Church. The central payroll is able to provide one paid minister for every three congregations and for many ministers the burden is greater. With membership at a low ebb in many places, ministers can find themselves managing administrative duties, overseeing building maintenance or single-handedly embodying the church's outreach to the community, and acting as social workers, as well as leading public worship and caring for the spiritual life of their church members. They deserve the encouragement of a fellow minister set apart specifically to support them.

However, if local ministers are working at full capacity to sustain existing causes, and synod moderators do nothing more than offer spiritual friendship and support to those ministers and their churches, the ongoing cycle of decline is inevitable. There is a need for the kind of oversight that reads the signs of the times, identifies the thriving causes, shares their stories, and encourages missionary imagination and experimentation. Where ecumenical opportunities arise for church planting or other creative endeavours, someone needs to have cultivated the relationships to enable the URC to participate. Someone needs to develop an overview of the big picture and the resources available so that myriad local circumstances can be built into a regional strategy. And, of course, there is a perpetually expanding body of legislation requiring local and regional compliance: someone needs to dangle the carrot and wield the stick to make sure that those responsible are fulfilling their legal obligations.

Synod moderators today typically admit that their pastoral work is largely confined to crisis response and they lament that there is not more time for the routine visiting of ministers, let alone retired ministers or their widows/widowers. Rather, their primary focus is the synod meeting, which takes place twice or three times a year, gathering ministers and church representatives together, because this is their greatest opportunity for encouraging visionary thinking and enabling inspiring stories to be shared. There is always plenty of 'business as usual' to fill the agenda, but they know that 'business as usual' will not lead to renewal.

Another core task of the moderators is the introduction of ministers to vacant pastorates. They are expected to conduct exit interviews with departing ministers and then serve as external consultants to pastorates preparing to call a new minister. This is rarely routine, not least because the number of ministers that the central payroll system can allow to any particular synod is continually reducing. Often the skills of a diplomat are required to persuade reluctant congregations to join together to share a minister. For years the denomination has pressed the advantages of team ministries of ordained and lay leaders operating across groups of churches, but the churches have been slow to warm to this model. Even where it has been embraced, it requires careful support and development.

In a previous generation, the moderators would gather to suggest the introduction of particular ministers to particular churches. As people of significant pastoral insight who between them had personal knowledge of every minister and church, their suggestions often carried the weight of 'call' for the individuals concerned. This system gave way several years ago to a preference for equal opportunities so that today it is usually the minister who requests an introduction to a particular pastorate, leaving the moderators as agents passing profiles back and forth. They retain a veto power, which they scarcely ever exercise.

The monthly Moderators' Meeting still happens, however, and it has taken on a life of its own, meeting more frequently and at greater length than any other group in the Church. Their prayer encompasses many of the pains felt across the Church. They are able to give in-depth attention to issues emerging within the synods and they often hold wide-ranging discussions about the state of the Church and where the future lies. Others vie for time on their agenda in order to test ideas with them or seek their support for some new venture, though the moderators are absolutely clear that they do not constitute a council of the Church. There have been times when they have overreached themselves in offering leadership in the wider councils on which they do sit, though the Church is quick to put them in their place. Normally they are heard with respect and gratitude. The value of the Moderators' Meeting as a forum for evolving vision cannot be overestimated.

In addition to the Moderators' Meeting, URC moderators embody the denomination's commitment to furthering ecumenical possibilities at every level of church life. Reviews of the role of the moderator are always quick to point out that there is no obligation for the moderator to be the person who engages in regional ecumenism. However, the reality is that some bishops will not do business with anyone but the person they perceive to be their 'church leader' equivalent. And URC members collude by scanning the ecumenical procession in the cathedral to spot whether 'our person' is there.

Moderators join up the thinking between their various committees, nurture their fellow synod workers into teams, respond to cries for help from local churches in distress and answer letters from members of the public complaining about the treatment they have received at the hands of ministers or churches. The policies and procedures of the denomination are readily available online, but in practice it is the moderator who knows they exist and refers people to the documents they need.

In addition to these synod-related duties, the moderators are members of the wider councils of the denomination. The Mission Council meets twice a year to carry out the wishes of the biennial General Assembly. Some moderators become deeply involved in Assembly work, chairing committees, serving on task groups or representing the denomination at significant ecumenical or international events.

In short, the job is impossible. But it is also glorious for the sheer wealth of opportunities it offers for an experienced minister to make a difference for the kingdom. It is a ministry under immense stress. Significantly, it carries enormous responsibilities without the attendant authority to make things happen. The moderator must be a master adept in the art of persuasion.

Some theological reflections

The Reformation was a vast movement transforming sixteenth- and seventeenth-century European culture and society through hundreds of separate manifestations. As a united Church, the URC can trace its origins to various times and places. However, there is a Reformed spirit underlying and infusing the disparate stories, and it was the recognition of this spirit in the lives of partner denominations that enabled the unions of 1972, 1981 and 2000 to happen.[1]

What matters is Jesus Christ, alive through the Spirit, calling followers, dwelling within and among them, nurturing them into abundant life and empowering them for participation in the mission of God. The URC declares Christ to be the only ruler and head of the Church. It listens for the voice of God through the Bible, emphasizing again that it is the Spirit who enables us to discern the Word in the words before us. Wherever the word of God is faithfully preached, and the sacraments rightly administered, we recognize the essential marks of the Church.

Pretty much everything else is provisional. Although we take our foundational documents seriously, we regularly assert 'our right and readiness, if the need arises, to change the Basis of Union and to make new statements of faith in ever new obedience to the living Christ' (Basis of Union Schedule D). The rules governing local church life, the shapes of ministries, the number and frequencies of councils – all can be changed if the Spirit so leads.

This means that the role of the synod moderator is not cast in concrete. The moderator has never been seen as part of the basic *esse* of the Church. The role was created for pragmatic reasons and a pragmatic people would have no hesitation in putting something different in its place. That the role has evolved over the generations and now bears little resemblance to the vision of the 1919 Congregational Assembly surprises no one.

Although it would be possible to overlay the role of the synod moderator with biblical texts on *episkope* or insights from Christian history and tradition, there seems little point in doing so. The focus belongs on God. What on earth is happening to the Christian Church in Western Europe in this new century? The indigenous Church we inherited is now a vibrant multicultural family as the world the missionaries went to serve moves in and establishes itself in our midst. Other great world faiths we barely knew about are now major players on the religious scene. We are increasingly marginalized from public debate and must earn the place at the table that we once took for granted. Secularism may well have the last word, at least for a while.

We live by the promise that God's purposes will ultimately triumph. Our duty is to be actively, unceasingly faithful. While it would be easy to lament the passing of influence and significance that we once enjoyed, it is far more interesting to scan the horizon to try to discern what will happen next. This is what local church meetings are meant to do, within a denomination that gives them almost total freedom to respond to what they see. And it is the primary justification for theologically savvy translocal ministry. This is a ministry that gathers up the local stories and analyses them to discern the woods beyond the separate trees. It is the networking that enables significant stories to be told and lessons to be learnt. It is the strategizing so that resources can support new experiments as well as sustaining existing work. It is the vehicle by which translocal partnerships can be negotiated and fostered for the good of all. And, as time allows, it is the comforting presence that enables beleaguered individuals and churches to find encouragement and affirmation.

Challenges and difficulties

The role of the synod moderator just about worked until the wider world intruded with its regulations and demands for accountability. Charity law requirements have affected every denomination. Each synod moderator is now well acquainted with a legal adviser and the bills run high. While in theory local church elders have always been the managing trustees of their congregations, now they need to be explicitly prepared to execute those duties. Risk management, accounting regulations, disability requirements, health and safety, the safeguarding of children and vulnerable adults all combine into an administrative burden that even the strongest local churches struggle to bear. Just the provision of authoritative advice is a major demand. The URC has never wanted the sort of wider structures that could dictate what local churches had to do. The synod moderators get caught in the middle.

Likewise, with the oversight of ministry. URC ministers are office holders who have historically been exempt from much employment law. However, the denomination is eager to provide a framework as protective and scrupulous as that of secular employment. Again, the moderators find themselves expected to deliver and report and ensure, sometimes to the detriment of their pastoral role.

It is often noted that ecumenical opportunities and expectations have multiplied beyond anything that the early moderators could have imagined. While it is not essential for the moderator to attend to all of them, the alternatives are not terribly satisfactory. An ecumenically minded denomination is keen for its regional leaders to be key players alongside leaders of the other denominations. And it is often in church leaders' meetings that the moderators themselves find the support they need from understanding colleagues.

Moderators are appointed by the General Assembly to serve in the synods. A synod may have representation on the nominating group for new appointments, yet the ultimate power of appointment lies elsewhere. Thus, it can be felt that a moderator has been imposed from the outside against the will of the synod. Without the support of the synod, a moderator cannot function. Until recently, nominating groups were responsible for identifying suitable candidates and inviting them to consider allowing their names to go forward. A change in procedures now means that ministers are free to submit their own names for consideration. Each candidate fills in an application form for scrutiny against specified criteria. It is a more open system, but it does alter the sense of 'call' that sustained many a moderator through many a difficult period in times past.

Looking ahead

Ultimately, the renewal of the Church can only happen from the grassroots. Many ministers and congregations feel isolated in the challenges they are facing, and almost universally their plea is for a return to a model of translocal ministry that focuses primarily on pastoral care. It would be a relatively straightforward, if expensive, strategy to relieve the synod moderators of the administrative duties they have acquired: no one intended for them to become administrators. However, balancing care for existing church life with the need to reach for the future through vision and strategic planning will not be so easy. That vision is the responsibility of the councils of the Church, but good conciliar life requires good leadership. Time will tell whether putting resources into pastoral care repays dividends in energy and vitality that will enable the denomination to continue offering an effective witness in the future.

Note

1 The URC was initially formed when the English Presbyterians merged with English and Welsh Congregationalists in 1972. The Churches of Christ then joined in 1981, followed by the Scottish Congregationalists in 2000.

9

The Salvation Army

Territorial Command Structures

MIKE PARKER

Introduction

The Salvation Army is a worldwide Christian church and registered charity. Under the leadership of the General of The Salvation Army, Territories around the world are responsible for the work of The Salvation Army in their country(ies). While the structure of The Salvation Army (TSA) is essentially the same throughout the world, there is room for flexibility with area or regional variations. For the purpose of understanding translocal leadership within TSA, it is better to consider just the ecclesiastical aspect of The Salvation Army, though in reality the full mission of TSA is undivided.

Biblical parallel

Taking into account the overall leadership of the General in the 'church' part of the ministry, there are essentially three command structures. First, the Territorial structure. This is led by a Territorial Commander who is responsible for the ministry in their Territory, which could comprise a number of countries. Second is a divisional structure into which each territory is divided and led by a Divisional Commander. Third are the local expressions of mission where a Commanding Officer (local leader) takes responsibility for a corps (congregation) or centre to which they have been appointed. While there are other roles and structures, this is the relevant framework that is replicated around the world.

The New Testament also appears to indicate an emergence of three such structures. The universal Church, which includes Christians all over the world, translocal church itinerant individuals, who minister among the various churches, and the local church, which is exactly what it says. With reference to the APEST (Apostle, Prophet, Evangelist, Shepherd, Teacher) leadership model, the essence of TSA's approach to translocal leadership, although wide-ranging, would not only incorporate the apostolic role but other leadership gifts and responsibilities to enhance mission in a local church. The 'leadership' list in Ephesians 4.11, as most commentators suggest, is not a list of diverse roles in the Church but of different aspects of the same function. The New Testament appears to indicate an overlap of roles, for example 1 Timothy 2.7, where Paul is identified as both an apostle and a teacher. In the early Christian treatise the *Didache*, the terms apostle, prophet and teacher are used interchangeably, suggesting that to be an apostle implies that you are also a teacher and likely a prophet and evangelist too. In 2 Timothy 4.5, Timothy is exhorted to do the work of an evangelist immediately after having been told to teach sound doctrine. The main emphasis is on equipping and mobilizing the body of Christ, whatever that takes.[1] This essentially correlates to the divisional structure of TSA, where a team, under the leadership of the Divisional Commander (DC), exercises spiritual leadership, gives pastoral care and brings strategic leadership to some, but not all, of the key dimensions of the role.

Recent developments in TSA in the United Kingdom Territory with the Republic of Ireland (UKI) have brought some radical changes to TSA's exercise of translocal ministry. Historically the Territorial Headquarters gave oversight to the work of the movement through departments that focused on overall strategic planning and vision. A divisional structure is where the Divisional Commander and their team are responsible for all the work of TSA in their geographical area. Such a wide-ranging responsibility was proving to be particularly challenging in the context of the UKI Territory, with TSA combining being a church and a major charity that focuses on areas such as homelessness with residential centres; older people's services including care homes; human trafficking including refuge centres for victims of modern slavery as well as women and children who have suffered abuse; emergency support in times of disaster; employment programmes for those out of work; centres for people with learning difficulties; and day-care centres. TSA passionately sees its social mission not merely as 'charity' but also as an expression of 'church'. So in these recent developments, which majored on a better focus and greater effectiveness, a significant element of the resulting restructure was a stripping out of the business administration from the divisions. It is also worth noting that the social mission was centralized many years ago, making it a multi-faceted enterprise with enormous demands on the corporate and administrative life of TSA. It is no surprise that TSA kept exploring whether our structures were both fit for purpose in the twenty-first century, and 'Fit for Mission', a title that would ultimately be taken up into our strategy for moving forward.[2]

Historical perspective

A brief historical overview provides the context out of which the influence of Methodist-style organization and structure shaped TSA and continues to be evident today. The Salvation Army was founded by William Booth in 1865 in London's East End. Originally a minister with the Methodist New Connexion, Booth had a deep desire to be set free to do the work of an evangelist. Feeling restricted and unable to follow God's way for his ministry, he resigned his position and became an itinerant preacher before commencing his work in the East End.

On his way home from a preaching engagement in East London, Booth came across a group of Christians leading an open-air service. He responded to an invitation to speak and the group immediately invited him to take on the leadership of their small mission. They started their ministry in a tent on a Quaker burial ground, calling themselves the 'East London Christian Mission' and developing further centres of ministry throughout East London. When they expanded to Croydon, the 'East London' designation in the title was dropped and the mission was simply called 'The Christian Mission'. It developed its structures and approach to evangelism in the following years until, in 1878, it was an army in all but name. Booth had already acquired the title of General because the use of 'General Superintendent' from his Methodist background had proved a rather cumbersome designation for everyday use. In addition, his number two, George Scott Railton, was his self-styled 'lieutenant'. The mission called people to join the 'Hallelujah Army'. Other ministers were often called Captains and they even held a 'War Congress'. In the same year that the Revd S. Baring-Gould gave to the world his stirring processional hymn 'Onward Christian Soldiers', the Christian Mission changed its name to 'The Salvation Army'.

> The Salvation Army – what a strange name! What does it mean? Just what it says – a number of people joined together after the fashion of an army; and an army for the purpose of carrying salvation through the land ...[3]

It was at the 'War Congress' that this transformation formally took effect, and within weeks the first edition of *Orders and Regulations for The*

Salvation Army were in print. Organizational structure became a challenge in those early days as the number of ministers (now called officers) in the UK increased from 120 (1878) to 2,260 (1886), and the number of corps (churches) increased from 50 to 1,006 over the same period. The social work was also growing rapidly, and work outside the UK moved from being non-existent in 1878 to 1,932 officers serving abroad in 743 corps by 1886 (Sandall, 1947, p. 338). A strong mission focus alongside pastoral care and a structure for the oversight of the movement's progress continued to develop and has been the pattern since the beginning. However, the focus on purpose has remained the plumbline when such developments occurred. Today that development has continued with the 'Fit for Mission' initiative.

Fit for Mission

From 2012 to 2014, TSA took a fresh look at itself, seeking to be more effective in God's mission. The call to be 'Fit for Mission' (FFM) was the challenge from TSA leadership in the UK. The outcome in 2015 was a renewed vision to deliver and support its core mission, 'To Save Souls, Grow Saints and Serve Suffering Humanity'. This new vision has four priorities, which were outlined by the Territorial Commander, Commissioner Clive Adams:

> What we learnt, from many months of discussion … has shaped this new strategy that builds on our central ministry. Working together as a Territory, we will commit to delivering four mission priorities that spell out the word TIDE: bringing about lasting Transformation in lives and communities blighted by spiritual and social poverty; engaging every aspect of our movement in our Integrated mission of physical, emotional and spiritual health for every person; nurturing and equipping people in their faith to commit to lifelong Discipleship; and Effectiveness in how we support and deliver mission.
>
> The commitment to move forward together as One Army with One Mission and One Message – a progressive, influencing and active movement that looks to the future, is bold, risk-taking and ready to cross boundaries!

Translocal leadership in The Salvation Army

The 11 principles of the present approach to translocal oversight within TSA are:

- Prioritizing local mission.
- Developing spiritual leaders.
- Reducing administration for local settings.
- Streamlining process and reducing duplication.
- Simplifying decision-making.
- Satisfaction in local settings at levels of service and support received.
- Communicating effectively across the Territory.
- Empowering people for mission in their local mission setting.
- Empowering people to develop their local strategy in alignment with the Territorial mission priorities (TIDE), through a new mission development planning tool (MDP) using faith-based facilitation (FBF).
- Enabling The Salvation Army to assess new and existing opportunities for mission using the Mission Opportunities Assessment Tool (MOAT).
- Enabling The Salvation Army to measure the impact of its mission and strategy and make decisions.

The new structure is shown in the following diagram:

Our mission – structure

DHQ
Enabling
Pastoral care
Relational support
Leader development
Mission focus groups
Equipping
MDPs

SERVICE CENTRES
Resource, support, encourage and train people to deliver mission
Business support

MISSION DELIVERY

THQ
Leadership
Vision
Developing leaders
Governance
Accountability

CENTRAL SERVICES
Operational and admin support
Resource production
Processing

Support for the mission at local level comes essentially from three areas.

First, there is the role that Territorial Headquarters brings in such areas as the administrative support and resourcing of 'Central Services' and the vision/strategy that are part of the cabinet-style leadership of the Territorial Headquarters (THQ).

Second, there is the regional structure provided through 'Service Centres', which take on the business and administrative duties of the charitable work to free up Divisional Head Quarters (DHQ) teams to better support corps and centres in local mission. These Service Centres provide support for mission and business particularly through matters related to property, human resources, finance and communications.

Third, in DHQs there are several roles that are part of TSA's translocal leadership. DHQs concentrate on providing pastoral care, enabling mission, developing spiritual leaders and supporting leader development at the front line. The Divisional Commander is the spiritual leader for mission in each division.[4] The position of a DC is one of the most influential in The Salvation Army. The DC's spirit and work has far-reaching effects on the work of the Army in the division and on the lives and activities of its officers and soldiers. Key attributes and responsibilities are:

- Dependence on the Holy Spirit
- Example of Salvationism
- Inspiring officers
- Love for souls
- Aggressive pacesetter
- Sacred responsibility
- Internationalist
- Leader and pastor
- Development of soldiers
- Family responsibilities.[5]

The DC is responsible for ensuring that mutual accountability processes are working well and for building good relationships with spiritual leaders. DCs also support the involvement of divisional and regional mission specialists at corps and centres. Other roles at DHQs enhance the relationship between the front-line and divisional teams.

Effective spiritual leadership is vital if TSA is to create healthy missional communities. Getting the spiritual leadership right will impact the whole movement. Without spiritual renewal, mission will atrophy and die over time. Without mission, spiritual renewal is a self-centred indulgence that will not impact our world or society.

In essence, the role of the Divisional Commander is seen as:

- Shepherd – pastoral care and equipping
- Seer – leader development
- Steward – enhanced relationship
- Supplier – increased engagement
- Support – effective mission support.

Other new roles put in place are dedicated to growing spiritually healthy missional communities and the development of spiritual leaders for local mission. The Divisional Mission Enabler (DME) is one such key appointment.

The DME supports the MDP process and holds people accountable for delivery. They are trained to work alongside corps, centres and every expression of mission. Rather than enforcing a one-size-fits-all set of rules, mission enablers help leaders to discover practical insights about what works and what does not in delivering transformational mission in their local settings.

The focus is on giving pre-eminence to the local setting and empowering rather than taking control. It is about developing ownership and resilience in the local church rather than creating or maintaining a culture of dependency. This is the driving principle of FFM that leads into new ways of enabling, resourcing, planning and measuring local mission in order to improve our ability to serve others. Those at the front line are supported in evaluating their current effectiveness. In essence the role of the DME is to:

- Facilitate the journey
- Support the mission as a 'generalist'
- Provide mission specialists
- Develop relationships
- Bring mutual accountability for the MDP
- Develop local resilience.

Spiritual reflection

> Time after time God reaches out to a lost world through the Church serving as part of its community. The first mission strategy of the Early Church placed the local setting at the centre, with people taking the good news about Jesus from Jerusalem to the ends of the earth. Improved planning tools will empower people to bring that same message of healing and salvation to our modern world.[6]

A further key role within this new translocal structure is the Divisional Leader for Leader Development. This role supports the development of spiritual leaders and encourages mutual accountability within divisions. The intentional emphasis on development in this new role enables spiritual leaders to have greater clarity about their role and how they might fulfil it. Officers and other spiritual leaders understand how their role impacts the mission of TSA and know what support and resources are available to equip them for the role. Spiritual leaders are supported in becoming aware of both their personal strengths and less effective behaviours, and of how to maximize their own capabilities and gifts. There is increased transparency, engagement and mutual accountability within these improved systems and processes.

To recap, although much of the work to resource and enable local mission occurs through DHQ personnel, regional mission specialists also offer support to corps and centres. Specialist roles in children's ministries, family ministries, music and creative arts ministries and older people's services resource, support, encourage and train centres and corps in delivering Christian programmes and worship that are inspiring and attractive. A specialist role in community services ensures the achievement of the Christian mission and professional management of social and community programmes within divisions by providing advice, support and resources as well as promoting continuous improvement in the quality of service provision. Overseeing this work is the renamed Mission Service – formerly the Programme Service – which has a greater focus on training, resourcing and enabling employees, officers, local officers and cadets (student officers) to be more effective in local mission. The Mission Service is there to:

- Enable, empower and equip effective front-line mission
- Provide an integrated and more client-responsive service facilitating delivery of effective mission
- Ensure an effective research and evidenced-based approach to mission
- Resource and train people in local settings
- Ensure integration is a high priority in the way mission is delivered.

As this demonstrates, the threefold resource structure for effective mission within TSA is deployed primarily through the ministry of the divisional team. However, this is augmented by the regional structure as described above, and the THQ role, which concentrates on executive leadership, governance, vision and strategy and, through the Central Services, helps with all centralized activities of operational and administrative support.

Conclusion

In respect of the FFM strategy, the commitments made at a senior level are pivotal to the effective transition to this new way of working. Here these commitments are expressed as a direct quote:

We will:

- Nurture a culture of mutual accountability so our behaviours match our values, leading to trust and integrity among our people.
- Give pre-eminence to the local setting and empower rather than take control. This driving principle of FFM leads to new ways of enabling, resourcing, planning and measuring front-line mission to improve our ability to serve others.
- Establish new divisional boundaries and staff structures to increase the ability of divisional teams to provide training, support and pastoral care.
- Reorganize and simplify operational and administrative services to be more responsive to the needs of front-line corps and centres.

Without resilient expressions of local mission, the danger is that TSA will continue to encourage dependency. This journey to more effective mission has only just begun, so it is too early to comment on how effective it is proving to be. However, the desire and commitment to be fit for mission is strong. Leadership at all levels passionately wants to ensure that every aspect of The Salvation Army is as effective as it can be in reaching out relevantly to people with the transforming message of the gospel. The future looks exciting.

Notes

1 See David Fitch at Missio Alliance, www.missioalliance.org/author/davidfitch/ (accessed 25.07.2019) and Hirsch, Alan and Tim Catchim, 2012, *The Permanent Revolution*, San Francisco, CA: Jossey-Bass, pp. 81–3.

2 This chapter draws significantly on unpublished internal documents that were part of the evolution and decision-making process for the Fit For Mission initiative. They are quoted by permission of TSA.

3 William Booth, www.salvationarmy.org.uk/files/transforming-livespdf/download?token=WeNtmK-x (accessed 25.07.2019).

4 Often, but not always, a married couple who are officers will be the Divisional Leaders. However, TSA also has single men and women in these roles.

5 *Orders and Regulations for Divisional Commanders* (internal Salvation Army publication).
6 Unpublished TSA document (see note 2 above).

References

Hirsch, Alan and Tim Catchim, 2012, *The Permanent Revolution*, San Francisco, CA: Jossey-Bass.
Sandall, Robert, 1947, *The History of The Salvation Army, Volume Two*, London: Thomas Nelson.

10

Pentecostalism

Translocal Leadership in UK Pentecostal Churches

WILLIAM K. KAY

Introduction: theology and legal frameworks

It is not widely appreciated that the structure of the Church both locally and nationally reflects a combination of theology and the underlying legal system in force. In Britain, where the ownership of freehold property is possible, and where charity law designed to alleviate poverty has a long connection with parliamentary statutes, the emergence of property-owning Pentecostal denominations is and was eminently possible. Added to this, the religious history of Britain, with its own Protestant Reformation and its long-established dissenting and nonconformist traditions, made religious freedom a companion of legal entitlements. Congregations could buy buildings and there was legal machinery to allow a group of religious individuals to own property jointly. The concept of a 'trustee' was legally defined and the position of religious groups in respect of banking and charity was either settled or open to settlement. There were, it is true, complaints about the amount of money flowing into Elim in the 1920s and this did cause charity law to be tightened up (Kay, 2017, p. 204). The point here is that the tax advantages of charitable status were long recognized and the legal framework sufficiently flexible to allow a variety of denominational structures to come into existence. In this sense, theology provided the motivating power and, ideally, a blueprint derived from Scripture, while the law was broad enough to accommodate the various options religious groups might eventually fix upon.

Pentecostal beginnings

The beginnings of the Pentecostal movement in Britain can be dated to the time of the First World War. The first Pentecostal church to be built in Britain was constructed and opened in 1908 and it took the name Apostolic Faith Church. From this group, as a breakaway, the (Welsh) Apostolic Church came into existence in 1916.[1] In 1915, George Jeffreys founded the Elim Pentecostal Church in Ireland which, from 1921 onwards, spread over to the rest of the United Kingdom. The Assemblies of God was formed in 1924. In terms of ethos, and to a lesser extent in terms of doctrine, these Pentecostal churches were all influenced by the Sunderland conventions (1908–14) called by the charismatic Anglican clergyman Alexander Boddy (1854–1930) (Kay, 2008, pp. 183–99). Boddy wanted the outpouring of the Holy Spirit to renew the mainline denominations to bring about revival. Yet the process of forming separate congregations, organized as denominations, began to assume a momentum of its own, partly because a significant minority of early Pentecostals were nonconformist pacifists (unlike Boddy) and partly because their tongues-speaking was not welcome in mainline churches. The acquisition of property as well as the need to train Pentecostal ministers and support Pentecostal missionaries added further rationale to the establishment of the new denominations.

All three groups – the Apostolics,[2] Elim and Assemblies of God – prospered, and the most obvious distinction between them was that the Assemblies of God specifically and deliberately prioritized the autonomy of the local church while Elim, growing out of the powerful healing ministry of George Jeffreys (1889–1962), was more centrally controlled. The Apostolics were insistent upon the restoration and reality of apostolic and prophetic ministry and, in this sense, they built the notion of translocal ministry into their earliest theological thinking. But they had no concept of the autonomy of the local church and, even today, the entire denomination has one charity number, and so local assemblies have no separate legal existence.

Pentecostal teaching was characterized by a distinctive doctrine and experience of 'baptism in the Spirit' and all the charismatic implications of this. Although ecclesiology was important, it was not made explicit or worked out by Assemblies of God or, to a lesser extent, Elim, at least until the end of the 1920s.[3] Here the concerns were largely with the harmonious functioning of the charismatic congregation with its free-flowing worship, rather than with translocal implications. The primary text from Acts 2 spoke of the outpouring the Spirit on 'all' flesh (v. 17), thus showing that the ministry of women in preaching and prophecy was divinely legitimated. More than this, the message was restorationist in the sense that many Pentecostals believed the Church would regain what had been lost in the years that had elapsed since the vibrant early days canonized in Acts.

There is surprisingly little discussion in early British Pentecostal literature of the governmental options historically available to start-up denominations in the UK. The probable reason for this is that ministers of local Pentecostal congregations had limited horizons: they wanted to be sure of a viable platform from which to conduct their ministries. They were practical people ready to receive encouragement leading to church growth or missionary success, but they did not want theological theory or lessons in church history. Psychologically, they wanted support for Pentecostal doctrine and some sense of collective identity and value, and this they could receive at an annual conference where, in large gatherings, they could overcome any sense of their minority status in religious and civil society.

Translocal practice in the British Apostolic Church

In the Apostolic Church the apostleship, both legally and in practice, has authority over any given assembly and may intervene at any point. If there is a problem, the area apostle does not need an invitation but can intervene if they so wish. There is an assembly presbytery (the pastor and elders) but the apostle, together with the area pastors' meeting, appoints the elders to each assembly presbytery, so that these elders owe their position to an agency outside the assembly where they serve. Only an apostle, however, can ordain elders and, even though the local pastor and presbytery have much more influence in the ordination of elders than they used to, it is still technically an appointment from above by the apostleship rather than an appointment from below by the local assembly. In keeping with this, the local assembly has no say in the choice of its pastor, as appointment is by the apostleship.

The area apostle is very much seen as the pastor of the pastors, although in some parts of the country there are complaints that pastors only see their apostles when there is a crisis. Contemporary Apostolics would be horrified at the suggestion that their apostles are essentially bishops, though this is exactly what they are. Indeed, D. P. Williams, the key figure in the founding of the Apostolic Church, wrote freely about the three orders of ministry (apostle, presbyter, deacon) in the same terms as an Anglican or Roman Catholic might do. Thus, although the Apostolic Church saw itself as restoring apostolic and prophetic ministry in line with the twentieth-century outpouring of the Spirit, it did reach back to the history of the early Church. According to Jonathan Black, whose scholarship has informed these insights, 'the one big difference between our apostles and the normal working of bishops in an Episcopal system is that the Apostolics have always stressed collegiality. Therefore, it is always the apostleship together who have any authority, rather than a single apostle.'[4] In line with this, the apostle, if present, has the prerogative to take the Table at the Breaking of Bread and, *in extremis*, the power to excommunicate or undo excommunication.

Translocal practice in the Elim Pentecostal Church

Historically, Elim is composed of churches of different categories, some more closely tied into the central administration and others less so. The ructions in Elim from *c.*1935 to 1940 over the eventual departure of George Jeffreys, the denomination's founder, were ostensibly concerned with local church autonomy. Having set up a centralized system, Jeffreys reversed his priorities and demanded autonomy be ceded to local congregations, including autonomy over the appointment of pastors and the disposal of buildings. Although he had set up a system of local superintendents, and although this system continued for over 50 years, his own new post-1940 vision was for a collection of autonomous congregations according to a pattern almost indistinguishable from that adopted by the Assemblies of God. The momentum of Jeffreys' reforming push continued after his departure and resulted in greater lay representation at the annual conference and greater involvement by church officers like deacons and elders in the running of local congregations. Elim mainly had deacons in local churches rather than elders until the 1980s. This was one of the problems identified by the Doctrine of the Church Committee (1970–76) and was further exacerbated by the challenge from the Restoration Movement, with their emphasis on apostles and elders. This balance between local empowerment and regional superintendency (overseen by an Executive Council and answerable to an annual General Conference) continued until revisions influenced by the neo-Pentecostal or restoration movement were introduced in the 1980s. These allowed churches to appoint elders and deacons by a method of their choosing (subject to the approval of Elim headquarters) and in other ways to enjoy greater autonomy in their style of worship. With regionalization in 1986, further changes followed (Frestadius, 2018, p. 251). Regional leaders were introduced, and these were seen as offering pastoral support to pastors. Although there was criticism that regionalization resulted merely in a bureaucratic structure, the intentions were spiritually creative

(Frestadius, p. 252). The Executive Council became the National Leadership Team in 2000. Whatever the force of these changes, however, the translocal effects – that is, on local pastors – did not alter much. In general, local churches, as long as no overt problems reared their heads, could run their affairs without much in the way of regional or national interference. Nevertheless, the appointment of pastors, especially in the category of Elim churches tied most closely into the central administration, required at the very least the approval of regional superintendents. As in all translocal matters, it was either at the moment of local pastoral appointment or in a time of contention or trouble that ministerial authority emanating from outside the local congregation became operative.

Translocal practice in British Assemblies of God

The Assemblies of God (AoG) is organized nationally. This means that each country where the AoG exists is independent of all the others. There is loose affiliation between these groups, but it is not true that what AoG does in one country is exactly the same as what it does in another, or that AoG in one nation is answerable to all the others. In Britain there is a sharp divide between the period from 1924 to 2007 and the period after 2007, the year the Constitution was changed. Prior to 2007, AoG was organized as a set of self-governing congregations grouped into districts, with between 20 and 50 congregations in each district, and later into regions, which were similar but larger groupings. The essential workings were the same. A district or regional chairman would be elected and the ministers would attend monthly or bi-monthly meetings to discuss matters of common interest. If a particular congregation got into difficulties (perhaps through immorality or financial mismanagement), then the district or region could be invited into help. The autonomy of the local church ensured that the district or regional ministers could not come in unless invited to do so by a substantial proportion of the congregation or a significant number of elders or trustees.

After 2007, the switch to 'apostolic' leadership led to a much more hierarchical system. The churches were assigned to areas, which were altogether bigger groupings containing perhaps 100 or 150 churches under an Area Leader, who was a member of the National Leadership Team and appointed by the National Leader. The area leaders appointed Zone Leaders, who were given groups of about 50 churches to look after, and they frequently subdivided these zones into fraternals (smaller groupings for fellowship but without any other function). The Zone Leaders carried out much of the day-to-day pastoral and training work within the denomination. They might be asked to help in anything ranging from pastors with marriage problems to structural and financial difficulties. The congregations still retained the right to resist the encroachments of the Zone or Area Leader although, in the years that followed 2007, the denomination tightened the rules on ministerial status to raise expectations that ministers would obey the instructions coming down from the National Leader and the National Leadership Team. In other words, although the autonomy of the local church was safeguarded by the trust deeds of the local congregations, the accreditation of ministers was tightened up and the trust deeds of the churches were made as uniform as possible to ensure buildings were likely to be surrendered to AoG's national leadership should a church have to be closed.[5] The post-2008 system might be called 'episcopal' in the sense that a hierarchy of authority was constructed (the National Leader related to Area Leaders, who related to the Zone Leaders, who related to the local church leaders), but it was done in the name of an unexamined doctrine of leadership: the presumption was that a denomination could be run in the same way as a local church, where the National Leader was equivalent to the pastor and the ministers of the independent churches were equivalent to the congregation.

Pentecostal denominations transplanted from overseas

Many Pentecostal denominations planted themselves in the UK from the mid-1960s onwards and most of these were of West African origin. So, for instance, the Aladura International Church arrived in 1970, the Celestial Church of Christ in 1974, Christ Apostolic Church Mount Bethel the same year, Church of Jesus Christ Apostolic in 1975 and Christ Apostolic Church of Great Britain came in 1976 (Goodhew, 2012, p. 109). The 1980s continued with the planting of the Church of Pentecost's first UK congregation in 1988, the same year as the Redeemed Christian Church of God (RCCG) (Goodhew, pp. 112, 129), and the trend continued into the next decade. Matthew Ashimolowo left the International Church of the Foursquare Gospel begun by Aimee Semple McPherson in the 1920s to start Kingsway International Christian Centre (KICC) in 1992, at a time when Nigerian immigration was on the increase: statistics give 47,201 migrants in 1991 and 88,380 in 2001, and about 80 per cent were resident in London (Goodhew, p. 129).

These churches held to various polities, some of which were a variant of the Apostolic Church – indeed, may have been founded in Africa directly or indirectly by the Apostolic Church – and others had a system of governance more akin to that of Elim or Assemblies of God. The arriving churches grew, especially among specific ethnicities – though they later broadened out – and they usually gave attention to the acquisition of property, vesting episcopal or 'apostolic' authority in a few senior individuals. Their translocal ministry followed along lines already practised by the classical indigenous Pentecostal denominations, a congruence facilitated and encouraged by the need to conform with British charity law.

The language of governance

The language of governance is theological, although in recent years, perhaps since the start of the 1990s, many of the underlying influences on its practice have been drawn from the business world. At least some denominational leaders have tended to see themselves as belonging to the management sector and thereby entitled to all the privileges that go with this status. They expect expense accounts, gym membership, car allowances, hotel and meal costs as well as business-class travel. Beyond the accoutrements of secular status, the ideas of management, often derived from corporate America, have also been utilized. National leaders may speak of the 'branding' of their denomination and local congregations may be 'franchisees' of the brand; translocal leaders may function like church-growth consultants, giving expert advice on mission statements, budgeting and advertising.

While there may be nothing intrinsically wrong with growth targets and professional competence within the running of a group of churches, the danger is that the church leaves behind the standards and values of the New Testament. Where the costs of translocal government account for 30 per cent or more of the income of the denomination, one may question whether the prosperity gospel has so radically altered the operation of the Church as to change its very nature.

As far as the actual words used to describe governance are concerned, there seems to be an interchangeability between 'overseer', 'superintendent' and even 'bishop'. The most generic term, 'leader', has become widely used although it is not closely connected with any precise New Testament terminology; but this, perhaps, is why it is favoured. It can mean whatever a denomination wants it to mean.

Conclusion

Translocal ministry in Pentecostal churches has evolved over time and is based partly on British law governing associations and denominations and partly on theological ideas dating at least as far back as the Reformation and probably to the New Testament. Given that Pentecostalism claims to be a restorationist movement attempting to restore the Church to its pristine New Testament beauty, it is not surprising that there have been attempts to recreate apostolic governance in the twentieth and twenty-first centuries. Even if we take the normal assumption that the emergence of monarchical static bishops in the second century AD is a straight historical development from the mobile apostles the first century, it is obvious that the current arrangements for translocal ministry within Pentecostal churches cannot easily be equated with very different conditions nearly two millennia earlier.

The apostolic networks formed in Britain in the 1980s attempted to begin afresh, to start from a new year zero. By contrast, the Pentecostal groups formed at the start of the twentieth century adapted ecclesiology from the portfolio of options engendered by the Free Churches in the period since the Reformation. Complications were bound to occur when hybrid systems were introduced, systems that took early democratic Pentecostal modes of governance and attempted to graft new and authoritative types of governance on to them. What we can say is that the legal ownership of buildings and the retention by denominations of property is a subterranean factor in the maintenance of coherent denominational identities. Equally, the idealistic notion of bright, young, new groupings of churches led by mature and wise apostles, while obviously attractive, is difficult to realize in practice. One might say that the bad, bureaucratic and inflexible systems that are sometimes developed by Pentecostal churches might be mitigated by the presence of good, godly and gracious people; and, equally, that wonderful systems of governance might be damaged by the presence of authoritarian, short-sighted and bungling regional or quasi-apostolic ministers. Perhaps the answer is that character matters more than structure or that the combination between holy and gracious character and biblical structure is still an elusive ideal.

Notes

1 This group prospered while the group founded in 1908 did not.
2 Despite its Welsh beginnings, the membership soon diversified through congregations in England, Scotland and Northern Ireland.
3 For a fuller account, see Donald Gee's writings referenced below.
4 Personal email (29 May 2018).
5 The Area Leadership Team now has the right to approve of the leader within a local (autonomous) church seeking to come into AoG. This approval seems to relate to the right of the church to nominate a leader to represent the church at the General Council. Over time, if this system persists, local church autonomy is likely to be eroded.

References

Evans, Eifion, 1987, *The Welsh Revival of 1904*, Bridgend: Bryntirion Press.
Frestadius, S. K., 2018, 'Whose Pentecostalism? Which Rationality? The Foursquare Gospel and Pentecostal Biblical pragmatism of the Elim tradition'. Unpublished doctoral dissertation, University of Birmingham.
Gee, Donald, 1928, *Concerning Spiritual Gifts*, Springfield, MO: Gospel Publishing House.
Gee, Donald, 1930, *Concerning Shepherds and Sheepfolds*, Nottingham: Assemblies of God.
Gee, Donald, 1952, *The Ministry Gifts of Christ*, London: Elim Publishing Co.
Goodhew, David (ed.), 2012, *Church Growth in Britain: 1980 to the Present*, Aldershot: Ashgate.
Hathaway, Malcolm, 1998, 'The Elim Pentecostal Church: Origins, Developments and Distinctives', in Keith Warrington (ed.), *Pentecostal Perspectives*, Carlisle: Paternoster Press.
Kay, William K., 2008, 'Sunderland's Legacy in New Denominations', *Journal of the European Pentecostal Theological Association* 28.2, pp. 183–99.
Kay, William K., 2017, *George Jeffreys: Pentecostal Apostle and Revivalist*, Cleveland, TN: Centre for Pentecostal Theology Press.

11

Apostolic Ministry in the New Church Streams

Personal Reflections from Newfrontiers

TERRY VIRGO

Beginnings

The development of the group of churches called Newfrontiers began in the 1970s when I, then the pastor of a Free Evangelical church in Seaford, Sussex, was invited to visit a small group of believers meeting in a private home in Scaynes Hill, a village some 25 miles away.

I was invited because they wanted to hear about the freshly discovered charismatic experience we were enjoying. I spoke on some related themes and was invited to come regularly, resulting in a commitment to visit this group on alternate weeks for an indefinite period. My visits included Bible teaching, practical instruction and praying for people.

Numbers attending the meetings multiplied considerably, leading to a room in the house being extended to accommodate the meetings. One couple from the group moved to another town and made a similar invitation, resulting in my visiting them on the alternate weeks. As a result, two house churches were formed. Gradually this number grew until about ten such groups were scattered across Sussex. I arranged a monthly event in Brighton at Hove Town Hall, which initially gathered around 300 people but ultimately grew to a thousand or so.

At my home church in Seaford we developed a team ministry of preachers so that, although I was still regarded as the pastor, I was free to be away frequently serving other churches. In these early days there was no formal recognition of what now might be called 'translocal ministry'. I simply responded to invitations to provide help in Bible teaching and practical instruction for these new churches.

When I was invited to help Allerford Chapel in Catford, South London, this was my first involvement in an existing church with its own history. The pastor invited me initially to bring a week's teaching ministry; this led to regular visits to help reshape the style of the church. The congregation was blessed with fresh vitality and growth and other churches in the neighbourhood began to invite me to help them as well.

As this network of relationships grew, from time to time I would invite the leaders of these churches to gather for prayer and fellowship. On one occasion a pastor saw a vision of a herd of elephants running together, breaking through undergrowth and forming a new path where one had not previously existed. He prophesied to those gathered, 'There are no well-worn paths before you, but together you can make a way where there is no way. You can accomplish more together than apart, and many will follow.'

Until that time we had no intention of forming a group of churches or 'movement'. I was simply helping individual churches where I was invited. We discussed the implications of this prophecy and came to the conclusion that we would work in association together. We agreed on a list of values and goals and settled on the title of 'Newfrontiers', though each church would retain its own identity and local name. By this time about 30 house churches had established eldership teams and released their own full-time or part-time pastor, or leading elder. They had outgrown private homes and were now meeting publicly in hired school halls or other venues. It is encouraging to observe that these congregations are now large churches that have acquired warehouses or other properties of their own.

We began the Downs Bible Week, an annual summer camp held at Plumpton Racecourse, modelled on a larger event that had been started in the north of England by a similar group, called The Dales Bible Week. We ran this for ten years and over that period it grew from 2,700 to 10,000 people in attendance. This was later replaced by the Stoneleigh Bible Week, near Coventry, which grew to a gathering of 28,000.

Meanwhile more churches were seeking our help and it became impossible for me to respond to all the requests. I asked men whose churches I had previously served if they would represent me and travel on my behalf. Gradually a 'team' of translocal men emerged within our ranks, all of whom were functioning as elders or pastors in their local churches. None were invited to be exclusively translocal.

The earliest churches were formed in a fairly spontaneous way, first by small informal groups asking me to teach them and growing to become congregations. New churches began to be born from them in nearby locations, much as a strawberry plant sends out runners and establishes new plants. Later, people moved intentionally to form entirely new churches in new areas. Training programmes for leaders were developed, and also year-long programmes for young people on a 'gap year' to serve and gain experience.

Biblical perspectives

Alongside this historical background was a constantly developing framework of biblical understanding to guide our programme. The early prophecy had mentioned 'no well-worn paths', and we certainly saw little precedent elsewhere. We knew we were blazing new trails, but as evangelical believers we were very serious about the need for our practices to grow out of clear biblical theology and orthodoxy.

We recognized that in the early Church there were clearly not only elders in local churches but also people who travelled among the churches, serving them in a different capacity. Apostles served churches by laying foundations and providing a fathering role to new congregations. The apostle Paul rarely travelled alone but gathered a team and would sometimes send others, such as Timothy or Titus, to represent him. The churches started by Paul would have had certain characteristics rooted in apostolic doctrine, common to all the churches he founded. The minutiae of local church oversight was principally the responsibility of local elders, although he might advise on points of practice and doctrine.

As we studied Scripture it became apparent that what Paul sometimes referred to as 'all the churches' did not include every existing church, but those Paul himself served within his God-given sphere (2 Cor. 10.13–16), and for which he felt a certain fatherly concern: the so-called 'Pauline churches'. The relationship was one of love and intimacy. He served the church at Thessalonica like a 'nursing mother' and 'charged them like a father' (1 Thess. 2.7, 11). A family atmosphere pervaded their relationships. Within Newfrontiers we have made it our goal to emulate this priority of warm fellowship, so that our style and language are strongly relational, rather than formal or hierarchical.

With regard to raising up itinerant ministry, much has been taught and imparted by means of inviting potential 'Timothys' to accompany us on translocal ministry trips; but we have also provided training programmes and a series of training sessions, entitled TIM (Training Itinerant Ministries), with conscious reference to Paul's companion and representative, Timothy. Here we taught on things associated with translocal ministry, such as the importance of establishing gospel foundations in local churches, the fundamental understanding of grace, community, worship, and corporate prayer.

The style of those working among the churches has always been based on influence rather than authority. Their role has never been imposed but welcomed and initiated by those being served. A weakness we have sometimes encountered is when, because of growth and multiplication, certain translocal leaders have moved on to a new geographical location and have handed over churches they had previously been working with to others. Some of our more long-standing churches have been 'handed over' more than once to the next man, which has threatened the relational factor and has proved unpopular and less effective.

Recent developments

More recently we have recognized and released a number of translocal teams and asked the churches we serve in the UK to choose which team they would like to work with, without geographical priority. Formerly, we formed regions based entirely on geographical location. This obviously had certain advantages, particularly when events and meetings were arranged in those geographical areas; for instance, pastors from certain regions would often gather for prayer and mutual encouragement. Now, however, with the formation of these new teams, churches are encouraged to build their main working relationships with a team of their choice, even though that team may be based in a different part of the country. Effectively we are prioritizing relationship over geographical convenience.

It seems from the New Testament that the apostles did not serve simply as regional supervisors but were very 'missional' in their perspectives, always wanting to reach 'regions beyond'. Paul involved the churches he worked with in his apostolic mission. The church at Philippi was, for instance, 'in partnership' with him and the church in Corinth was urged to resolve their internal problems with a view to his being released from being preoccupied with them and freed to extend his sphere of influence.

People fulfilling translocal ministries among us are encouraged to train leaders and develop church-planting strategies across the UK and overseas. This has now resulted in our involvement in over 60 nations around the world. We are also encouraging the criss-crossing of gifted people among the different teams; so, for example, a prophet may be based in one team but will be invited to use his prophetic gift to benefit churches in another; and this will also apply to the other ministries listed in Ephesians 4 that are recognizable among the churches. Each of those serving translocally continues to be based in a local church, and that is where he will find his home, where his family will be nurtured and where he finds accountability; but he may well be asked to serve in other spheres from time to time.

The more experienced translocal ministries tend to be freed increasingly from 'hands-on' responsibility in their home church in order to give themselves more effectively to translocal work. In Newfrontiers we have found that these translocal ministries have played a very significant role in our growth, in numbers as well as in maturity.

Relationships based on friendship and gifting are the most fruitful. Genuine gifting is vital to bring vision, change and progress; but it is most effective when allied with the trust that comes with already existing friendship. So we aim for both excellent relationship and God-given skills to bring help to the churches.

Further Reading

Virgo, Terry, 2001, *No Well-Worn Paths*, Eastbourne: Kingsway.

Personal Reflections from Pioneer

GERALD COATES

Stirrings

It is almost impossible to predict when an 'incident' will become a movement, never mind an apostolic movement! But this is what has happened. I was in my mid-twenties, newly married and living in a small terraced house in Cobham, Surrey. There was no such thing as a House Church Movement and the charismatic movement at the time was primarily in a small but growing section of the Anglican Church. This was led by Michael Harper, who was the founder and moving force behind the Fountain Trust.

Pentecostalism was separatist, loud and legalistic and there were no Pentecostal churches in the area where we lived. Meanwhile the Fountain Trust organized many large events in London and at Surrey University based in Guildford. One of these events was addressed by Dennis Bennett, an Episcopalian minister from the USA. He wrote of his baptism in the Spirit, speaking in tongues and prophecy in his widely read book, *Nine O'Clock in the Morning*.

I had concluded that there had to be more to Christianity than I was experiencing. A Christian bookshop opened in Cobham High Street and there I discovered the work of Watchman Nee and A. W. Tozer. These challenged my mediocrity. One day while riding my bicycle I was singing and praying. Suddenly without warning an unexpected verbal ejaculation occurred. '*Keyarunda Saddavesto*.' I had never heard anyone else speak in tongues. I asked a new friend with a Pentecostal history to visit me, explain and pray. This he did and the verbal stream of ecstasy became an amazing torrent of thanksgiving.

Following this my wife Anona and three young friends were also baptized in the Holy Spirit. As a result, we spoke to our local church leaders in the Plymouth Brethren. They believed that the gifts of the Holy Spirit had ceased once the canon of Scripture had been completed. So what were we to do? All the other churches in our immediate area were both traditional in their outlook and liberal in their theology. Some hardly believed in the Scriptures never mind gifts of the Holy Spirit.

A new beginning!

We no longer felt comfortable in the Gospel Hall, despite the fact it was full of many fine people. So one Sunday a tiny group of us met in our small living room. Initially I endeavoured to replicate what I had experienced in our former church. An open Bible sat on our coffee table along with a loaf of bread and grape juice. I realized I had brought the Gospel Hall into my front room! I cleared it all away.

We realized that the old model of church would not take us forward, but we had no other models, and becoming a new model is quite different. Development of personal and corporate growth was slow, but we became broader, inclusive and less religious.

As we struggled to find our identity, word was out. People found their way to our terraced home. Many were baptized in the Holy Spirit, others made rededications, while others were born again. Eventually 37 people crammed into our living room, hallway and up our stairs. We moved our meeting place to a local hall and midweek we met in the home of a former commander of HMS *Ark Royal*. Their son had joined us and when his parents were away we found ourselves in his home with a packed-out room, and sang in tongues for 45 minutes. It was a warm evening, so all the windows where open. The next morning two neighbours knocked on the front door. Edwin assumed they had come to complain about the cars and the noise. As he began to apologize they stopped him and explained they were fascinated by the singing and had opened their own windows to listen. They wanted to ask where the choir came from!

We remained in our terraced house, Anona gave birth to our first son, and I was working in nearby Epsom, but I found it impossible to do my job and care for this growing group of people, so I left and became a local postman, up at the crack of dawn and working in the mornings while using my afternoons to read Scripture, prepare talks and care for individuals. Later on, as the work progressed, the church decided to support us financially.

We then began to hear of other experiments in Romford, south-east London and groups that gathered around the author Arthur Wallis, speaker Denis Clark and church leader Lance Lambert. We visited each of these and, as a result, went back to Scripture to help us shape what was happening spontaneously in various locations. That was when the issue of apostles and prophets arose.

Emerging issues

Our reading of Scripture helped us understand that there are only three spheres of church that matter: church in the house, church in the locality and the universal church. There was no national church. There were no centralized denominations. Instead there were relational organizations.

Elders or overseers cared for these three spheres, while apostles (sent ones) went both to the Jews and the Gentiles. Peter became the lead apostle to the Jews and Paul spearheaded a movement into the non-Jews. However, the role of the apostle was not a fixed position like a general in an army or a managing director of a business organization. Paul acknowledged he was not an apostle to everyone. This was not a rank that he or others carried with them.

For us the question arose, 'What do apostles do?' Pastors pastored and cared for the Church. Evangelists evangelized. Teachers taught and prophets prophesied. It became obvious to us that apostles were sent and went off on a mission to preach the gospel and build the Church. A key to understanding the apostolic for us was found in the image of a hand. It seemed that the apostle was the thumb and could bring together evangelists, pastors, teachers and prophets and enable them to work together. All were needed to build up the Church and establish its identity.

Apostolic authority

Initially the early Church only had a record of the old arrangements contained within the Old Testament, with the creator God and a promised Saviour. It would have been easy to centralize, codify and assume ultimate authority would be found in the written account of these old arrangements. Paul's letters to the churches, however, were to change all that. He has no fixed personal authority to operate, but rather is given authority by those who realize that Jesus was the promised Saviour. As he writes he instructs, prays, pleads and implores, but he cannot fine or imprison people who do not obey. That remains the model for us. Apostles are wholly concerned with reconciliation: being reconciled to God and to those who believe in Jesus.

Back to the 1970s

Forming and shaping a model of church is quite different from simply following a pre-existing one. In the early years we were pioneering, cutting through cultural nonsense and our received understanding of church and theology, which was different from that of the apostle Paul. Feeling on our own, when we heard about an experiment in Romford led by John Noble, we asked him and his friends to help us. These visits and conversations became foundational as our local church grew to several hundred people and a network developed across the UK and beyond.

Originally known as the House Church Movement, I coined the phrase 'the New Church Movement' to replace what had become a misnomer. The movement was still highly relational, and I chaired what was rather grandly called the Charismatic Evangelical Round Table for nearly 20 years. Although denominational leaders participated, those who attended were primarily from the New Churches. I do not regard my ministry as apostolic as my main gifting is in the realm of the prophetic. Much of this is retold in Ralph Turner's recounting of my life and ministry, *Gerald Coates Pioneer*.

A sell-out?

Decades after we started in our little front room, I remain strongly convinced of the necessity and validity of the path we took. However, we have also had to face how we relate to those who pursue their discipleship in the historic denominations. Having given these denominations a hard time, especially the Church of England, I have since come to know successive Archbishops of Canterbury, especially George Carey, Rowan Williams and Justin Welby. Identity precedes function. I have learnt that it is almost impossible to influence people or movements if you have nothing to do with them.

Today we find ourselves in the strange position of having individuals and teams, still locked into denominational frameworks, who are apostolic, evangelizing and planting Fresh Expressions of church or even Messy Churches. One evening Rowan Williams and Bishop Graham Cray were explaining why these expressions of church were necessary. Suddenly one of them stopped and commented, 'Of course you were doing this in the 70s, Gerald!' Well, that was true. The difference was that we hardly knew what we were doing, but they had watched us for decades, took the best of what was done and learnt from it.

One more thing

There is one final point it is important to make. Apostolic charismatic evangelicalism has changed both the heart and the face of the Church over five decades. This has not only been done through church planting, evangelism and the writing of many books. There is also the circulation of thousands of talks given at Spring Harvest and other Bible weeks and special events, listened to by large numbers who, like us, were looking for something more for their Christian faith and fruitfulness. Tens of thousands were drawn into the apostolic movement through initiatives that were not branded by new church names such as Pioneer, Ichthus or Ground Level. These have included the 'March For Jesus' movement that attracted tens of thousands for more than a decade. Every year we took to the streets to pray for our nation, culminating in 75,000 in Hyde Park, drawing on Christians from denominational structures and outside of them. Apostolic reconciliation was taking place among groups who had often felt threatened by each other.

ACET (AIDS Care Education Training), founded by Pioneer's Dr Patrick Dixon, ended up caring for more AIDS sufferers dying in their homes than all the other charities put together. ACET was staffed primarily by people from the new churches. It is now found in many nations and has played a major role in slowing down the spread of AIDS in Uganda.

Fusion is a response to other Christian groups on university and college campuses who were anti-charismatic. It is estimated that almost 75 per cent of Christians who are currently studying at university are charismatic. In Fusion there is a far greater openness to draw in speakers from the new churches to teach on the kingdom, church, gifts of the Holy Spirit and relationships.

The Champion Of The World event took place at Wembley Stadium in 1997, attracting around 45,000 people. The day consisted of hours of worship, prayer and music from Noel Richards, Graham Kendrick, Delirious and Matt Redman, and I was privileged to speak. I was told 2,000 made a response to the gospel that day.

The Charismatic Evangelical Round Table began at Waverly Abbey House in Farnham, Surrey. The house was an important part of CWR (Crusade for World Revival), which was then led by Selwyn Hughes. CWR ran a very successful publishing company, which included among its publications the daily devotional *Every Day With Jesus*. The CEO asked if I would go and help them with issues they were facing regarding the house, which slept over 40 people. It was shortly after this that the theme of reconciliation emerged again, and twice a year for over a decade, leading figures of the new churches and denominations met for two days to discuss relevant issues, pray and support each other at Waverly House. Fellowship mellows judgements. It is easy to caricature a person you may never have met. This is more difficult when you are spending a couple of days together twice a year. Grace and understanding emerge at such times and help the focus on more important issues like the Great Command and the Great Commission.

These events and initiatives furthered the apostolic message of Church and kingdom, the gifts of the Holy Spirit, and especially prophecy. And long may it continue!

Further Reading

Turner, Ralph, 2016, *Gerald Coates Pioneer: A Biography*, London: Malcolm Down.

12

The Black Church and Episcopacy

R. DAVID MUIR

The remarks occasioned much laughter from the full room of Redeemed Christian Church of God (RCCG) ministers. 'Was it something funny that I said, or had I put my foot in it?', I found myself asking. Luckily for me it was not the latter. It was obvious that serious discussions had taken place before my arrival at the 2000 Birmingham leadership conference about ecclesiology and the various titles and offices in the Church; so when in my introduction I conferred the designation of 'Bishop' on RCCG's international leader, Pastor Enoch Adeboye,[1] there was much good-natured hilarity. Of course, RCCG does not have 'bishops' in its ecclesiology and I suspect that I would have been greeted with a similar response had I used the term 'Apostle' when referring to the leader of this global Pentecostal Church.

Engaged in formal theological training in higher education, I have the privilege of visiting ministerial theology students at their place of worship as part of their ministry placement. I witness enormous diversity in their theology and ecclesiological practice. One soon learns the protocol in how to address church leaders in African and Caribbean Pentecostal churches. It's important to get titles right and address office holders correctly. In some churches, great umbrage is taken if one gets this wrong. Sometimes it is taken as a lack of respect for the 'ministry' or 'anointing' of the individual; it can also be interpreted as a form of ecclesiological imperialism, where leaders feel that the UK churches are trying to mould them into their ecclesial image with all of its accompanying rituals and regimes of ministerial formation.

The growth and proliferation of black Pentecostal and charismatic congregations has, undoubtedly, changed the religious landscape in the UK and some of our perceptions about 'ministry' and episcopacy. Indeed, there is a view that these churches – Black Christianity – 'may well prove to be a key in the re-evangelization of Christian Britain' (Bradley, 2007, p. 198). Yet there are those from this tradition who question this proliferation. For example, Aldred (2013) asks:

Does it seem like ecclesiological discipline that there are so many independent Pentecostal churches operating, often in isolation from each other and the rest of the body of Christ? ... Does this pass for diversity or fragmentation? (p. 21)

In this chapter, I will attempt to do three things briefly. First, make a few general remarks about episcopacy in the New Testament. Second, look at an exciting but long-overdue development in one of the leading Pentecostal churches in the UK, the New Testament Church of God (NTCG),[2] as they grapple with episcopacy and the nomenclature of 'bishop' and the ordination of women as bishops. I will conclude by considering the ministry of a 'bishop' and an 'apostle' in two leading black Pentecostal churches.

In Paul's Pastoral epistles to Timothy and Titus the terms 'bishop' (*episkopos*) and 'elder' (*presbuteros*) are used interchangeably. According to Berger (1975, pp. 142–4), Titus 1.6–9 and 1 Timothy 3.1–13 belong to the same literary genre as Acts 20.18–23, where the ideal *episkopos* is illustrated. In antiquity, the term *episkopos* was a generic description for a responsible office. It is probable that the Christian 'presbyteral model' was influenced by the Jewish synagogue model with its 'elders', whose duties included giving direction to the community, along with guiding policy decisions and supervising finances (Brown, 1997, pp. 645–6). It was, therefore, a natural title for Christians to use to denote their officials (Dillon and Fitzmyer, 1968, p. 104). The idea of 'monarchical episcopacy' is certainly a post-apostolic phenomenon, given credence by St Ignatius' threefold ministry of 'bishops', 'presbyters' and 'deacons' in his letter to the Magnesians; and in his letter to the Ephesians, where he makes a distinction between 'bishop' and 'presbyter'. In the former letter he says:

> I exhort you to study to do all things with a divine harmony, while your bishops presides in the place of God, and your presbyters in the place of the assembly of the apostles, along with your deacons, who are the most dear to me ... (Roberts and Donald, 1986, p. 61)

The injunction that all things in the Church should be done 'decently and in order' (1 Cor. 14.40), along with the healthy commendation of the desire to be a bishop, has enormous implications for how we do church and view ministry, lay or ordained. Indeed, as John Stott reminds us, it would be difficult to think about the life and renewal of the Church without giving serious thought to its 'ordained ministers'. From the New Testament, he argues, it is plain that God 'has always intended his church to have some form of *episkope*, that is, pastoral oversight' (Stott, 1992, p. 270).

Believing in the flow of the Spirit, early Pentecostals were, as Kay states, 'resistant to any form of organization' until they came to terms with church structures in the New Testament and the need to organize for effective local and international evangelization (Kay, 2009, p. 55). As the pioneering leader of the Pentecostal movement that started at Azusa Street, Los Angeles, William J. Seymour had a novel take on credentialization and the office of bishop: he believed that ministers should rightly receive credentials from the 'visible church', but that the main credential is 'to be baptized in/with the Holy Ghost' and to see the Holy Ghost as the 'bishop' presiding over the 'entire work of God on earth' (Espinosa, 2014, pp. 185–6).

Unsurprisingly, with the growth of independent black Pentecostal churches in the UK there is the potential for enormous ecclesiological diversity. The question of what is a 'bishop' and what constitutes effective episcopal and pastoral oversight is interpreted variously by these leaders. On the one hand there are, of course, churches governed by strict rules and formal accountability structure like the New Testament Church of God and the Church of God of Prophecy, while on the other hand there are churches with self-appointed 'bishops' and much looser ecclesiological structures. In both cases, biblical texts and examples are invoked to justify their status and formal ecclesiology. Although the ecclesiological practices differ in many of these churches, and they often eschew many of the trappings of the established churches, it does not mean that there is widespread ecclesiological antinomianism. Indeed, within these churches one will find elements of episcopal, presbyterian, congregational and what Erickson calls 'nongovernmental' forms of church polity (2013, p. 1004).

While Erickson commends the nongovernmental form for 'accentuating the role of the Holy Spirit and the need to rely on him', there is the danger that the 'degree of sanctification and sensitivity to the Holy Spirit they posit of the members of a congregation is an unrealistic ideal' (2013, p. 1002). The desire to eliminate as much structural organization as possible (ecclesiological minimalism) in their ecclesiology (the 'postmodern mood') risks making a virtue out of a necessity, especially in light of the biblical evidence. Most African and Caribbean Pentecostal churches would recognize the fivefold ministry of apostles, prophets, evangelists, pastors and teachers. While very few Caribbean churches would adopt the title of 'prophet' or 'apostle' for their leaders, several independent African churches currently use these appellations.

In the UK, the New Testament Church of God is on the verge of a significant development in its ecclesiology. A debate has been ongoing regarding changes to titles and offices in the governing institutions of the

Church of God in America, namely, the International General Assembly and the International General Council. Most significant was the 2016 proposal to re-examine the title of 'bishops', with a view to reporting back in 2018. Along with issues of episcopacy sits the gender equality theme. In the Church of God, the latter might not be too dissimilar to what Cardinal Walter Kasper referred to as a kind of 'Copernican Revolution' (2015, p. 231), a Second Vatican Council moment.

As with many major denominations and ecclesial traditions, the debates about the role of women in ministry have been both theological and political. Indeed, in the wider socio-political discourse on equality some churches are woefully behind; and this is not about trying to bring the church 'up to date' or conformity with the zeitgeist and some of the inherent dangers in this approach for Christians; rather, it is because it is felt that there are doubtful biblical and theological grounds for the subordination of women in Christian ministry and service. In the NTCG there are no women on the National Executive and no women district bishops. Women are now officially permitted to be members of the Church and Pastors' Council (passed at the 73rd IAG in 2010), but the exclusively male Executive Council will only change when women's ministerial status is upgraded – when women can be 'ordained bishops' in the Church of God.

Ironically, for a church that privileges Scripture in the formulation of its practices and 'doctrinal commitments', it appears that the long march through the denomination for gender equality in ministry has had more to do with tradition than with biblical theology. In the report presented to the IAG in 2018, the role and contribution of women was recognized thus:

> Since the early history of the church, women in ministry have garnered contemplation, discussion and debate regarding their role and engagement in ministry. A review of the Church of God reveals women believers in the many phases of ministry outreach have demonstrated strong support to growth and development throughout our 130 plus years of existence.[3]

The report calls for a 'thorough assessment and reflection' on the role of women in the Church's ministry. Given the prominence of women in the early years of the Azusa Street Pentecostal revival under the African American leader William J. Seymour, it is ironic that women's advancement in this organization is taking so long. The contribution of women to Pentecostalism and their 'spiritual giftings' were similarly debated over two decades ago in another leading global Pentecostal organization, the Assemblies of God (AoG) (Cavaness, 1994, pp. 49–62).

What is, therefore, due to return to the 2020 General Assembly is both instructive and encouraging: instructive in that some of the anomalies surrounding the use and title of 'bishop' will be fully addressed biblically and theologically; encouraging in that the gender equality issue will open up places and spaces for women to contribute and participate fully in the highest level of Church of God governance.

Formally, the 2020 proposal calls for two main sets of ecclesiological matters to be reported on, namely the main one dealing with the nomenclature of 'bishops' ('ministerial' and 'ordained', especially how they are perceived in the USA) and the related issues, including women in ministry. The formal proposal is as follows:

1. Better address whether it is necessary to change the current nomenclature in order to clarify and fulfil the intent of the International General Council with respect to the designation of the ministerial rank ('bishop') in the Church of God.
2. A detailed look at the title of 'Ordained Bishop' and any effect it has on the legal and cultural issues of the international church and on the IRS (USA, Internal Revenue Service) rulings concerning the national church (USA).
3. That the following issues and relatedness of these issues be part of this report: titles for all ranks of ministry, qualifications of ministry, women in ministry.

Bishops in the New Testament Church of God, like those in the USA, are regulated by the *Minutes* of the International General Assembly. In Paul's letters to Timothy and Titus, the qualifications/qualities of a bishop include such things as having a blameless moral character, teaching ability, a hospitable nature, sobriety, leadership skills in the home and the community. Doubtless, there is also the need for good administrative abilities.

These qualities are mirrored in what is required of an 'ordained bishop' in the Church of God. According to the *Minutes*, such a person making an application for ordination as bishop 'must meet the biblical requirements as set forth in 1 Timothy 3:1-7'. While Paul does not specify the age one should be to occupy this office – though there is caution about being a 'novice' – the *Minutes* state that an applicant may be ordained when he is 25 years of age, 'provided he has had at least eight (8) years of active ministry', or when he is 30 years of age, 'provided he has had at least five (5) years of active ministry'.[4] In addition to the requirement that those seeking ordination as bishops in the Church of God must have 'the baptism of the Holy Ghost' and have duly passed the ministerial examination, which is mainly comprised of the 'areas of church government, doctrine, and general bible knowledge'. There are also implications for the bishop's wife. According to the *Minutes*, the wife of bishop 'must be grave, not a slanderer, sober, and faithful in all things'. Like other Pentecostal churches, the duties and authority of a bishop in the Church of God, not dissimilar to that of a 'senior pastor' or 'apostle' in other churches, gives them the right to preach, teach, baptize, administer the sacraments, ordain ministers and establish and organize churches.

As more independent black Pentecostal churches spring up in the UK the question of 'episcopal' and 'apostolic' oversight will become critical. Although many of these leaders, as Sturge argues, look to the USA for their ecclesiological model of 'leadership styles and organisational methodologies' (2005, p. 102), they still want their churches and fellowships to come under the umbrella or 'covering' of established churches, denominations or parachurch organizations like Churches Together in England (CTE) for accountability and ministerial development. Doubtless there are also pragmatic reasons for seeing this form of oversight, especially when it comes to the question of getting children from these churches into church schools where 'church affiliation' is critical.

Ruach City Church (RCC) is a good example of a black independent Pentecostal church now seeking oversight and membership of CTE. Before starting this London-based church, John Francis was part of one of the leading global Pentecostal denominations, the Church of God in Christ (CoGiC). Consecrated to the office of bishop in 1998, he is the founder and senior pastor of this megachurch. Along with his wife – and this is the model of leadership adopted by many independent Pentecostal churches – they run RCC and give what one may loosely call episcopal oversight to the Ruach Network of Churches. The vision of the Church includes reaching people for Christ and equipping members to become 'successful Christians' who are 'emotionally stable' members of society able to develop to the 'highest degree of spiritual endowment attainable'.

In terms of the Church's organizational structure, there are 44 'elders', including four 'resident elders' under Bishop Francis with responsibility for a range of services and ministries. Bishop Francis functions as the 'presiding' (international leader) bishop for the churches under him. Independent Pentecostal churches with a similar international reach, like New Wine, Woolwich or Kingsway International Christian Centre (KICC),[5] where the title 'bishop' is not part of their ecclesiology, would designate Bishop Francis' counterparts as senior pastors. RCC operates in five locations: Brixton (South London), Kilburn (North London), Walthamstow (East London), Birmingham and Philadelphia (USA).

The need for 'spiritual covering' and accountability is both a theological and a practical issue in many independent Pentecostal churches. The use of titles like 'apostle', 'bishop' and 'prophet' in these ecclesial communities often sits uncomfortably with leaders in established churches. The ecclesiology of many of these Pentecostal churches is still developing; and some, like Chan, might share the view that they exhibit a characteristically weak ecclesiology and 'sociological concept of the church' (2000a, p. 98 and 2000b, pp. 177–208). For Chan, this has the negative consequence of seeing the Church 'as essentially a service provider catering to the needs of individual Christians' rather that seeing individuals 'as existing for the church'. Bishop John Francis and Apostle Alfred Williams of Christ Faith Tabernacle, however, advocate the 'fivefold ministry' set out in Ephesians 4.11–12 of apostles, prophets, evangelists, pastors, teachers.

How one assesses one's ministry and the call to high office in the Church is both subjective and objective; and what ecclesial titles one has conferred upon them or self-designate is informed and influenced by a range of factors, including tradition and culture. Along with biblical prescriptions, there are also social and political constructs shaping our ecclesiologies. A significant element for black Pentecostal leaders is their testimony of God's call, echoing that of the Apostle Paul's 'Damascus Road' experience.

Apostle Alfred Williams tells of being called to ministry, and called to be an 'Apostle' through a vision he had of Jesus Christ in February 1984 in Nigeria. In the vision he recalls Jesus taking him to London and other parts of the UK, showing him preaching to thousands of people. He records what he describes as an out-of-the-body experience:

> I instantly saw my spirit depart from my physical body as we both began to glide through clouds into more clouds. ... The sea of faces listening to me stretched all the way down to Trafalgar Square with an overflow extending to Buckingham Palace Road ... Among the people I was preaching to were blacks in tens of thousands but they were only 1% of those present. (2011, pp. 22–3)

For Williams, this experience was life-changing; it was, he states, receiving 'a divine call into ministry ... from the Lord Jesus himself' to go 'back to London and start the work'. Since that encounter, Apostle Williams has planted churches in the UK, Europe, America and Africa, providing leadership and 'apostolic' oversight for them.

Unlike 'Apostle Williams', who officially uses the title for himself, Bishop Francis is also looked upon as an 'Apostle' by those under his immediate ministry and the churches in the Ruach Network of Churches for which he provides 'spiritual cover'. The theology of the fivefold ministry and its practice today is controversial. Churches like Ruach, Christ Faith Tabernacle and New Wine subscribe to the view that all these offices and the charismatic gifts of the Holy Spirit are available to the Church today. Given the fact that they also believe in the 'priesthood of all believers', it means that any individual can 'operate' in these gifts and offices. Others who take a 'cessationist' position would be wedded to a more established ecclesiology and understanding of episcopacy and would disagree that 'prophets' and 'apostles' were for today. The 78th International General Assembly of the Church of God scheduled for 2020 will do well to take note of Calvin's argument that for the office of bishop, Paul 'includes generally all pastors ... that this word is of the same import as if he had called them ministers, or pastors, or presbyters' (Calvin, 2009, p. 75). Calvin was also of the view that the office of 'Prophets, Apostles, Evangelists' was temporary and only 'Pastors and Teachers' were of 'perpetual duration' (Calvin, 1979, p. 686).[6] While the Church of God will, undoubtedly, take some note of Calvin on the meaning of episcopacy, many independent African Pentecostal churches will continue to ignore him on the 'temporary duration' of Apostles, Prophets and Evangelists.

Notes

1 Pastor Enoch is the General Overseer and Chairman of the Governing Council of the RCCG. He was named as the world's 49th most influential person by *Newsweek* magazine in 2008. In the UK, the leader of RCCG is Pastor Agu Irukwu of Jesus House.

2 The NTCG is part of the global Church of God with headquarters in the USA. NTCG was established in the UK in 1953, with Bishop Oliver Lyseight as its first General Overseer.

3 See Church of God, 2018, *Further Study, Report: Meaning and usage of the Term 'Bishop', presented to the 77th International General Assembly*, p. 19.

4 See Church of God, 2002, *69th General Assembly Minutes*, S57. Church of God, *Ordained Bishop*, Cleveland, TN: Pathway Press.

5 KICC's leader is Pastor Matthew Ashimolowo. It is one of the largest independent black Pentecostal churches in Europe. There are no 'bishops' in this organization; there are pastors and senior pastors.

6 John Calvin, 1995, *Institutes of the Christian Religion*, Henry Beveridge (trans.), Vol. II. (Aphorism, No.71), Grand Rapids, MI: Eerdmans, p. 686.

References

Aldred, Joe, 2013, 'The Challenges of Black Pentecostal Leadership in the UK in the Twenty-first Century', in Phyllis Thompson (ed.), *Challenges of Black Pentecostal Leadership in the 21st Century*, London: SPCK.

Berger, Klaus, 1975, '"Bishop" in The New Testament', in Karl Rahner (ed.), *Encyclopedia of Theology: A Concise Sacramentum Mundi*, London: Burns & Oates.

Bradley, Ian, 2007, *Believing in Britain: The Spiritual Identity of Britishness*, London: I. B. Tauris.

Brown, Raymond, 1997, *An Introduction to the New Testament*, New York: Doubleday.

Calvin, John, 1979, *Institutes of the Christian Religion, Vol. II*, trans. Henry Beveridge, Grand Rapids, MI: Eerdmans.

Calvin, John, 2009, *Commentaries, Vol. XXI (Commentary on 1 Timothy)*, trans. William Pringle, Grand Rapids, MI: Baker Books.

Cavaness, Barbara, 1994, 'God Calling: Women in Assemblies of God Missions', *Pneuma: The Journal of the Society for Pentecostal Studies* 16.1.

Chan, Simon, 2000a, *Pentecostal Theology and the Christian Spiritual Tradition*, Sheffield: Sheffield Academic Press.

Chan, Simon, 2000b, 'Mother Church: Toward A Pentecostal Ecclesiology', *Pneuma: The Journal of the Society for Pentecostal Studies* 22.2.

Dillon, Richard J. and Joseph A. Fitzmyer, 1968, 'Acts of the Apostles', in Raymond S. Brown, Joseph A. Fitzmyer and Roland E. Murphy (eds), *The Jerome Biblical Commentary*, Englewood Cliffs, NJ: Prentice Hall.

Erickson, Millard, 2013, *Christian Theology* (3rd edition), Grand Rapids, MI: Baker Academic.

Espinosa, Gaston, 2014, *William J. Seymour and the Origins of Global Pentecostalism: A Biography & Documentary History*, Durham, NC and London: Duke University Press.

Kasper, Walter, 2015, *The Catholic Church: Nature, Reality and Mission*, London: Bloomsbury.

Kay, William, 2009, *Pentecostalism*, London: SCM Press.

Roberts, Alexander and James Donald (eds), 1986, *The Ante-Nicene Fathers, Vol. 1 (The Apostolic Fathers)*, Edinburgh: T & T Clark.

Stott, John, 1992, *The Contemporary Christian: An Urgent Plea for Double Listening*, Leicester: IVP.

Sturge, Mark, 2005, *Look What the Lord Has Done! An Exploration of Black Christian Faith in Britain*, Bletchley: Scripture Union.

Williams, Alfred T. B., 2011, *My Encounters with Jesus and His Angels*, London: Revival House Publishing.

13

Oversight and the New Monasticism

Episkope *and Being a Leader in the New Monasticism in the Church of England*

IAN MOBSBY

And thus, nothing from old times will meet our exigencies. We want a rule which shall answer to the complexity of our own age. We want a discipline which shall combine the sovereignty of soul of Antony, the social devotion of Benedict, the humble love of Francis, the matchless energy of the Jesuits, with faith that fears no trial, with hope that fears no darkness, with truth that fears no light. (Wescott, 1902, p. 14)

For nearly 200 years the religious life and religious communities – both monastic (monks and nuns) and mendicant (friars, nuns and sisters) – have been reincorporated into the Church of England. It is often forgotten that during the carnage of the industrial revolution and its calamitous effects on working-class people across the UK, the religious life erupted into the Church of England in response to, and as part of, the Oxford Movement. At that time it was largely Benedictine- and Franciscan-inspired women and men who fought for the rights to bring Anglican mendicant and monastic communities back into the Church after nearly 500 years of absence caused by Henry VIII and the dissolution of the monasteries. Many of these new Anglican communities were involved in mission with and among the new underclasses that populated the slum housing areas that had sprung up near the factories. It was in this context that a more 'ancient:future' approach to Christian spirituality found renewed resonance, one that Bishop Westcott described as a fusion between Franciscan, Ignatian and Benedictine spirituality (Mobsby, 2012).

Now, in the early twenty-first century, in the heady days of our increasingly post-secular, post-enlightenment and it seems almost post-everything culture, the language of a New Monasticism has again arisen (Mobsby and Berry, 2013), this time in the context of mission and Fresh Expressions of church in our new apostolic age of forming ecclesial communities out of contextual mission. Now that increasing numbers of de- and unchurched people have either given up or have no interest in Christianity and any expression of church, new forms of 'missional community' have again taken shape in response to our current cultural crises. These Anglican New Monastic Communities[1] appear to be in two differing groups, drawing on different wells of the Christian tradition – and therefore two different approaches to unpacking Christian spirituality in the context of an increasing post-secular search for the spiritual. Roy Searle writes, following this, about the movement that calls itself Celtic Christian Spirituality as expressed through the Northumbria Community. The other grouping, which is akin to the nineteenth-century Anglican orders, draws on a fusion of Benedictine, Franciscan and Ignatian spirituality. Indeed, there is a deep resonance between the founding vision of Bishop Westcott and these newer expressions, such as the St Anselm Community in Lambeth Palace and many small New Monastic Communities popping up in various places, including the Moot Community, which I helped found in the City of London, and the Wellspring Community, of which I am now the elected Prior in Peckham, South London.

Leading and giving oversight to these emerging New Monastic Communities is not easy, in my experience. Indeed, leading any form of residential or intentional community is one of the hardest things to do because in such an atomized individualistic contemporary culture, we struggle with the required interpersonal skills of tolerance, humility, self-awareness and self-control. In the early days of the Fresh Expressions initiative in the UK, a number of these communities that bubbled up had pioneer leaders who called themselves names like 'Abbot' and 'Abbess'. Apart from causing great afront to leaders of traditional communities who had gone through years of preparation and experience of the religious life before using such terms, it soon became apparent that while these leaders may have been great pioneers, they did not possess the skills and knowledge to exercise such a ministry and had not been properly authorized to use such terms. As with the nineteenth-century romantic movement about all things Celtic, there was a definite and naive romanticism at the turn of the twentieth-first century concerning the religious life that did not do justice to how hard it is to live in, let alone lead and give oversight to. Many of these early new communities failed because of this romanticized idealism and the fact that leadership of such communities was really hard to sustain. However, some, like the Moot Community of which I was a part for 16 years, muddled through and now form part of a well-established network of New Monastic Communities within the Church of England. Many of these emerging Christian communities rightly see themselves as an ongoing element of the religious life and therefore seek to situate themselves as part of that tradition and its terminology. This may lead to the use of traditional terms for their leaders, and this may be appropriate in some cases. What matters is that the impact of those choices is considered and understood. The use of 'Prior' has begun to become popular in the New Monasticism because it situates the role within the ongoing religious life. Terms such as 'leader' are used by some communities, but for many it is too secular a term. Rightly, terms such as 'Abbot' are largely avoided.

We remember that in the early Church, when Christianity became the state religion of the Roman Empire, Christian monasticism began as a reaction against this, with Christians going into the Alexandrian and Syrian deserts to live as isolated hermits. This movement quickly coalesced into radical and deep Christian communities with a rhythm of life consisting of prayer, worship, study, work, rest and fellowship. Out of the lives of these communities were born new forms of leadership and oversight, with the heads of these communities called Father (Abba) and Mother (Amma). These were charismatic individuals like Antony, Theodora and Melania from the desert communities who, with the many who came after them, were seen as having authority over their communities and as equal to bishops and their dioceses.

It is from such an understanding that the Church of England takes inspiration, following the Roman Catholic Church and the Greek Orthodox Churches, which have seen the Abba and Amma leaders of monastic communities as equal to bishops. We have seen parallel streams – first bishops overseeing a diocese, parishes and local churches, and then abbots, abbesses, priors and prioresses overseeing radical Christian communities and orders with communities in more than one location.

Being leaders of religious communities requires a different skill set from that of a bishop because of the particular challenges of leading residential communities and orders. Leaders of emerging and new religious communities need to sustain a mission-focused and communitarian approach to a Rule or rhythm of life, the charisms of a community or order, and sustaining a living constitution in the governance of interpersonal residential communities and orders. A further challenge to leadership within these new emerging New Monastic Communities is also their fluidity, where people make commitments as seasonal vows once a year. In my experience, most stay around three years or so before moving on, particularly in urban contexts, so that many communities feel more like chaplaincy in an educational setting, where the student body changes every year, rather than a stable long-term religious community. This is the reality of a market-driven society where life is commodified. Being part of an emerging or New Monastic community can be a counter-cultural choice and, being led by the Holy Spirit, reorientates people to the importance of Christian spirituality and human ecclesial community.

Many of the emerging New Monastic communities within the Anglican context are happening as part of a diocese rather than being separate like the traditional communities that formed during the nineteenth century. The use of the term 'prior' is therefore an effective acknowledgement of the accountability of a prior to the bishop, as a prior would be to an abbot or abbess in larger religious communities with more than one house or monastery.

For over 20 years I have been an ordained Pioneer Priest and the leader of two very different New Monastic Communities. Sadly, very little has prepared me for this leadership role in my training as an ordained priest, Pioneer and now Prior. The Moot Community (www.moot.uk.net) emerged out of a missional endeavour to reach unchurched spiritual seekers in Westminster, where I was an ordained mission-focused curate. Now in Peckham, I have two differing ministerial roles, including being the part-time Priest-in-Charge of an urban deprived inner-city parish, where I have helped establish the small but significant New Monastic community called the Wellspring Community (www.wellspringpeckham.net). At Wellspring we seek to promote the practice of a deep contemplative spirituality and missional living, while giving time to various projects.

The role of leading both of these New Monastic Communities has required me personally to have a deep level of contemplative prayer alongside highly developed interpersonal skills that have been crafted from the raw material of practical experience. To these can be added the bruises of having been a participant in a dispersed and residential community, and the complex skill set that accompanies consultative governance and the practice of authority. In short, in my leadership role, there have not been many opportunities to acquire these translocal skills of leadership that are required for overseeing New Monastic Communities, as models from business management or the average ordination training course – pioneer training or otherwise – do not fit what is a very different context. This is perhaps why so many New Monastic Communities start well and then have real problems shifting from start-up to enduring sustainability.

In my own short career in leading New Monastic Communities I have made some of the biggest mistakes of my life, causing real pain as a consequence in direct relationship to how hard it is to lead such communities well. Such leadership is never easy and often occurs in very demanding contexts where there is much stress, little money and high expectations.

After 20 years I am beginning to feel I have begun to acquire some of the skills necessary for such a role. It is increasingly clear to me now that to be an elected leader of a New Monastic Community requires an evolved experience of leadership formed from having lived in radical New Monastic Communities under a Rule or 'rhythm of life'. The insights gained from living in some form of New Monastic community over a period of time lead to wisdom and understanding rather than idealism and 'guesswork'.

It is very difficult to appoint external ministers to be leaders of New Monastic communities, which increasingly consist of lay or ordained pioneer ministers, and expect them to have the skills to lead these emerging communities. This immediately creates a problem, not least because there are still so few New Monastic communities from which to identify and form potential leaders to fulfil this ministry of oversight. This challenge has directly led to some of us forming the Society of the Holy Trinity as a particular collaboration or umbrella New Monastic community to support and encourage the planting, developing and leading of New Monastic Communities in the UK and the wider Anglican Communion (https://societyoftheholytrinity.co.uk).

In my time as a leader of the Moot and Wellspring communities, 16 people have been called from within to become leaders, of whom all have been ordained. However, only three of these are involved in leading emerging forms of New Monastic or missional communities. In practice this means that the emerging communities are being deprived of these new leaders who, as a consequence of Church of England polity, are mostly required to go elsewhere to develop ordained or pioneer skills. New Monastic Communities are therefore being denied the ministry of those who could be effective leaders or overseers emerging out of the life of their own community to sustain the greater good of the Church of England. Leadership of many of the emerging New Monastic Communities is therefore coming from parish priests, lay pioneers and missionally minded curates, who are often excited by the idea of New Monasticism but have little experience of living in such a community or its particular approach to Christian discipleship. So what is the way forward?

The Church of England is at last exploring how to discern, train, support and deploy Lay Pioneer leaders, especially for the apostolic missional endeavours now needed in our post-Christian and post-church context. We remember that the original desert monasticism was also a reaction to the over-clericalization of the Church, and that Abbas and Ammas, such as Antony in the desert, were heavily critical of those who started out as monks and then became ordained priests. There are stories of such newly ordained priests literally being thrown out of these desert communities for daring to become ordained. Monasticism has always been a lay movement of ordinary people unsettled by the Holy Spirit to turn to a life of prayerful contemplative action. We remember that in the nineteenth century it was largely lay women who had to fight bishops and archdeacons in the Church of England to start religious communities.

Now the Church has to relearn that the answer to many of the problems it faces today will not be solved purely by training and turning out more ordained priests. Instead, what is needed is an approach that embraces many differing vocations, and where some will be called to give oversight and lead individual New Monastic communities or groups of communities as orders that will not necessarily require ordination. It is my sincere hope that some of these recognized lay pioneers will not only birth new emerging communities but will also help lead those that have been previously established; likewise, that it will be possible for those who are formed in New Monastic Communities to remain part of the laity and be trained and supported to lead New Monastic Communities through new processes of discernment and learning, rather than just being ordained to established forms of parish ministry. This requires Diocesan Directors of Ordinands, Diocesan Missioners and Fresh Expressions Enablers to be acutely sensitive to the needs of communities that have already been established, and the emerging opportunities for founding New Monastic missional communities that seek to reach out to the de-churched and unchurched. So rather than just talking about ordination with those exploring vocation who are part of New Monastic communities, such individuals would also be encouraged to explore Lay Pioneer ministry to build an increasing pool of experience, skills and competency to be effective servant leaders of Anglican New Monastic communities.

In my experience, many choose to be ordained because this creates a more sustainable lifestyle with properly paid roles and proper work contracts whereas, for those who have families, lay pioneering comes with enormous uncertainty and lack of job security and ongoing career pathways. This is a very real problem given the challenging context of contemporary society with the lack of affordable housing, well-paid jobs and the increasing weakness of the Church. In my own career as a leader of New Monastic communities I have had to self-fund my role for many years, as I could not raise enough money to cover my costs and had to remortgage my flat, face the scourge of debt and, at one point, almost become insolvent. Just to be able to keep going as a pioneering leader was difficult, with very little support at that time from the diocese of which I was a part. At that stage I was very grateful for the traditional religious communities who saw my plight and helped keep me going by covering some of my costs.

The new religious communities founded by Anglicans in the nineteenth century were set up to be self-governing charities with independent financial means. They were sponsored by rich benefactors who endowed them with sufficient funds not only to establish sustainable communities but also to provide the resources needed to support and grow indigenous leadership to oversee these communities. The irony is that these traditional communities often have quite large financial charities supporting their work but few joining them, while the emerging communities are attracting lots of new participants but have little funding. This substantially restricts their stability and sustainability let alone the formation and support of those called to leadership. This is why I stayed on as the Community Leader of the Moot community for 16 years, as it took that long to set up and develop a café and small market to fund its life and ministry. That it was still fighting to cover its costs after 16 years goes to the heart of the matter.

To even begin to think about the appropriate oversight of several emerging communities, or the effective leadership of a particular community, requires these communities to have developed the security and sustainability to support such leadership. If this is not the case, the stresses and strains of fighting to keep projects financially viable create an environment of unhealthy and unsustainable forms of leadership. At one point in my own career, the working environment for leading the community of which I was a part was so stressful that my own mental health was deeply challenged, reducing my effectiveness and leading to poor decisions that affected the life of the whole community. Looking back, I can see that this was because I did not have the stability or support necessary for such a demanding role. There was a high cost to being one of the leaders of the first wave of Fresh Expressions projects in the Church of England, where many had to fight for recognition and adequate support. Many of these projects failed because this support had not been built into the system. Listening to the stories and voices of many who are seeking to develop and lead New Monastic communities, it remains a problem that in some dioceses there is still an unhealthy culture of high expectations and neglect. I am now so grateful to the Diocese of Southwark for enabling me to thrive as a leader of a New Monastic community. With the right systems and support structures in place, I am released to support and encourage the founding of new emerging projects in the diocese and beyond.

I do believe that New Monastic communities will grow in our current cultural context, driven by a resurgent interest in spirituality and human community. The challenge will be how to lead and found these New Monastic communities with the right leadership and right structures in place to support those with a call to apostolic and missional leadership.

Note

1 Elsewhere (www.ianmobsby.net) I have talked of the four factors that make a community a Christian New Monastic Community:
   1 a commitment to a shared rhythm of daily life;
   2 a commitment to contemplative forms of prayer and meditation;
   3 a commitment to spiritual practices and radical community;
   4 a commitment to missional loving service as an individual and as an ecclesial community.

References

Mobsby, Ian J., 2012, *God Unknown: The Trinity in Contemporary Spirituality and Mission*, Norwich: Canterbury Press.
Mobsby, Ian J. and Mark Berry, 2013, *A New Monastic Handbook: From Vision to Practice*, Norwich: Canterbury Press.
Westcott, Brooke Foss, 1902, *Words of Faith and Hope*, London: Macmillan.

Episkope and the New Monasticism in the Celtic Tradition: The Northumbria Community

ROY SEARLE

> I hope you will abandon the urge to simplify everything, to look for formulas and easy answers, and begin to think multidimensionally, to glory in the mystery and paradoxes of life, not to be dismayed by the multitude of causes and consequences that are inherent in each experience – to appreciate the fact that life is complex. (Peck, 1998, p. 14)

Leading the Northumbria Community has been a challenging and remarkable privilege. From 'the few' in 1990 the Community has grown to 'the many', with over 3,000 Companions and Friends across the world. The Community came into being through courageous prophetic insight allied with apostolic ingenuity and the ability to translate its ethos and form lasting relationships. The contemplative and apostolic streams of the Community's life together form the monastic and missional elements that are foundational to our New Monastic calling. The Community has journeyed through seasons of joy and pain, failure and achievement, and in the process encountered setbacks and successes along with the misunderstandings that accompany many new, experimental and emerging movements.

Mistakes have been made in leading the Community: inappropriate structures, unrealistic expectations, unwise decisions and bad behaviour all contributing to the struggles, particularly in our early years. It is testimony to the courage and perseverance of the first and second generations to follow God's radical call that the foundations were laid for those who followed and have gone on to bear fruit across the world.

Appreciating some of the dynamics of chaos theory has shed light on how the Community is led. We have learnt to recognize the need for authority without becoming authoritarian, understanding the nature of power in relationships and tempering it with the spiritual disciplines of self-awareness, humility and accountability. We've had to look for patterns and discern trends in order to respond appropriately to what is emerging. This highly complex yet creative and very different way of leading has required us to take risks and entrust ourselves to God.

Leadership is much more about shaping and influencing than about determining; it requires a continual adjustment to respond to what happens and emerges. Driving through strategies rarely achieves anything and tends to undermine relationships. Instead, setting the tone, creating the space for people to grow and fostering imagination produces more meaningful outcomes and better relationships.

We have found the insights of Frederic Laloux very helpful. The old secular organizational models – Impulsive, with its division of labour and top-down authority; Traditional, with its replicable processes and stable organizational charts; the Achievement mode of innovation, accountability and meritocracy; and the Pluralist model with its empowerment, values-driven culture and stakeholder value – all seemed ill-fitting to us as a community and to the leadership we needed.

Finding what Laloux describes as a 'Teal' or 'Evolutionary' view of organizations has helped us to match our vocation with the organizational aspects of our Community. It has been liberating to operate in ways that intentionally disempower the ego, build trust and create an environment in which self-awareness and spiritual formation, together with the well-being of individuals and the Community collectively, are encouraged.

Consequently, there continue to be various evolving expressions of leadership. Drawing principally from Celtic monasticism, with its roots in the desert tradition, the early expression of leadership was modelled on that of an abbot and bishop(s). The terms were rarely spoken and we avoided using them publicly to avoid misunderstanding. Nevertheless, these terms gave coherence in our formative years and still provide a useful means of understanding what leadership is and how it works today.

An important transition came as the founding abbot appointed his successor, formerly the Community's prior, Trevor Miller, who was tasked to 'build the new on foundations of old', guarding our ethos and building 'home' for Companions and Friends. Rooted at the Mother House, his task was to lead by example and to oversee the Community in all aspects of its life and work. He brought stability from the wisdom he possessed and allied his pastoral and teaching gifts and with the apostolic, creative and missional ministry I brought; thus, monastery and mission were embodied in the Community's leadership. Guarding one another's hearts and watching each other's backs, with trust, accountability, kinship and support we worked closely together in serving the Community. Our lives and friendship, woven together in a common vocation, have given expression to an integrated monastic and missional way of life.

The two of us continued until Pete Askew joined the Overseers team in 2009, bringing his gifts, which incorporated both abbot and bishop qualities. Consequently, we have evolved to a team of three leaders, while still being committed to both the monastic and missional nature of our Community.

The role of the abbot(s) is primarily about guarding the Community's vocation, rooting people and all aspects of the Community's life and work in the values of our Rule of life. This is not about maintenance; rather, it is about guarding the heart and protecting the Community in the way a good parent supports and encourages, protects and blesses their children. The role of abbot carries great authority within the community, yet the abbot is not the sole arbitrator but shares with other Overseers the responsibility of leadership, thus protecting them from becoming 'guru'-type figures. They exercise authority without claiming it; never asking for allegiance or loyalty but acting out of compassion, pointing people back to God who is the source, inspiration and reason why the community exists. They encourage the formation of people, alone and together, around the practices and disciplines of the Christian life.

The bishops within the Community share oversight and are essentially missional and apostolic people, forming and establishing relational connections and encouraging people to live out their vocation outside of the 'monastery'. If abbots represent stability, the bishops represent movement. They are more visionary in outlook, exploring new horizons, breaking new ground with creativity, innovation and experimentation. If the abbot is a story-keeper, the bishop is a story-teller and story-maker. The roles are different in expression yet one in heart, and it's easy to see the value of both for the Community. They provide a necessary antidote to the one-person leader with all the inherent dangers of isolation, insecurity and scant accountability. The two roles, monastic and missional, hold together the Community's vocation and provide an expression of our call to be 'alone together', seeking God and the willingness to journey for the love of him.

Power and authority lie not in any individual but in a partnership that models diversity, not uniformity. Our strong relational emphasis is rooted in a communal understanding of the Trinity. This is reflected in our leadership pattern and practice, which is unity in diversity. The early Church Fathers, wrestling with the nature of relationships within the Trinity, used the term *perichoresis*; Father, Son and Holy Spirit, co-equal and co-eternal, three persons comprising one God, relating to one another as in a 'divine dance'. We all, being made in the image of God, should be reflecting God's nature and ways of relating.

Pete Askew's appointment followed a thorough discerning process and commitment to succession planning that helped pave the way for others to both emerge and eventually be recognized as leaders, as the Community moved from second to third generation.

Ten years on from the formation of the Community, we witnessed significant growth in numbers, many connecting with us from near and far. In the light of this we formed a General Chapter, with other Companions taking responsibility for various aspects of the Community's life and work. This led to the emergence of a leadership network where Overseers, Provosts and Provincials, along with trustees, carried the overall leadership responsibility.

Provincials carried a specific responsibility for a geographical area or specific aspect of the Community's life. They reported to the Overseers on all aspects of their 'province' and were often invited to attend the quarterly Chapter meetings when issues relating to their province were being considered. Use of social media has made communications and organizational structures possible that would have been unattainable in the early years.

Provosts worked closely with the Overseers, most living not far from the Mother House, and took specific responsibility to manage certain areas of the Community's life; for example, business, trading and finance, resources, communications and the Mother House, managing the weekly responsibilities for the Community's life and work.

That organizational pattern operated for several years but after further growth and development we have had to explore different ways of leading. From the Community being centred on the founders and their successors, initially a very small, strongly directive team, we have evolved to the creation of teams and a leadership network which, while continuing to be proactive, is much more consultative in its style.

Pete Askew, still a Companion, concluded his time as an Overseer of the Community when he accepted the post of Bishop's Chaplain with the Newcastle diocese in 2017, something that was unexpected. His leaving saw the Community enter another season of review and transition. An interim leadership team worked closely with our trustees, embracing a new leadership framework which, after 18 months, resulted in a significant transition. The appointment of three new Overseers saw the handing over the baton of leadership as both Trevor and I stepped down. We remain very much part of the Community and the emerging Council of Elders, described as 'oak trees of the Community, helping the new leaders get their bearings and providing support, encouragement, wisdom and advice as appropriate'. The roles of the Overseers are now described in the following way:

> their collective purpose being that of holding the heart of Community, sustaining the ethos and creating life-giving spaces for transformational learning that enable us to live out the Rule and be a kingdom-presence in the world.

The first women to be appointed as Overseers have carried the whole-hearted affirmation and support of their predecessors and have been received with joy from the wider Community. Catherine Askew, as Monastery Lead, creates, guides and leads on spiritual formation. She holds primary responsibility for the Mother House, Nether Springs, and leads the team there alongside overseeing all its activities and the thriving Novitiate programme. Sarah Hay is School and Process Lead and carries a vision for creating and enabling the School for Monastic Living and managing the operational aspects across the Community. Sarah Pillar is the Dispersed Community Lead, overseeing the dispersed global network of Companions and Friends and helping to find ways to experience more tangible connections with each other.

Leaders emerge through various channels, so that potential leaders, after a discerning process, principally involving the existing Overseers, are then interviewed and appointed by the Community's trustees. Calling and character are as essential as competence and gifting. Recognizing hierarchy, we seek not to be hierarchical. Strong emphasis is placed on spiritual formation and the need for individuals to be living the Community's Rule of life. Integrity and authenticity demand an intentionality that seeks to live what we teach.

There is an inevitable tension between the priorities of being the relational, loosely knit and geographically dispersed 'community of the heart' and the challenges of being an efficient and coherent organization that complies with statutory bodies and regulatory requirements. It is no easy task to reconcile the Community's charism of a relational and flexible structure with the organizational demands of a growing network. It is a tension that is seen in the desire to exercise 'low control, with high accountability'.

Trustees carry the legal and financial responsibilities on behalf of the Community. They are all Companions, endorsing and affirming the appointments made throughout the leadership network, having delegated the day-to-day responsibility for the Community to the Overseers. They meet monthly by video conference and gather quarterly for a weekend at the Community's Mother House.

Over the last 20 years we have also cultivated and strengthened our relationships with the wider Church by appointing Community Visitors from outside who can speak into our life. Their visits, reflections and insights are much appreciated. We enjoy good relationships with both established and emerging churches, though we are not 'owned' by any of them. We have also invited people to journey with us, particularly during periods of transition – people whose knowledge and experience have helped us considerably. All these outside 'voices' have guarded us from being overly parochial in our attitudes and given expression to that part of our Rule that embraces 'a willingness to be accountable to others in ordering our ways and our heart in order to effect change'.

In conclusion, reflecting on modes of ministry, given the growing numerical size of the Northumbria Community and its geographical dispersion, we have adopted a leadership and governance pattern that is episcopal in nature. As someone who adheres to a more baptistic form of governance that seeks together to discern the mind of Christ, I have found three factors have helped me to see the value of a more episcopal model in our Community context.

First, it helps us to appreciate gifts of leadership, particularly the apostolic and prophetic, which are not always recognized or affirmed within the local church. In my own Baptist denomination, we are having to come to terms with growing numbers of people who are called to translocal ministry. This requires a broadening view of the minister, who has traditionally been seen as the pastor/teacher of a local church. This has huge implications and challenges both for our churches and for our theological colleges. The post-Christendom missional context we find ourselves in is not best served by a Christendom model of church with its bias towards teacher/pastor ministries. A recognition of the fivefold ministries of Ephesians 4.11–12 would in my opinion not only serve the renewal of the Church and enrich its life but provide needed momentum and understanding to be a missional movement.

Second, drawing from the example of the Celtic saints, there is a strong emphasis within the Community on its missional and apostolic calling; that is, less towards the Church and more towards culture, living out the gospel in ways that both challenge and contribute to the shaping of human life in society.

And finally, pragmatism determined that in order to work across such a geographically dispersed network, we needed to adopt a pattern that not only serves the Community but also provides means of governance that work well. The influence of the wisdom from the desert tradition, together with the monastic emphasis on spiritual formation, has helped to keep us from expressions of episcopacy that can lead towards power, hierarchy and clericalism. We have sought diligently not to be a centralizing Community, giving edicts from those who occupy the roles of leaders, but rather to encourage Companions and Friends to live out their calling, alone together, in their differing cultural and ecclesiastical contexts.

In order to guard against uniformity, we have avoided categorizing the Northumbria Community by geography, region or diocese. A more ad hoc way of governing helps us to maintain community as relationship by adopting a more spontaneous Celtic pattern than the more institutional Roman pattern of organization allows. What for some would be chaotic and disorderly has been for us creative, liberating and life-giving. Apostolic or translocal leadership operates freely within, across and beyond the Community, enabling us to relate to people, churches, communities and the wider society from a relational rather than institutional starting point. We have avoided a committee-based structure and endeavoured to be institutionally and organizationally light in order to create both the space, time and freedom for people to discover their monastic missional calling.

Of course, there are limitations on our ability to respond immediately and personally to people in need when they are geographically distant from us. The reality of being isolated and experiencing 'the alone' is very real for many, but herein lies both the gift and mystery of Community: a sense of deep connectedness, of being together. Companionship and a very strong sense of bond and covenanted relationship.

I have pondered why I have been able to enjoy a depth and quality of relationship with people whom I don't see every week as in a congregational setting. There is something of quality, depth and authenticity that exists within a group of people, be they church or community, who cohere together around common values and a shared vocation. By contrast, running services, programmes, projects and strategies offers no guarantee of forming deep and meaningful relationships.

We've been privileged in leadership to see how the values of the Community have not only shaped and transformed people's lives but have also been a major building block in constructing relationships between Companions and Friends across the world. There is also, when the emphasis is on those values, less dependence on leaders to feed, nurture and pastor people in their faith. The Community has encouraged people to seek God for themselves. Those who have bought into a consumerist mentality, with its demands for goods and services, find themselves disappointed or disillusioned very quickly with the Community and its leadership.

We endeavour to keep open access as a leadership network to Companions and Friends. Nether Springs is a key listening and discerning place, together with Community teams, gatherings, groups and happenings 'on the road'. It is an impossible task for the leadership network to personally know everyone now within the Community. What we have sought to do is to model covenant relationships among the leadership that we pray will be realized in the lives of others. Thus the gift of community, which is both mysterious and wonderful, is the arena in which trusting, safe, deep and meaningful relationships can flourish and where leadership is exercised in ways that are empowering and transforming for others.

Reference

Peck, M. Scott, 1998, *Further Along the Road Less Travelled*, New York: Simon & Schuster.

Further Reading

Harle, Tim, 2011, *Embracing Chaos: Leadership Insights from Complexity Theory*, Cambridge: Grove Books.
Laloux, Frederic, 2016, *Reinventing Organizations*, Milton Keynes: Nelson Parker.

PART 3

Practice

14

Episkope, Identity and Personhood

ROGER STANDING

> To be a leader without a very real and developing spirituality is to face extreme vulnerability. The marketplace and the desert are the life-blood of every leader struggling to retain their integrity and lead with a divinely-guided sense of purpose. (Grundy, 2011, p. 197)

Those who are experienced in the ministry of translocal oversight know only too well the vital importance of holding together the bustle created by the marketplace of the active ministry to which they are called, and the quiet place of reflection and waiting upon God. If the former is evidence of a commitment to get things done and make a difference for the sake of the kingdom of God, it is the latter that leads to deeper self-awareness and insight into the purposes of God. This is imperative given the insatiable demands and opportunities that translocal ministry presents, and the accompanying dangers and snares that can compromise effective and fruitful ministry.

One of the most fundamental mistakes for those transitioning from church-based ministry in a particular locality to the translocal oversight of churches is to over-presume their familiarity with what they are being called to do. This vocation is the missio-pastoral ministry of Christ after all, and is ministry in an ecclesiological setting and theological context that can best be described as an individual's spiritual home. As a consequence, it is a context in which relationships are well established, ministry gifts have been identified and affirmed, and the trust of the Church invested. Indeed, these are the prerequisites for authentic and effective *episkope*. Yet for all of the commonalities between them, translocal ministry is not local ministry writ large. The gospel may remain the same, but the ecclesial location, geographical range, organizational requirements and spiritual responsibilities of that translocal oversight can prove very different.

So to begin at the beginning: as the Lima document of the World Council of Churches affirms, the exercise of ordained ministry is personal, alongside also being collegial and communal (p. 23). If the collegial and communal aspects of ministry draw on the riches contained within the body of Christ and the Christian tradition within which it lives, the personal mode flows out of the character, experience, wisdom and spirituality of the individual. As well as being a representative embodiment of the wider Church, as they minister, they do so out of the substance of who they are as a disciple of Jesus Christ.

It is therefore of first importance that those who are called to exercise *episkope* give ongoing attention to their own well-being, spiritually, socially, physically and psychologically. The relentless nature of translocal ministry will exact a heavy toll on those who neglect themselves, exerting pressures that can easily begin to open up potential fault lines in their life and ministry. As one bishop reported:

> I joke, though not really, and say that in my first year as bishop I lost my prayer life, my family life, and my exercise life. It took me several more years to get those things back in line. (Martin-Hanley, 2015, p. 17)

Personal authenticity, integrity and well-being

If genuine, authentic Christian spirituality is about the integration of faith with the whole of life, personal and professional, our self-understanding and contextual awareness, our relationships, loyalties, passions, problems and challenges and all of the elements that make up the life we live, then it is good to make time and space to ponder these things. If Grundy is right, that those in leadership who do not have such a developing spirituality leave themselves extremely vulnerable, it is essential to pause and think what such questions might look like through the lens of translocal oversight.

The six questions below have been refined over the years with those new to exercising a ministry of *episkope*. In one sense there is nothing particularly profound about them, neither are they unique to those in translocal ministry or even the only way such questions might be formed. The objective was simply to provide a straightforward framework for individuals to use in reflecting on their personal experience, and to sensitize them as to how their new role might exercise power to shape and reshape them. They can be used privately or with a spiritual director, supervisor, mentor or coach. Used over time, along with a contemporaneous record of reflection, they can help provide robust foundation for an integrated life of spiritual authenticity and integrity – the holy life.

1 Who am I before God? The question of faith and relationship with God

This is the most fundamental question, however we conceive the substance of our ongoing relationship with God. This is the wellspring out of which our ministry flows. The problem is that for many involved in translocal ministry, the very ministry they have embraced is disruptive of the rhythms and structures of ministerial life that become the devotional superstructure that is supportive of faith. The lack of routine and the uneven nature of translocal ministry can easily destroy an established life-giving habitus of the spiritual disciplines, patterns of private prayer and study, commitment to lead the weekly round of worship services, Bible studies, gatherings for prayer and sermon preparation. Indeed, for many local ministers, the preparation of a new weekly sermon or homily is an unrecognized yet vitally important dimension of their ongoing spiritual discipline and health. In a translocal context where such an investment of time in sermon preparation may be inappropriate, a significant dimension of the minister's spiritual life is thus diminished. The necessary stepping back from the day-to-day life of a local church also has a material impact on a minister's spiritual life. In one study less than half of responding bishops reported spiritual growth as a positive experience of their time in episcopal ministry (Martin-Hanley, 2015, p. 30).

Discerning a sustainable pattern of spiritual discipline that is compatible with the demands of translocal ministry and fits an individual's own personality and needs is therefore of the utmost importance. While this may be stating the obvious, naming it and acknowledging its significance is the necessary prerequisite to addressing it. The truth is that there is no one answer with regard to the pattern or form this might take. What has worked in the past? It is likely that something akin to this will work in the future if it takes account of the translocal nature of ministry.

Some of the strategies that have been found helpful to those in translocal ministry include:

- proactively establishing an appropriate 'rootedness' in your local church;
- planning regular retreat days and blocking dates in the diary;
- spiritual direction;
- agreeing the shape and substance of a devotional commitment with those who share in translocal ministry;
- spending time considering how the spiritual disciplines might be incorporated into your pattern of life as a translocal minister;
- redeeming travel time for prayer and reflection.

2 Who am I at home? Questions of marriage and family[1]

'Why is it that bishops have a call and their spouses have a role?' This is a revealing question, not least because it indicates a significant difference between local ministry and translocal ministry for the spouse, with the possible exception of The Salvation Army. As part of a local congregation, being married to the minister confers an identity and place at the centre of the community's life. The spouse of a translocal minister has a very difficult transition to make from the outset. In one move they lose their role, status and identity as an honoured member at the centre of the life of a local church. The sense of dislocation is further exacerbated by the need to establish themselves within a new congregation where someone else is the minister, they are no longer the minister's spouse and a shared experience of being at the centre of a worshipping community is missing.

Though often experienced in ministerial transitions with the accompanying disruptions caused by moving to a new area and the sense of loss and grief they bring, those called to translocal ministry discover that this transition is harder and the struggles more persistent. Indeed, evidence suggests that it is harder for the spouse as less of life is shared, time apart is more frequent and time together is more often marked by the 'absent presence' of the tired or preoccupied translocal minister. A sense of isolation on the part of a spouse is an altogether too common experience. Given that research has indicated that those in these roles identify their relationship together as their most important source of support (Martin-Hanley, 2015, p. 74), the significance of the health of this relationship cannot be overestimated.

Life situation also contributes to the challenges of home life by providing fresh and often unanticipated situations to be addressed. Given that those called to exercise *episkope* tend to be older and more experienced, the issues of late middle age kick in. What are the implications of being 'empty-nesters' or grandparents? How are aged parents to be supported? Then there is age itself – as one bishop remarked, 'The job doesn't change, but you get older!' Energy levels and the capacity to work long hours diminish and, of course, age itself brings a greater likelihood of other health matters to be addressed or coped with.

Every translocal minister needs to find a pattern of family life and maintaining healthy relationships that works for them, but these are some of the insights shared by those engaged in this ministry, and intentionality appears to be the common denominator:

- 'We deliberately plan a family time each week and fiercely guard it.'
- 'In normal circumstances I only commit to preaching on Sunday mornings.'
- 'Diary, diary, diary … plan and diary special occasions as far ahead as possible.'
- 'I use my diary as a tool to remind me to do things as well as book appointments. It particularly helps me deal with inappropriate or unwanted requests.'
- 'We regularly block Sundays throughout the year so that we can worship together as a family.'
- 'I always have an eye to when we can piggyback something I'm doing with a family trip like going to a seaside church or one near a local beauty spot or attraction.'

3 Who am I in the church? The question of the religious professional

It is good to reflect on the nuts and bolts of our vocational experience, not least because of the significant differences between local church ministry and that exercised in the translocal sphere. How is this work of ministry influencing me and my self-perception? How is it subtly affecting what I do? What challenges is it presenting me with? For example, the impact of travel on perceived levels of productivity. As a Baptist Regional Minister, I regularly invested 20–30 hours a month getting from one place to another on my patch in south-central England. Consequently, my reduced capacity and output made it feel like I was significantly underperforming. But to have a realistic understanding of my situation meant both recognizing and acknowledging the impact of the investment of time to get from A to B.

Or again, and rather obviously, as with all ministers who work from home, the unfinished nature of the task means that it is impossible to get away from. The temptation will be to invest time off in seeking to clear the backlog of mail, email, phone calls and other administrative tasks that are all too accessible. In addition, the intensity of the crisis-management work that falls to those exercising *episkope* is significantly more 'draining' than that experienced as a local church minister.

Of course, there is also the shift from working with a local congregation that is by its very nature more relational and organic, to working within a denominational infrastructure or organizational network. The latter is far more institutional and, whether structured along charitable or entrepreneurial lines, far less relational and controlled by organizational policy and structural processes. Clearly, the difference between working with volunteers and employees is significant, as is the move from being a 'solo' minister or small team in a local church to being part of a much larger enterprise with well-developed and established team working. Even if there is experience of working in such an environment outside of the Church, to encounter it within the context of faith can still be a culture shock.

Irrespective of the demands of translocal ministry, not to comprehend this very different working environment properly is to set up an ongoing cause of friction that will be both frustrating and energy-sapping. Indeed, acknowledging it is vitally important for a translocal minister to flourish and make the contribution they are capable of. By contrast, avoiding or neglecting to adapt to this ecclesial reality is to sow the seeds of future stress, overwork and disillusionment.

All of the above are, of course, triggers for the conversation about what work/life balance looks like for those ministering in translocal oversight. The struggle is how to disentangle discipleship, vocation, service, self-sacrifice, institutional leadership, organizational management and a personal life! The truth is that it is impossible. Interestingly, David Whyte, the poet/philosopher who is an Associate Fellow at the Said Business School in Oxford, observes that rather than pursuing some mythical and unachievable work/life balance between the competing commitments to work, self and other, we should see them both as non-negotiable commitments[2] and expressions of how we relate to the world. Rather than striving to bring them into balance by taking from one and giving to another, Whyte proposes that we see them in a dynamic relationship together where each can converse with, question and embolden the other two (Whyte, 2009, pp. 10–11). Working with a professional accompanist, supervisor, mentor or coach who understands the dynamics of translocal oversight and ecclesiological context is a helpful way to explore and tease out these issues.

4 Who am I in my ministry? The question of calling and a sense of vocation

In a more general sense, vocation is talked about when an individual feels particularly attracted to a certain occupation, or for which they appear particularly well suited. In ministry it is more specifically related to God's call, and especially to ordination. The question of 'Who am I in my ministry?' explores issues of spiritual self-awareness and self-understanding, as viewed through the grace of God's gifts in the Spirit, natural abilities and aptitudes and the discernment of God's guidance. Chapter 15 will examine this more thoroughly, but here it is sufficient to include this within the overall framework that is being suggested as helpful in understanding the relationship between *episkope*, identity and personhood. What we intuit as the substance of God's call on our lives has a central role to play in defining our identity. Insofar as the ministry of translocal oversight enables this call to be expressed, there is an experience of harmony and fulfilment. If, however, it is overlaid with other tasks and responsibilities and opportunities are limited, the result is frustration and a deep sense of misfit. If individuals are called to translocal oversight for the person they are, it is wholly appropriate to expect an outlet for their vocation and passion. There are important questions to ask in this regard:

- What is my particular gifting?
- What energizes and renews me in my service of Christ?
- What is central/integral to my calling as a minister of the gospel?

Alongside this it may be helpful to:

- examine the overall balance of your diary and seek to ensure there are opportunities to minister in the area of vocational passion;
- openly share with colleagues those things that bring a particular sense of fulfilment in relation to your sense of call, so that when opportunities arise they might be directed appropriately.

5 How am I and I? The personal question, 'love others as you love yourself'

'I and I', the Rasta-influenced, Jamaican street-speak that identifies our physical self and our spiritual self – the person we are, whether we are thriving or struggling, flourishing, stable or striving to hang on. The question echoes John Wesley's interrogative, 'How is it with your soul?' where he expected the inquiry to connect spirituality with lifestyle, holiness with personal habits, well-being with well-doing.

Translocal ministry has a number of challenges where personal health and welfare are considered. A sedentary lifestyle that is fed by liberal quantities of junk food, with erratic sleep patterns and a disproportionate level of tense and conflictual situations to be dealt with is a recipe for ill-health. What does a healthy lifestyle look like in the context of such a ministry? What are the issues that need to be addressed and what are the means by which to address them?

A brainstorming session that looked to identify how to establish and maintain the practicalities of a healthy and accountable lifestyle produced some interesting results:

- Exercise regularly:
  - join a gym;
  - go swimming regularly;
  - take a brisk walk (plan it strategically when you're out and about);
  - buy a bike (and use it!);
  - racquet sports – tennis, badminton, squash;
  - bat sports – cricket and table tennis.
- Consciously change your eating habits – limit fast food and sweet things.
- Commit yourself to follow a hobby or outside interest:
  - crafting, woodwork, metalwork, philately;
  - join a club (photography, Lions, Rotary, golf, bowls) or a choir;
  - learn to play a musical instrument – join a band or orchestra;
  - follow a local sports team (or a professional one) and go to matches.
- Read books – fiction or non-fiction – for pleasure. Join a book club and meet people.
- Form a support group who know you well, to whom you can be accountable.
- Be prepared to seek professional help if necessary. This is a sign of responsible leadership, not of professional failure.

In such discussions proverbial wisdom abounds: 'Fallow seasons lead to productive land', 'Even the ocean has its shallows', 'All work and no play makes the bishop a dull priest!' None of this is exclusively applicable to those exercising translocal oversight. None of the suggestions is particularly novel. However, all are potentially life-giving in the quest to sustain our loving of others, by adequately loving ourselves. Yet their simplicity is all too easily lost sight of in the welter of activity and responsibility that comes with the ministry of oversight.

6 Who will I be in 18 months' time? Adapting the CPD question

Churches have been slow to adopt annual appraisals or reviews, not without some justification. The uncritical embracing of secular business practice would frequently benefit from robust theological scrutiny, not least to avert or mitigate unintended consequences. So often related to performance-related pay, such an approach is clearly anathema on so many levels. However, to sit down annually and think about personal and professional development, with the necessity to draw up a plan and follow it to completion, has much to commend it. With the accepted constraints of translocal ministry, any hope of addressing such issues requires an intentional approach.

Ask yourself: What are my present strengths and weaknesses, my concerns and passions with regard to my spirituality, my family life, my professional life, in my calling and in my personal life? Which of these do I need to address? How will I address them? Over what time-frame can they realistically be addressed and what are the intermediate steps to accomplish them? This is about the whole of life, not just a higher education degree or providing impressive substance for an ecclesiastical CV.

In the ministry of *episkope*, the familiar elements of who we are, the Church of which we are a part and life in general all come together, but in unfamiliar, unexpected and unusual ways. A translocal minister's identity and personhood are intimately connected and intertwined with what emerges from this complex set of dynamics, and care needs to be taken both to establish and to maintain personal well-being. This is not a task that is completed once the role has been understood and the ministry bedded-down, but rather is an ongoing and continual realignment of identity and personhood with the heart, mind and nature of God. It is about enabling and sustaining a life that epitomizes for the churches what it is to 'love God and live generously'.

Notes

1 Of course, not everyone in translocal ministry is married and living in a family home. Some, like Roman Catholics, embrace singleness as a doctrinal expression of their ecclesiology. Others are single for a variety of other reasons, including bereavement, separation/divorce or because they have never married. The opportunity to explore their experience and insights is not possible within the limitations of this volume.

2 Whyte talks about them as 'three marriages'.

References

Grundy, Malcolm, 2011, *Leadership and Oversight: New Models for Episcopal Ministry*, London: Mowbray.

Martin-Hanley, Marla, 2015, *Fulfillment of Mutual Affection: Bishop and Spouse Partnerships in the 21st Century*; www.collegeforbishops.org/bishop-spousepartner-study?rq=marla (accessed 17.12.2019).

Whyte, David, 2009, *The Three Marriages: Reimagining Work, Self and Relationship*, New York: Riverhead Books.

World Council of Churches, 1982, *Baptism, Eucharist and Ministry*; www.oikoumene.org/en/resources/documents/commissions/faith-and-order/i-unity-the-church-and-its-mission/baptism-eucharist-and-ministry-faith-and-order-paper-no-111-the-lima-text/@@download/file/FO1982_111_en.pdf (accessed 17.12.2019).

15

The Shape of Translocal Oversight

ROGER STANDING

Shaped by character and spirituality

A sixth-century controversy over titles would seem a strange place to start in exploring the shape of translocal oversight in contemporary Britain. However, Gregory the Great (c.540–604) is an influential figure in church history, and his run-in with John the Faster led to Gregory's adoption of the epithet for his own role as Pope and Bishop of Rome as *Servus, servorum Dei* ('servant of the servants of God'). This was in pointed contrast to John who, as Archbishop of Constantinople, had adopted the title of 'Ecumenical (or universal) Patriarch', which Gregory asserted was a 'diabolical arrogance'.[1]

It was Gregory, of course, who also dispatched Augustine on a missionary expedition to Britain and set in motion the sequence of events that led to Augustine becoming the first Archbishop of Canterbury. More importantly in this regard, however, is Gregory's *Liber Regulae Pastoralis*, or *Pastoral Rule*, which was effectively the first ever handbook on being a priest and a bishop. Concerned with both the inner life and outer responsibilities of vocation, Gregory wrote of the bishop:

> The conduct of a prelate ought so far to be superior to the conduct of the people as the life of a shepherd is accustomed to exalt him above the flock. For one whose position is such that the people are called his flock ought anxiously to consider how great a necessity is laid upon him to maintain uprightness. It is necessary, then, that in thought he should be pure, in action firm; discreet in keeping silence; profitable in speech; a near neighbor to every one in sympathy; exalted above all in contemplation; a familiar friend of good livers through humility, unbending against the vices of evil-doers through zeal for righteousness; not relaxing in his care for what is inward by reason of being occupied in outward things, nor neglecting to provide for outward things in his anxiety for what is inward. (Ogg, 1972, pp. 91–6)

From the earliest days of Christianity, attention has been given to those qualities of character, behaviour and spirituality that someone called to oversight in the Church should display. The Pastoral epistles have served as foundational documents in this, whatever the differences of time and space in the exercise of *episkope*. In Titus, for example, this is articulated as the blamelessness of someone who, by contrast, is not arrogant, quick-tempered, addicted to wine, violent or greedy for gain but is rather hospitable, a lover of goodness, prudent, upright, devout, self-controlled and with a firm grasp of the faith that enables them to preach with sound doctrine and refute those who contradict it (Titus 1.7–9).

The shape of translocal oversight, then, begins with the individual concerned; that is, the kind of person they are, not so much concerning their personality type or psychometric profile as their character and spirituality. It is about maturity and wisdom, self-knowledge and an empathetic understanding of the other, of a life under the mastery of the values of the kingdom – what has traditionally been named as holiness or Christ-likeness. This is not special to, or different from, the life that all disciples are called to live, but it is the expectation of a life that will exemplify such a quality of living. As such, it is a significant and formative influence on the shape of the *episkope* that is practised by those called to exercise it.

Shaped by a different context

Those called to a ministry of translocal oversight are almost invariably drawn from the ranks of those engaged in local congregational or parish ministry. While they may be experienced in the wider structures and counsels of their denomination or network, such participation is almost invariably experienced and understood through the lens of the local church. While this perspective is vitally important, translocal ministry is a changed perspective because the location of ministry has shifted.

Ecclesial location

Translocal ministry is not the local church. The functions, roles, emphases, responsibilities and relationships are different because the context is different from congregationally based service. The translocal leader is not in the same worshipping, discipling, serving congregation day by day, week by week, month by month and year by year. While translocal ministry may organize times of shared worship, participate in Christian service and engage in explicit dimensions of discipleship, and even though the shape of translocal oversight may involve a small cohort of fellow travellers in the ecclesial structure who share the journey, it is not ministry in a local church. Indeed, many of the fellow travellers, though brothers and sisters in Christ, are employees of a legally constituted organization and formally regulated charity. Rather than being volunteers in a believing community of relationships with the freedom to regulate their participation, engagement and financial links to the shared work, they may well be paid members of staff with job descriptions, formal responsibilities under charitable law and the protection of employment legislation.

Proximity

By and large the work of ministry in a local church is just that, local. Translocal ministry changes ministry on the most practical of levels because it is translocal. At the very least, such oversight stretches across a self-contained city and its hinterland. For most the area is much larger. As a Baptist Regional Minister serving the Southern Counties Association of churches, the team I led had oversight of 175 churches in Oxfordshire, Berkshire, Hampshire and most of Dorset, and included churches in seven other counties and the Channel Islands. This was more churches than most of the churches had worshippers. At the most basic level this affected so many of the core elements of ministry: availability, regularity of contact, the development of meaningful relationships, the fellowship of shared activity and experience. Not to mention the investment of time, especially when this involved a long drive home after a late evening finish.

Representative role

In a very real sense local church ministry is representative, as a minister represents their congregation in the local community, their denomination ecumenically and, within the congregation they lead, Christ himself. Yet the nature of this representative role is primarily relational, and the minister acts out of who they are as a disciple of Christ. However, on undertaking translocal ministry there is a subtle change and the representative role shifts to being primarily institutional. Of course, it is not that locally based ministry does not have such dimensions, or that translocal ministry does not benefit from strong relational ties, it is just that the primary locus of the representative function is different. The exception to the rule is highlighted in the experiences of Terry Virgo and Gerald Coates as their respective networks grew out of their personal ministry and influence. But therein lies the explanation. An established denomination or network has a pre-existent identity that those serving translocally within it are automatically perceived, if not required, to represent.

The impact of this is felt immediately for a minister who is used to a more relationally based ministry in a local church. From invitations to civic events and the engagement with the wider community, to meetings with clergy and lay people alike, who they are is most often second to what they represent. Indeed, preconceptions of the institution, and past experiences with it, can dramatically shape the nature of encounters, meetings and conversations. What can at first seem a highly personal response or reaction may be no such thing. Rather than being about the translocal minister themself, it is about the institution, authority in general or even past experiences with previous incumbents projected into the present.

While the translocal minister is the same person they were before, now clergy and church members respond differently to them because of the representative nature of their role, as they are a physical embodiment of the diocese, province, district or denomination. The reality is that the default position in engaging with someone exercising *episkope* is institutional rather than relational.

Authority

Not unrelated to the representative nature of translocal ministry is the issue of authority. Here ecclesiology is important, but not as important as might be first expected. Congregationally organized denominations tend to see the differences between themselves and more hierarchical systems in stark contrast. They are not 'episcopally led and synodically governed' as is the state Church. Indeed, the Baptist Union of Great Britain does not have a lengthy rule book, not even a shared statement of faith, merely a three-part, 134-word 'Declaration of Principle', which forms the basis of the Union.[2] Even so, the dynamics of day-to-day reality are much closer across the spectrum.

While contemporary analysis and commentary identifies many differing categories of authority, suffice here to note Max Weber's classic outline of three main types: traditional authority that is rooted in the past with its traditions and customs; legal-rational authority that is legitimized by rules and laws; and charismatic authority that is based in the personal attributes of the individual (Renwick and Swinburn, 1993, pp. 61–2). Translocal oversight can be a complex interaction between all three and, while the nuances of action will be shaped by the immediate ecclesiological context, there is a strange paradoxical and ironic symmetry between them.

Given the representative nature of translocal oversight, ecclesial authority appears to be clearly rooted in the traditional sphere of church history and its biblical foundations. While such authority may be acknowledged in theory, in practice it does not deliver much clout. This is reserved for the legal-rational application of rules and laws. However, these tend not to be in the gift of a translocal minister and are only there to be bureaucratically applied. The exceptions are those areas of church life where those in translocal oversight are 'gatekeepers' to resources and processes. In areas like the distribution of grants, the deployment of ministers or access to ordination training, the level of legal-rational authority can be very high indeed.

Mostly, however, it is the 'soft' power of a Weberian charismatic authority that most translocal ministers, of almost all Christian communities, find themselves most dependent on. Of course, the ironic paradox is that this is made more difficult by the institutional nature of the representative role.

Marginality

While there are times when the translocal minister is deeply involved in the lives of the churches and ministers they oversee, the very different nature of the ministry that is required of them tends to make the experience one that is lived more on the margins. That is not to say that relationships are not real, meaningful or good, or that the opportunities for ministry are not welcomed, rich and significant. Indeed, they are often indicative of key moments of celebration or crisis. But in the normal ongoing life of the Christian communities they oversee, the wider life of the denomination and those who exercise *episkope* will not figure highly in their consciousness or list of priorities. Many, if not most, worshippers would not recognize their bishop, district chair or regional minister if they saw them, and many would struggle to name them even if they even understood something of their wider ecclesiastical setting. And it is probably true that the greater the inclination towards a congregational ecclesiology, the greater the sense of the marginality. But that is how it must be. A minister providing translocal oversight cannot be intimately involved with the churches and ministers under their care on a consistent basis like someone in local ministry because it is simply not possible.

Shaped by the role

Translocal oversight in the twenty-first century is more defined by job descriptions and documents outlining various roles and responsibilities than was ever the case in the past (though many would be swift to add that such documentation is an indicative rather than exhaustive account). To the degree to which they exist, are kept up-to-date and are actively used for organizational management and to guide annual reviews, they supply a significant superstructure for the exercise of *episkope* along with the theological understanding that informs them. Significant too is what is brought to the role by the incumbent in terms of their own gifts and passions and the ecclesiological convictions within which they are embedded.

In seeking to understand how the role operates in the life of the churches, various attempts have been made to identify either the tasks that are performed, such as those of chief pastor, successor of the apostles and leader in mission (Avis, 2015, pp. 17–32), or the different approaches to the role, like that of a missionary, a reformer and the intriguing model of 'enslaved liberator' (Grundy, 2011, pp. 52–69).[3] However, it is perhaps more helpful to think of both the tasks and approaches as a series of different dimensions to the role.

The pastoral dimension

Historically speaking, the priority given to the pastoral dimension of the role has been consistent over the centuries and is illustrated by the symbolism of the bishop's crozier shaped like a shepherd's crook in Western Christianity or the designation of a diocesan bishop as its 'chief pastor'. This richly biblical theme is also echoed in the shepherding and pastoral language contained within the ordination service of bishops in *Common Worship*.[4] However, pastoral ministry in the context of translocal oversight has its own gruelling demands. Frequently it is the more serious or intractable issues that cannot be dealt with elsewhere that need to be addressed.

Issues of discipline or conflict resolution, heightened in intensity to the point of escalation, do not lend themselves to quick fixes. Much will depend on the resources to hand as to whether the translocal minister must tackle the situation themselves or whether they can deploy others under their authority. To have appropriate policies and procedures in place in such trying circumstances is vitally important to be able to demonstrate both the transparency of process and the fairness and justice of its application.

I quickly discovered, in dealing with a conflict between minister and congregation, that it was a 'no-win' situation. The result was that I learnt to preface all such work with observations that named this invidious dynamic that was prone to automatically dismiss an outcome that did not favour the preferred convictions of one side or the other. In such minister–congregation conflicts I would say:

> If the outcome appears to favour the minister then unhappy congregants will murmur, 'Of course they would, wouldn't they, they're all ministers in it together!' Whereas, if it is perceived that the congregation's position has prevailed, the pastor and their supporters would reflect, 'Of course they would, wouldn't they, because ministers come and go, but the authorities always have to relate to the congregation!'

The pastoral dimension of translocal oversight can easily be subverted too, as the Church's shameful failure in too many child abuse scandals has frequently demonstrated. In attempting to recalibrate the pastoral ministry into a translocal context, the notion of being 'a pastor to the pastors' is an obvious and not illegitimate perspective to develop. Yet this has all too easily slipped into collusion as abusers have been successful in recruiting those in positions of oversight to their cause. Thankfully, issues of safeguarding are now very much in the forefront of people's minds, and pastoral responsibility is recognized as being for the whole people of God, and not just the clergy. Sadly, given the extent of the cover-ups regarding child abuse, one suspects that issues of spiritual abuse, bullying and the range of behaviours that were historically identified as 'conduct unbecoming of a minister of the gospel' may also have been passed over. In an excellent example of the strategic level of pastoral oversight required of translocal leaders, the bishops of the Blackburn diocese wrote a compelling letter to their clergy, lay readers and safeguarding officers following the publication of the report of the Independent Inquiry into Child Sexual Abuse:

> But we need to understand also that safeguarding is not just about ticking boxes and following rules. It is about a much deeper awareness, especially for clergy and church-leaders, of where power lies in relationships and how easy it is to abuse that power. The report has a great deal to say about 'clericalism' and about an inappropriate culture of deference to clergy, especially senior clergy, which has resulted in cover-up and in the voices of the vulnerable being silenced.[5]

The missiological dimension

In the oft-quoted observation of the theologian Martin Kähler, 'mission is the mother of theology' (Guder, 1998, p. 7). Rather than being 'a luxury of the world-conquering church ... [theology] was generated by the emergency situation in which the missionizing church found itself'. Kähler's observation was that as Europe Christianized and Christianity became an established religion it became dislocated from its missionary roots (Bosch, 2003, p. 489). Without the *missio Dei* there would be no Church, and, as the body of Christ, the Church's life, identity and calling are indistinguishable from its participation in the *missio Dei*. To quote another theologian, Emil Brunner, 'Where there is no mission, there is no church' (Brunner, 1931, p. 108).

The later decades of the twentieth century witnessed the seemingly inexorable decline of the churches in Britain and a growing realization that mission was not just meant to be conducted overseas. The influential writing of Lesslie Newbigin and others helped the reintegration of missiology into the centre of contemporary theological dialogue and paved the way for significant developments that were to affect the churches profoundly. Within the Church of England, for example, the emergence of the 'five marks of mission' out of the Anglican Consultative Council and Lambeth Conference in the 1980s, and the *Mission-Shaped Church* report of 2004, paved the way for the revolutionary Fresh Expressions movement.[6] Among Baptists the missional impetus was grasped by David Coffey, the General Secretary, as a denominational restructuring was undertaken in 2002 with the objective of facilitating mission. Coffey himself looked to articulate what this missional thinking looked like in a Baptist context with his 'Six Marks of a Missionary Union', the sixth of which he identified as the significance of the recognition and encouragement of 'apostolic leadership' upon which the other five hinged (Wright, 2014, pp. 97–112). A similar move in The Salvation Army is narrated by Commissioner Mike Parker earlier in this book.

There is no doubting the critical importance of those in translocal oversight to both encourage and facilitate missional momentum in their jurisdiction. As Coffey himself concludes, 'We offer ourselves in prayer to our missionary God ... [and] develop intentionally those apostolic leadership teams which will prepare the whole of God's people for their works of service' (Wright, 2014, p. 111).

The ecclesiological dimension

The Methodist Conference, in a very insightful report on the nature of oversight in their own context, helpfully define their terms in the following way:

> the Greek word *episkope* which, with its related verbs, is used in the Bible to describe God visiting people and 'keeping an eye' on what is happening ... involves aspects of watching over, watching out for, monitoring, discerning, disciplining, directing, guiding, encouraging and caring. These in turn can be grouped under headings which can appropriately be described as **governance** (exercising formal authority in formulating the policies and ordering the practices of the Church), **management** (implementing strategies to enact the policies, deploying people and other resources to that end, and monitoring the results) and **leadership** (inspiring, discerning and articulating vision, and providing models of giving guidance and exercising power with authority, justice and love). (Methodist Conference, 2005, p. 1)

In many ways this is the nuts and bolts of translocal oversight. Governance and management are impossible to avoid if anything is to be accomplished. While some resist, decry and seek to side-step them, they are organizational necessities that cover legal obligations, administrative requirements and systems of accountability for getting things done. Many in positions of translocal oversight tend to gravitate to the leadership function, but without appropriate levels of governance and management their leadership can be quickly compromised or corrupted.

There is much that the Church can learn from the experience of business and the charitable sector regarding governance, management and leadership. Personally, for example, exploring the nature of leadership I have benefitted a great deal from the insights of Warren Bennis and Burt Nanus with their account of transactional and transformational leadership, along with Simon P. Walker's trilogy on 'the undefended leader'. Of course, there is a seemingly endless supply of leadership theories and resources that can be profitably mined for insight and truth. Yet any adoption of such insights needs to be done in the presence of rigorous theological scrutiny. Just because a particular process is widely deployed and universally acknowledged as best practice does not mean that it is theologically or spiritually appropriate. Take, for instance, the practice of equal opportunities recruitment. To create a level playing field for every applicant to a role is clearly in accord with the principles of natural justice. However, the outcome is predicated on a principle of institutional self-interest, of getting the best-qualified person to do the job that we want done. By contrast, seeking to call someone to *episkope* is about answering the question of who God is calling to this role. It involves the humility of recognizing who might have gifts and abilities to contribute what we do not yet see the need of, to shape the future for a context that we do not yet fully comprehend. Indeed, the person best suited to the task we presently think needs doing may actually be called by God, and better deployed, to serve elsewhere! As such, the issue for recruiters is how to sharpen their sense of spiritual discernment and mitigate the potential for personal bias and prejudice.

It is no coincidence that a debate along these lines was released into the Church of England when, in the wake of the Green Report on *Talent Management for Future Leaders and Leadership Development for Bishops and Deans*, various recommendations sought to adopt the insights of business and the third sector, such as the provision of an outsourced MBA that bypassed the theological colleges. Martyn Percy, Dean of Christ Church, Oxford was one among a number of critics, including the educators and bloggers Ian Paul and Mike Higton.[7] Percy, while acknowledging sound ideas in the report and the need for competent management, was stinging in his criticism. For him the lack of origination of ideas and strategies in theological or spiritual wisdom; the control of a 'talent pool' by executive leaders who have already pre-established strategic priorities; the assessment of potential candidates of 'outstanding', 'high' and 'strong' performance in ministry against measurable 'growth factors' was indicative of a subversion of the Church into what he calls 'ecclesionomics' and 'ecclesiocracy' (Percy, 2017, pp. 33–6).

The shape of translocal oversight is affected by many things, and those highlighted above are far from providing an exhaustive list, but in my experience, they are at least indicative of what someone engaging in the ministry of *episkope* will experience and wrestle with. Of course, we have not begun to explore the impact of expectations and how to manage them. As for everyone in ministry, this is a potential minefield where responsibilities, priorities and expectations engage in a dynamic, three-dimensional dance through the diary. However, that is a practical and interactive seminar for another day. The short answer is that there is no hope of maintaining balance, and the only way through is by self-awareness and spiritual discernment, laced with the wisdom of Solomon!

Notes

1 For a fuller account of the controversy, see www.catholic.com/encyclopedia/john-the-faster (accessed 20.12.2019).

2 Though, of course, as a legally constituted charity it does have a detailed constitution. An explanation of the Baptist Union's 'Declaration of Principle' and full copy of the text is available at https://baptist.org.uk/Groups/220595/Declaration_of_Principle.aspx (accessed 22.12.2019).

3 Grundy also identifies 20 different models of *episkope* under the three headings of Organic, Directional and Authoritarian (pp. 111–28). See also the generic job description for a bishop published by the Church in Wales, www.churchinwales.org.uk/en/clergy-and-members/clergy-handbook/generic-job-description-bishop/ (accessed 23.12.2019).

4 See www.churchofengland.org/prayer-and-worship/worship-texts-and-resources/common-worship/ministry/common-worship-ordination-services#mmo15 (accessed 23.12.2019).

5 The whole letter is worth reading and will reward reflection. It can be found at www.blackburn.anglican.org/news/274/letter-from-senior-clergy-reflecting-on- (accessed 23.12.2019).

6 The Five Marks of Mission:
    The mission of the Church is the mission of Christ
    To proclaim the Good News of the Kingdom
    To teach, baptise and nurture new believers
    To respond to human need by loving service
    To transform unjust structures of society, to challenge violence of every kind and pursue peace and reconciliation
    To strive to safeguard the integrity of creation, and sustain and renew the life of the earth.
See www.anglicancommunion.org/mission/marks-of-mission.aspx (accessed 23.12.2019).

7 Mike Higton is a Professor in the Department of Theology and Religion at Durham University and his blog addresses this issue at http://mikehigton.org.uk/2015/02/ (accessed 23.12.2019). Revd Dr Ian Paul is a theologian, author and member of General Synod who runs the awarding-winning blog *Psephizo*, which responds to the Green Report at www.psephizo.com/life-ministry/should-bishops-come-from-a-talent-pool/ (accessed 23.12.2019).

References

Avis, Paul, 2015, *Becoming a Bishop*, London: T&T Clark.
Bennis, Warren and Burt Nanus, 2005, *Leaders: Strategies for Taking Charge* (2nd edition), New York: HarperCollins.
Bosch, David J., 2003, *Transforming Mission: Paradigm Shifts in Theology of Mission*, Maryknoll, NY: Orbis Books.
Brunner, Emil, 1931, *The Word and the World*, London: SCM Press.
Grundy, Malcolm, 2011, *Leadership and Oversight: New Models for Episcopal Ministry*, London: Mowbray.

Guder, Darrell L. (ed.), 1998, *Missional Church*, Grand Rapids, MI: Eerdmans.
Methodist Conference, 2005, *The Nature of Oversight: Leadership, Management and Governance in the Methodist Church in Great Britain*; www.methodist.org.uk/about-us/the-methodist-conference/conference-reports/conference-reports-2005/ (accessed 17.10.2019).
Ogg, Frederic Austin (ed.), 1972, *A Source Book of Mediaeval History: Documents Illustrative of European Life and Institutions from the German Invasions to the Renaissance*, New York: Cooper Square Publishers.
Percy, Martyn, 2017, *The Future Shapes of Anglicanism: Current, Contours, Charts*, London: Routledge.
Renwick, Alan and Ian Swinburn, 1993, *Basic Political Concepts*, Cheltenham: Stanley Thornes Publishers.
Walker, Simon P., 2007a, *Leading out of Who You Are: Discovering the Secret of Undefended Leadership*, Carlisle: Piquant Editions.
Walker, Simon P., 2007b, *Leading with Nothing to Lose: Training in the Exercise of Power*, Carlisle: Piquant Editions.
Walker, Simon P., 2009, *Leading with Everything to Give: Lessons from the Success and Failure of Western Capitalism*, Carlisle: Piquant Editions.
Wright, Nigel G. (ed.), 2014, *Truth That Never Dies: The Dr. G. R. Beasley-Murray Memorial Lectures 2002–12*, Eugene, OR: Pickwick Publications.

16

Translocal Ministry and Scholarship

PAUL GOODLIFF

One of the strong biblical roles for those who are translocal as bishops or superintendents is defending or guarding the faith: the *regula fidei*. Some who offer this will do so from the perspective of theological education, and may already be 'professional theologians', which will often mean coming from a university appointment. Allied to this is the role of forming and educating those seeking to become ministers, and thus another context from which those offering translocal oversight may come is the theological seminary.

I want to suggest that there is a particular role, among the various 'colours' of translocal ministry mapped out elsewhere, for 'the scholar bishop', or their ecumenical equivalent. What they lack in local church or parish experience is compensated for by their experience in teaching the faith and guarding the gospel. This may not be the most common route into regional oversight but adds a vital element to the collegial character of a bench of bishops or superintendents.

It may be appropriate to make distinctions between those who become bishops or equivalent from the background of a professional scholar or academic, and those whose ministerial background has included some tutoring in a theological setting, such as on a ministerial training course or in the context of a college. While most academics will remain in the academy, and most bishops and their equivalents will have a conventional ministerial career in the parish and congregation, it is the combination of the two that makes for the unusual 'hybrid', the scholar bishop. Historically this was not so unusual. Of theologians, Jaroslav Pelikan observed that:

> During the years 100 to 600, most theologians were bishops; from 600 to 1500 in the West, they were monks; since 1500 they have been university professors. Gregory I, who died in 604, was a bishop who became a monk; Martin Luther was a monk who became a university professor. Each of these life styles has left its mark on the job description

of the theologian, but also on the way doctrine has continued to develop back and forth between believing, teaching and confessing. (1971, p. 5)

However, today this creature is increasingly rare, and I will argue for its conservation, and indeed, the possibility of a rare-breed breeding programme too! First, however, a historical and empirical survey.

The Church of England

There is a strong tradition of some of those exercising oversight in the Church of England coming to this ministry from the academy. A century or more ago this was likely to be as headmaster of a public school – that is, an independent school, not a state school or grammar school – but this background has been almost entirely absent in more recent years. More often today it is the university sector that provides the background for 'scholar bishops'. The Bishop of Durham has been a professional academic theologian twice in recent appointments: David Jenkins, who was Professor of Theology at Leeds, and Tom Wright, who came to the post in 2003 having been a university lecturer at Oxford and elsewhere.[1] On his resignation from the post of Bishop of Durham he returned to the academy as Research Professor of New Testament and Early Christianity at St Mary's College in the University of St Andrews in Scotland.

A similar pattern emerged in the case of Rowan Williams, whose career prior to his appointment as Bishop of Monmouth in 1992 and Archbishop in Wales from 1999 had been entirely academic.[2] After his time as Archbishop of Canterbury, to which see he was translated in 2002, he similarly returned to the academy in 2012, having been appointed as Master of Magdalene College, Cambridge. Both Wright and Williams combined writing and research while serving as bishops, and one suspects that such were the demands on their energies as bishops that research and writing was a helpful retreat from those pastoral and political demands. It certainly brought their work as a bishop into a wider context.

A similar story might be told about Stephen Sykes, who was a Cambridge academic (Regius Professor of Divinity at Cambridge 1985–90) before his appointment as Bishop of Ely. Once again, an early retirement from that post saw a return to the academy in his appointment as Principal of St John's College, Durham, having previously served as Van Mildert Professor of Divinity at Durham from 1974 to 1985.

A wider group of Anglican bishops have pursued research without holding a university chair but serving in the context of a theological college. Michael Scott-Joynt was chaplain and tutor at Ripon College,

Cuddesdon from 1967 to 1971, his first appointment, followed by a conventional career in parish ministry, cathedral appointment and Diocesan Director of Ordinands in St Albans and a suffragan post prior to the see of Winchester (1995–2011). John Hind, Bishop of Chichester 2001–12, had been Principal of Chichester Theological College from 1982 to 1991, although without taking any postgraduate award. Richard Harries, Bishop of Oxford 1987–2006, had held college posts at Wells Theological College before becoming Dean of Kings College, London, from 1981 to 1987. In retirement he was appointed Gresham Professor of Divinity in 2008. Ian Cundy, Bishop of Peterborough 1996–2009, had held posts at Oak Hill College and Cranmer Hall, Durham, where he was Warden, and died in office. Peter Selby (Worcester), Stephen Platten (Wakefield) and David Atkinson, among others, all had experience tutoring in theological colleges.

This route from the academy is clearly not the most frequent career path for preferment to the bench of bishops within the Church of England at present, as the route from parish ministry is more common, but it has yielded some very significant candidates for Anglican translocal ministry as bishops. A separate route for preferment lies in the Deaneries of the Cathedrals, and here also experience of the academy is present. For instance, the current Dean of St Alban's, Jeffrey John, was Fellow and Dean of Divinity at Magdalene College, Oxford prior to his appointment as Canon Theologian at Southwark, while his predecessor, Christopher Lewis, who moved from there to be Dean of Christ Church, Oxford, had been previously tutor and Vice Principal of Ripon College, Cuddesdon. The presence of canon theologians on the staff of many cathedrals perhaps provides the stronger route for some who bring scholarship to aspects of translocal ministry, although, strictly speaking, a cathedral appointment is local, not translocal.

The trend for the appointment of diocesan bishops has been criticized for being too closely tied to suffragan appointments, and the tendency has been to appoint suffragans from archdeacon or parish posts. This may now make the appointments of significant scholars like Tom Wright and Rowan Williams to diocesan posts more unlikely, neither having served as suffragan bishops. Indeed, the appointment of Justin Welby (the man of action) to replace Rowan Williams (the man of ideas), and the criticism of Williams as being 'just a bit too clever', accompanied by the cry for an Archbishop who the man or woman in the street might understand, might suggest that such an appointment again is quite unlikely. The criticism of Williams was, I think, unfounded and the press had a strong bias against him, as they do with other intellectuals, because of his supposed eccentricities ('a bearded Welsh druid' was how he was portrayed) and for the fact that he refused to be glib and offer cheap soundbites. But that is the nature of a man of such intellect, and such is the trend in the Church today towards an ever-increasing managerial mode inimical to the scholar. Equally, the description of Archbishop Justin as 'the man of action', if that implies a lack of intellect, is unfounded as he too has an acute mind.

The Free Churches

Among Methodists, the two recent General Secretaries have previously served in theological education: Brian Beck was Principal of Wesley House, Cambridge, and his successor Martyn Atkins, Principal of Cliff College. The *Methodist Handbook* does not give the history of appointments of its ministers, so it is hard to see where District Chairs held posts, but what is clear is that of the 33 District Chairs, five have doctorates (15 per cent). This is a much higher percentage than in either of the other two Free Churches, the United Reformed Church and the Baptist Union. Currently there are two Baptist Regional Minister/Team Leaders with a doctorate and none are widely published authors. Historically this had not always been so, with Roger Hayden and Pat Took, historians; Roger Standing, a missiologist and Paul Goodliff, a pastoral and systematic theologian, engaged in doctoral research in their respective fields.

Of the 14 URC Synod moderators, only one has a doctorate (7 per cent). David Peel, analysing the appointees to the posts of Congregational provincial moderators (1919–71) and those as United Reformed Church provincial and synod moderators (1972–2010), notes how moderators had a higher level of academic qualification in the URC period than in Congregationalism (Peel, 2012, p. 126).

At national levels of translocal oversight the trend is more favourable to appointments from the academy. We have noted already that both of the most recent appointments as Methodist Church General Secretaries came from theological education. In the United Reformed Church, David Cornick was Chaplain of Robinson College, Cambridge, 1984–7, held a translocal post as South-West Provincial Training Officer, 1987–92, and was then tutor, and Principal, of Westminster College 1996–2001 before his appointment as General Secretary of the United Reformed Church, 2001–8. He had never been a synod moderator.

In the Baptist Union of Great Britain there had been a period mid-century when General Secretaries were significant scholars, in the persons of Ernest Payne and David Russell, although thereafter, from Bernard Green, who was appointed from the pastorate, David Coffey, who had held a national BUGB post, Jonathan Edwards, who had been South-West General Superintendent to Lynn Green, a Regional Minister, their previous ministries had not included significant appointments to a college, and only Lynn Green had a research degree. Other senior national appointments have similarly been made from a range of backgrounds, but Malcolm Goodspeed was appointed Head of the Department of Ministry (1991–2004) from a post at Regent's Park College, Oxford, and I succeeded him, already a published pastoral theologian and engaged in doctoral research that was completed in post. Stephen Keyworth from Northern Baptist Learning Community became Faith and Society Team Leader in 2012. It appears that there are two distinct streams within Baptist translocal experience: regional oversight and college tutoring, with very little transfer between the two, reflecting perhaps a suspicion of the academic often discerned among Baptists.[3] It is for their practical and pastoral or missional gifts that Regional Ministers are appointed, not their scholarship. That remains tied firmly to the academy. Not since Dr David Russell's appointment as General Secretary in 1967 from the Principalships of Rawdon College (1953–64), then Northern Baptist College (1964–7), has any College Principal been appointed to a national or regional translocal post, and only one college tutor to a regional post, Ernie Whalley from Northern Baptist College to the Yorkshire General Superintendency. Indeed, the movement has mostly been in the other direction: Myra Blyth was Deputy General Secretary of the Baptist Union (1999–2003), and moved to be tutor and Fellow at Regent's Park College; Roger Standing was Southern Area General Superintendent and moved to become tutor at Spurgeon's College, and later Principal; and Keith Jones, Deputy General Secretary (1990–8) moved to become Rector of the International Baptist Theological Seminary from that appointment. None had come into translocal roles from the academy, unlike their Anglican counterparts, Stephen Sykes and Tom Wright, who returned to the academy from the episcopate.

Colin Podmore observes in his contribution to the Perry Report (2001, p. 136) that by the mid-seventies, Michael Ramsey wondered if the diocesan influence on the appointment of bishops, formerly too weak, was not now too weighty: 'The system now put the needs of the diocese first, but what about the needs of the national church as a whole for intellectual and political leadership?' The same might be said of the appointment of Baptist Regional Ministers. Largely devoid of a national perspective, or indeed much of a national contribution, the perspective becomes pragmatic and parochial. The contribution to the intellectual leadership of the Baptist Union, while widely dispersed, lacks sufficient participation at regional levels. This may be a pragmatic response to local pastoral and missional needs, but in the current structures, the regional perspective carries significant weight and therefore requires the contribution of 'scholar regional ministers' to those wider national concerns.

The scholar and oversight

We have sought to trace something of a historical and empirical background to the phenomenon of the 'scholar bishop' and equivalents. The ecumenical scene demonstrates differing levels of valuing this kind of *episkope*, with perhaps the Church of England most likely to appoint such a bishop, and Baptists least likely (notwithstanding the editing of this book by two Baptist scholars who have exercised regional oversight).

What is the value of such appointees in this day of missionary challenge in a post-Christendom culture? I would argue that while the majority of those appointed to regional oversight should have pastoral and missional gifts as the primary reason for their appointment, there is a case on the grounds of a national perspective for some at least to bring gifts of intellect and scholarship as their contribution to the national 'bench' wherever collegiality is significant. Clearly, if there is no sense of collegial action or reflection, their contribution becomes merely local, but this is not the case for all of the mainstream churches,. Those exercising regional and national oversight work in councils of various kinds, and so the contribution that theological scholarship should make to national ecclesial debate is ensured, as well as other areas of intellectual life. Furthermore, in a church culture that emphasizes pragmatism and activism, the contribution of the scholar, as of the saint, is to ensure some depth of debate and policy.

However, perhaps most significantly, if a major role of the bishop, the moderator or the regional minister is to guard the faith in a secular age, then theological scholarship put to the service of apologetics is vital. Mere repetition of the faith in language that does not connect with the culture will avail little, while faith bent to the spirit of the age will not stand the test of time. What is required is the *regula fidei*, the faith once given, the faith enshrined in Scripture and the creeds, to be articulated in ways that answer the questions of the culture with the answers of the great traditions of the Church in every place and in every age. This requires scholarship and intellectual ability. This is the calling for every 'guardian of the faith', from parish or congregational minister to national leadership, and the particular challenge for the scholar bishop is to embody that calling at regional levels and in national councils. Mere pragmatism and a shallow understanding will not suffice.

Notes

1 Fellow and Chaplain of Merton, 1975–8, during which time he researched a DPhil; Chaplain and Fellow of Downing College, Cambridge, 1978–81; Assistant Professor in New Testament Studies at McGill University, Montreal, 1981–6; Chaplain and Fellow, Worcester College, Oxford and University Lecturer in Theology University of Oxford 1986–93, then the first of two cathedral theological appointments, Canon Theologian at Coventry Cathedral, 1992–9, then Lector Theologiae and Canon Theologian at Westminster Abbey, 2000–3.

2 After doctoral research at Wadham, Oxford, he had been a tutor at the College of the Resurrection, Mirfield. Following his ordination as deacon in 1977 he was a Tutor at Westcott House, a theological college in Cambridge (1977–80), combining this with parish ministry in Cambridge; Lecturer in Divinity at Cambridge, and Dean of Clare College, Cambridge (1980–6) and then Lady Margaret Professor of Divinity at Oxford (1986–92).

3 Baptists are not alone in this. In the mid-nineteenth century, the Prime Minister, Viscount Palmerston, relied on the advice of his step-daughter's husband, Earl of Shaftesbury, who showed a clear evangelical bias and did not favour academics. In 1860 Queen Victoria felt moved to ask Palmerston not to confine his selection to safe parish priests since the bench should not be devoid of some university men of acknowledged standing and theological learning.

References

Peel, David R., 2012, *The Story of the Moderators*, London: United Reformed Church.
Pelikan, Jaroslav, 1971, *The Christian Tradition: A History of the Development of Doctrine, Vol. 1, The Emergence of the Catholic Tradition (100–600)*, Chicago, IL: University of Chicago Press.
The Perry Report, 2001, *Working with the Spirit. Choosing Diocesan Bishops*, London: Church House Publishing.

17

Episkope and Gender: An Anglican Case Study

ANNE HOLLINGHURST

This book is about the theology and practice of translocal oversight, in which, as a bishop, I am deeply interested. From my own perspective, my gender isn't an issue, but that is not true for everyone given that female bishops are still a recent development in the Church of England. Our first female bishop was Libby Lane, consecrated as Bishop of Stockport in January 2015.[1] I was consecrated in September that year, along with Ruth Worsley, Bishop of Taunton. Four years later there are currently 19 female suffragan and five diocesan bishops out of a total of 130 in the College of Bishops. Some may be struck at the speed with which women have been appointed to episcopal roles. However, it should be remembered that the long period between the ordination of women to the priesthood and the legislation to enable women to be consecrated as bishops meant that there were plenty of experienced women around. Female episcopacy may be recent, but women have been exercising all kinds of significant oversight roles as area/rural deans, deans, archdeacons, overseeing multi-site chaplaincy teams or multi-parish benefices.

While some provinces of the Anglican Communion were ahead of the Church of England in consecrating women as bishops, in others women are currently still not ordained as either priests or bishops. This is also true of the Roman Catholic and Orthodox Churches and is why a chapter on *episkope* and gender is necessary, given the variety of practice across the churches, and why the issues need to be identified and explored. In my own day-to-day ministry my gender is not a preoccupation and I simply get on with the work to which God has called me. However, it has shaped and inevitably continues to shape my experience and that of female colleagues.

EPISKOPE AND GENDER: AN ANGLICAN CASE STUDY

Theological debate and living the journey

When the General Synod of the Church of England voted to open the priesthood to women in 1992 it did so separate from a decision to open the episcopate to women. While many have argued this made little sense theologically, it almost certainly enabled the vote that passed the legislation whereby the first women were ordained priests in 1994. The provision subsequently agreed through the Act of Synod was developed to hold those opposed to female priests within the Church. Arrangements to enable female episcopacy appeared beyond reach at that time and would take another 22 years. It was a long wait, but while the theological arguments around women's priestly and episcopal ministry are similar, there are distinct challenges around provision for those unable to accept the episcopal ministry of women that have a particular significance for how we understand the nature of the Church and its unity.

The day of the Synod vote in 1992 to open the way for women to be priests I was at home in Nottingham. Aged 28, I was an inner-city youth evangelist along with my husband. Having been through a local discernment process, I was filling out the paperwork for a national panel to test my vocation to the diaconate.[2] My sense of call was not especially to the diaconate, but to ordained ministry and leadership in the Church. It had been shaped throughout my young adulthood and almost eight years of varied parish ministry. Despite the seeming impossibility of this call, lack of role models and attempts to dissuade me by those with conservative views, I realized I would have no peace unless I tested the call. On the day of the vote, I suddenly found myself ticking the box that said I was offering for the priesthood and realizing that I was among the first to be able to do that.

It had been a long journey to that place of self-offering, during which I had needed to work through the arguments against women's priestly ministry and leadership. It was on holiday in Greece, having badly injured my ankle, that I immersed myself in books expounding the traditional catholic and conservative evangelical cases. I wanted to understand them and be sure I was being obedient, and not disobedient, to God. There are worse things than sitting by a hotel pool in the Greek sunshine wading prayerfully through such reading, but the injured ankle ensured I could do little else.

One thing my reading convinced me of was the sincerity and integrity of those who argue for an all-male priesthood, episcopate or church leadership. What became clear to me was that there were several main strands of argument that I would need to wrestle with and feel satisfied about.[3]

For those from the traditional catholic position, the fatherhood of God and the maleness of Jesus in the incarnation are vitally important. It is held that the symbol of a male priest at the altar presiding at the eucharist is so significant that it cannot be replaced by a priest who is female. That the twelve apostles were male, and the priesthood and apostolic episcopate are held to have been always and only male, are also key tenets of the argument. Indeed, there is concern about the efficacy of the apostolic succession if somewhere along the chain someone has been involved in ordaining women by the laying on of hands. This position is not that of all traditional Catholics, as for others the key barrier is a belief that only the Church universal, the Roman Catholic Church certainly and the Orthodox churches ideally, can decide to ordain women. They are not 'impossibilists'. It is not a 'never' to female priests and bishops, but that their adoption cannot proceed ahead of this. The unity of the Church is the core of this argument.

From the conservative evangelical perspective, the issue hinges on the interpretation of key biblical passages. Male headship is a significant principle, with the language being derived from passages addressing the relationship between husbands and wives (1 Cor. 11.3 and Eph. 5.23). Other references to leadership among Christians gathered for worship are also drawn in to support this.[4] This picture of male headship is held to be rooted in a creation ordinance supported by the story of Adam and Eve in Genesis. Alongside this concept of headship is an understanding of what has more recently been called 'complementarianism', in which it is argued that while men and women are equal, they have different characteristics and accordingly different roles. Women must not exercise authority over men. Teaching of other women and children is permissible but public preaching in a mixed gathering is a divinely given male activity.

As I read, prayed and engaged with those who held these views I was not convinced. Some of the arguments are based on significant assumptions about 'the tradition' of the Church being uniform and uninfluenced by historical and cultural traditions around gender. If the concern is unity, then, as many argued throughout the debate and as commentators such as John Barton noted, this view looks only to the Roman Catholic and Orthodox traditions. In terms of other ecumenical relations, the problem was not having ordained or consecrated women. Other denominations have had women in translocal oversight roles for some time and the Lutheran Church has had female bishops. It is not a view that makes for wider unity if it is suggested that churches that are reformed but have preserved the historic catholic threefold order have no genuine share in the apostolic succession because women have received the laying on of hands.[5]

There is also some ambiguity around many of the biblical passages that form the basis of the complementarian evangelical case, including the interpretation of the Greek word often translated 'head' in English.[6] For me there is need for careful hermeneutics to bridge the gap between the world of the text and the contemporary world. Without this our reading of the Bible may be prone to a reader-response interpretation that lacks knowledge of the biblical context. There are other ways of seriously looking at history, tradition and Scripture that argue persuasively that women's exclusion in the past has been more about human sin and patriarchy, cultural contexts, gendered-role construction and a failure to see how the freedom and new creation found in Christ transforms the relationships between men and women and means there is 'neither male nor female'.[7] In addition, missional priorities in the New Testament epistles sometimes urge accommodation to the prevailing culture in order to win a people for Christ.[8]

Being female and exploring a call into priestly/oversight ministry has involved many women in thinking deeply about the witness of Scripture and tradition. There has had to be a journey of discovery that has shaped our understanding of the gospel and of the activity of the Holy Spirit today in calling and equipping both women and men – a journey of discovering that both sons and daughters are to prophesy and exercise the full range of the Spirit's gifts (Acts 2.17–18), of discovering that the New Testament itself names women prominent in apostolic and teaching ministries.[9] The discovery has included journeying through the Old Testament, which although rooted in a culture in which women's leadership was not the norm, nonetheless has examples of women leaders like Deborah. The journey continues with the uncovering of early Church tomb inscriptions and of iconography depicting women exercising various ministries.[10] It has been a journey of seeing that God calls and equips women and that it makes no sense to deny the Church their considerable gifts because of particular interpretations of Scripture and tradition which, when examined more closely, can be shown to be flawed.

From female priests to female bishops

The long deliberation about the ministry of women has formed the backdrop to most of my adult life. The debates gained momentum throughout the early twentieth century,[11] and then while the General Synod voted in 1975 that 'there was no fundamental objection to the ordination of women to the priesthood', the motion asking for legislation 'to remove the barriers to the ordination of women to the priesthood and their consecration to the episcopate' fell in 1978.

There were various working parties and reports between 1992 and the 2014 vote to open up the episcopate to women, with the debate steadily shifting its focus from core theological issues towards devising arrangements that enabled the minority opposed to it to continue to have a full and honoured place within the Church of England. I was a member of General Synod when the first legislative package fell in 2012, to the dismay of many, but two years later a different approach enabled new proposals to go through. The House of Bishops' Declaration on the Ministry of Priests and Bishops, along with the Five Guiding Principles, enabled the Church finally to embrace the episcopal ministry of women. What had often sounded theoretical and abstract, a debate about an 'issue', started to be enfleshed as the first women were appointed, myself among them.

Transition to episcopal oversight ministry within the context of the Five Guiding Principles

There are new challenges for any minister transitioning to translocal oversight, but for women becoming bishops there are some additional ones. These concern the nature of the settlement achieved within the Church of England. I suspect that other challenges are more generic to women in translocal oversight in other denominations, including how such oversight and leadership are received. The fact that women continue to face some unhelpful responses to their leadership should perhaps be no surprise as it mirrors the situation in our wider society. However, the Church has a duty to model something better.

The 2014 settlement made clear that the Church of England remains committed to ensuring that those who cannot receive the ministry of female priests or bishops on genuine theological grounds are able to flourish within it. This potentially raises questions around the episcopal oversight of female bishops and whether this is in any way restricted or undermined. The House of Bishops Declaration and Five Guiding Principles do not intend this to be the case but attempt to put in place what is necessary for the building of good relationships and trust. Those who cannot personally accept female episcopal ministry on grounds of theological conviction are still to relate to their bishop and accept that she has been 'duly ordained and appointed to Office' and is a 'true and lawful holder of the office which she occupies and thus deserves due respect and canonical obedience'. The Five Guiding Principles are:

1 Now that legislation has been passed to enable women to become bishops the Church of England is fully and unequivocally committed

to all orders of ministry being open equally to all, without reference to gender, and holds that those whom it has duly ordained and appointed to office are true and lawful holders of the office which they occupy and thus deserve due respect and canonical obedience.

2 Anyone who ministers within the Church of England must be prepared to acknowledge that the Church of England has reached a clear decision on the matter.

3 Since it continues to share the historic episcopate with other Churches, including the Roman Catholic Church, the Orthodox Church and those provinces of the Anglican Communion which continue to ordain only men as priests or bishops, the Church of England acknowledges that its own clear decision on ministry and gender is set within a broader process of discernment within the Anglican Communion and the whole Church of God.

4 Since those within the Church of England who, on grounds of theological conviction, are unable to receive the ministry of women bishops or priests continue to be within the spectrum of teaching and tradition of the Anglican Communion, the Church of England remains committed to enabling them to flourish within its life and structures.

5 Pastoral and sacramental provision for the minority within the Church of England will be made without specifying a limit of time and in a way that maintains the highest possible degree of communion and contributes to mutual flourishing across the whole Church of England.

'Pastoral and sacramental provision' can be requested by a Parochial Church Council (PCC) passing a resolution in the following recommended form:

> This PCC requests, on grounds of theological conviction, that arrangements be made for it in accordance with the House of Bishops' Declaration on the Ministry of Bishops and Priests.

There need to be clear theological grounds articulated with this request, which is made to the diocesan bishop herself. This ensures that she and any parishes petitioning her are to work out any arrangements in relationship. The bishop can invite a suitable male bishop to take on certain functions and roles while she retains the 'ordinary' jurisdiction. This is intended to avoid any sense of a separate 'church within a church' and to maintain the highest possible degree of communion – the unity that episcopal ministry is called to hold. Female colleagues who are diocesan bishops indicate that this is usually worked out on the ground with grace and with every effort to maintain relationships. This may involve a female diocesan bishop being present but delegating certain functions at services, making visible the reality of the impaired communion and yet clearly indicating that we remain one in Christ and committed to sharing together in Christ's mission. It takes significant generosity and personal security to exercise such episcopal oversight.

The picture is complex and challenging, but the aim has been to make the arrangements as simple as possible. 'Simplicity' is one of the values enshrined in the House of Bishops' Declaration alongside 'reciprocity and mutuality'. Simplicity may have been the goal, but there is still some concern about how the Five Guiding Principles work in practice. This concern was particularly sharpened when Philip North, Suffragan Bishop of Burnley, was appointed to be the Diocesan Bishop of Sheffield and then chose to withdraw following an outcry against his appointment, as he neither personally accepted women's ordained ministry nor ordained them. While many female priests in his current diocese speak highly of him, there was anxiety around how ordained women in Sheffield could truly 'flourish' with a bishop holding his views. It became clear that there was some difference in interpretation of how the Five Guiding Principles work in practice, and what 'mutual flourishing' implies. Following an independent review by Sir Philip Mawer, several fault lines were identified in the process and an Implementation and Dialogue Group with broad representation was commissioned to explore how better to understand and embed good practice, of which I have been a part.

Living the complexity

Undertaking this work with the Implementation and Dialogue Group, combined with my own experience and conversations with female episcopal colleagues, reveals that there is much good practice being developed and positive relationships being forged between clergy, parishes and episcopal colleagues who in conscience cannot accept our priestly or episcopal ministry. An example of this for myself would be an invitation to preach at the Patronal Festival of a church with a traditional catholic history and accepting that the parish priest would preside at the eucharist given that my sacramental ministry would not have been received by some. I was welcomed most warmly. The congregation was delighted to have the relationship with me, and I with them. A particular test of the willingness to foster such partnership in the gospel has been the appointment of Sarah Mullally as Bishop of London, as the diocese has a significant traditional catholic and complementarian evangelical presence. Bishop Sarah is winning much respect with the clarity and generosity of her episcopacy in a diocese that found itself most surprised to be receiving a female diocesan bishop.

Other female colleagues have shared stories that mirror my own largely positive experience. A female suffragan describes an encounter with a cleric and his wife who wrote to her on her appointment to make clear they could not receive her episcopal ministry. When the time came for him to move on from his parish, he hadn't changed his theological view but suggested to my colleague the name of a female priest to succeed him. He also expressed real appreciation for my colleague's episcopal ministry, saying he was so glad she is there. Shared mission and respect for one another's ministry and difference is possible.

Though many experiences are positive and joyful, there are still painful times where the novelty of one's gender is deeply uncomfortable. Additionally, as a suffragan bishop I have discovered that such an office provides its own tricky paths to negotiate. While clergy and parishes may be required to relate to their diocesan bishop because she holds the legal jurisdiction, there are instances of clergy and parishes choosing not to build relationships with a female suffragan. There are examples of separate ordination services being requested where the handling of the request by the diocesan bishop has been felt to be undermining of the female suffragan's own episcopacy. There have also been occasions when male complementarian evangelical curates have refused to meet a female suffragan who, as sponsoring bishop, has been given responsibility in this area, and when no opportunity has been given to reflect together on what such action models. There are also experiences of the choreography of major diocesan services not being thought through clearly regarding the symbolic messages conveyed regarding a female suffragan's episcopacy.

The Church of England is clearly modelling some good practice, but we still have much to learn about living out the Five Guiding Principles. Female bishops often find themselves at the sharp end of this. It remains an extraordinary experience to be frequently reminded that the whole of womanhood can be judged for good or ill through one's own ministry. As a female bishop you carry around an awareness that you are still forging new ground, powerfully and symbolically representing something vitally important. Yet there are moments when this symbolic representation is not so obvious. On one occasion I arrived at a church to conduct a service to license a new priest. I was warmly ushered into a large vestry by a lady who appeared to be a churchwarden. I was looking around the room a little perplexed as to where the archdeacon and priest to be licensed were, when the lady came rushing back in and announced to the amusement of the other clergy gathered that she hadn't realized I was the bishop – this despite my arriving in full purple cassock, large pectoral cross, with my pastoral staff slung over my shoulder. With a twinkle in my eye I suggested that purple was the usual giveaway. A strong sense of humour is clearly an absolute prerequisite for women in translocal oversight!

Summary reflections

A theological question we are still wrestling with is 'What does mutual flourishing look like?' The image of the Good Shepherd features prominently in our services of ordination for both priests and bishops.[12] It is an image of oversight modelled on the ministry of Jesus for the Church and its welfare. We follow a Good Shepherd who laid down his life for the sheep. Here is a call to see the flourishing of the whole Church, the whole body of Christ. Such flourishing means good pastoral care and guarding of the faith and the faithful, but it also involves actually leading the flock somewhere. On retreat in the Sierra Nevada mountains in southern Spain, I was fascinated to witness the work of Mediterranean shepherds, bringing to life for me the model of shepherding with which Jesus would have been familiar. In order to ensure that the flock continued to be well-fed and well-watered, the shepherds had to keep moving the sheep on to new pasture. For the Church to flourish, pastoral care is important, but a Church that is truly healthy is a Church on the move – a Church engaged in the mission of God, a Church that is confident in witness and evangelism, and deeply involved in service and the work of transformation in the world. The task of episcopal ministry is that of leading the Church in this.

By contrast, the concept of 'mutual flourishing' can sometimes be talked about as if all that matters is 'my flourishing', rather than asking what makes for the flourishing of the other, or indeed of the whole body of Christ. Commitment to the flourishing of the other is especially challenging for us when we find ourselves in disagreement, because 'flourishing' implies growth and vigour, not a dwindling away – an intentional positive promotion of the other's health and well-being, not simply a toleration.[13]

In terms of the exercise of translocal oversight in the Church of England, this perhaps comes best into focus around the area of vocations and appointments. I am among those bishops who have a responsibility as sponsoring bishop. This means that I find myself meeting with prospective male ordinands who cannot accept my episcopal ministry. Yet I am there to encourage and support their vocation to ordained ministry. This I do and do gladly if their call and gifts are evident. We need all the gifts that the Holy Spirit is pouring out upon the Church if we want the whole body of Christ to flourish in its life and mission. Our meeting is also a helpful opportunity to explore their understanding of the Five Guiding Principles, and explore how they will exercise their ministry among female colleagues and relate to me as a female bishop. It isn't territory that is always easy to negotiate. We should consider what it means for the practice of translocal oversight by women when, for example, as Lee Gatiss writes in the Church Society's *Crossways* magazine, the guidance (that is, the Five Guiding Principles):

> commits the Church of England to the continued flourishing of complementarians within the life and structures of the Church ... It is acceptable not to agree with women bishops. We may recognise that they fill certain offices legally, but still not accept their ministry spiritually.[14]

I hope that through the positive conversations and personal engagement female bishops seek to foster we are at least laying helpful foundations for our future working together.

The attempt to appoint Bishop Philip North to Sheffield highlighted a question that still disquiets many. In the same way that a sponsoring bishop must promote the flourishing and ministry of someone with whom they disagree, can a bishop who does not ordain women, and whose theological convictions mean that he cannot accept their priestly or episcopal ministry, still nurture their vocations, enable the flourishing of their gifts and be willing to sponsor them for senior roles in translocal oversight, including the episcopate, if he sees in them the gifts and call of God?

If 'flourishing' speaks of health, growth and fullness, it becomes clear what it cannot mean. It cannot mean pretending we are not part of the same Church. We cannot desire and act to enable the flourishing of another unless we are in relationship. It cannot mean a female bishop in her ministry of oversight limits the call of someone who does not believe in her ministry of oversight. It cannot mean that a male bishop who has not been able to accept theologically the inclusion of women in the full threefold orders limits the ministry of women within his diocese or jurisdiction. We are in a Church that is 'fully and unequivocally committed to all orders of ministry being open equally to all, without reference to gender'. This challenge of building trust is a significant factor in the practice of translocal oversight by those of us who are among the first female bishops.

What needs to be highlighted is that the path to translocal oversight ministry for many women has been a rather different experience from that of many men. It has been an experience that has demanded great resilience, strength, understanding and grace – all rather helpful qualities in regard to translocal oversight.

This debate has been the backdrop to my ministry, and I now rejoice to see the gifts of so many talented women being exercised for the flourishing of the Church. I also continue to have genuine respect for, and enjoy friendship with, many of those who have not welcomed this development. They are people of integrity, and sharing with them in the mission of God is something I am committed to do. We are going to need to learn with humility more of what this means as we journey together in our mutual discipleship.

Do I long to see young women able to follow their vocation into ministry, into episcopal ministry, unencumbered by opposition to their ministries and free to develop confidently into the fullness of what God has for them? Yes, I do.

Birmingham Cathedral held a service to celebrate the 25th anniversary of women's ordination. For me it was an experience of great hope. Along with some young female ordinands, I was chatting with Bishop Mark Santer, who had ordained the first women there. One of these ordinands suddenly said, 'I was born in 1994, the year when the first women were ordained priests, and I've never known a Church in which women couldn't be priests.' It made me feel old, but also helped me see the long view. In 25 years from now there will be new young ordinands, male and female, who have never known a Church without female bishops, women exercising translocal oversight because of their gifts and calling and whose gender is no longer an issue.

Notes

1 Later to become the Bishop of Derby.

2 Open to women since 1985.

3 I cannot do justice here to the substance of the arguments. See the Further Reading section below.

4 Though some seem to forbid women speaking at all during worship, others seek to order arrangements around it. See 1 Corinthians 14.33–36; 1 Timothy 2.12; 1 Corinthians 11.5.

5 Barton (2004, pp. 17–20) develops this point.

6 There is scholarly debate as to whether Κέφαλος (*Kephalos*) should be translated 'head' or 'source' – as in head or source of a river (compare 1 Cor. 11.3 and 1 Cor. 11.12). This makes the interpretation about origins rather than authority.

7 Galatians 3.28.

8 See 1 Corinthians 9—11.

9 For example, Junia, Prisca, Phoebe.

10 For further reading, see Charlotte Methuen (in Rigney and Chapman, 2008, pp. 23–30) and Wijngaards (2002).

11 See the brilliant summary in Furlong (1991).

12 For the ordinal for deacons, priests and bishops, see www.churchofengland.org/prayer-and-worship/worship-texts-and-resources/common-worship/ministry/common-worship-ordination-services (accessed 31.03.2020).

13 The Faith and Order Commission study guide to the Five Guiding Principles puts it this way: 'To "flourish" has connotations of to prosper, to thrive, to grow – not to shrink out and die. It means prayerfully encouraging all within the Church of England, that they might prove fruitful in proclaiming the kingdom of God, not wanting any to dwindle or fail. It means not corralling some within the boundaries of their own parishes or networks, but providing space generously for all to flourish in its common life and in structures shared by all' (2018, p. 29).

14 https://churchsociety.org/crossway/page/principles_of_flourishing (accessed 28.11.2019).

Reference

Barton, John, 2004, 'Why Not Have Women Bishops? Meeting the Arguments Head-on', in Harris, Harriet and Jane Shaw (eds), *The Call for Women Bishops*, London: SPCK.

Further Reading

The Faith and Order Commission of the Church of England, 2018, *The Five Guiding Principles: A Resource for Study*, London: Church House Publishing.
Furlong, Monica, 1991, *A Dangerous Delight*, London: SPCK.
Harris, Harriet and Jane Shaw (eds), 2004, *The Call for Women Bishops*, London: SPCK.
Kirk, Geoffrey, 2016, *Without Precedent*, Eugene, OR: Wipf & Stock.
Podmore, Colin (ed.), 2015, *Fathers in God?*, Norwich: Canterbury Press.
Rigney, James and Mark D. Chapman (eds), 2008, *Women as Bishops*, London: Mowbray.
Ware, Bruce, 2007, *Summaries of the Egalitarian and Complementarian Positions*, on the website of the Council on Biblical Manhood and Womanhood, https://cbmw.org/uncategorized/summaries-of-the-egalitarian-and-complementarian-positions/ (accessed 08.12.2019).
Wijngaards, John, 2002, *No Women in Holy Orders?*, Norwich: Canterbury Press.

18

Episkope and Supervision

PAUL GOODLIFF

I wonder if on reading the title of this chapter you anticipated reflection on the way in which those exercising regional or national oversight offer supervision to others? Certainly, oversight involves supervising others – perhaps immediate staff offering administrative or chaplaincy support. In both Baptist and Anglican oversight teams there will be team members – Regional Ministers and suffragan bishops – to supervise, while for Methodist District Chairs there may be Circuit Superintendents. In some cases, this is intentionally a version of pastoral supervision, the recent decision of the Methodist Conference to enable all presbyteral ministers to receive pastoral supervision, rolled out throughout the Church in a hierarchical manner, being the most thoroughgoing example to date. I suspect, however, that in many cases it is more akin to line management than supervision, at least in the sense that supervision has taken on in the world of the 'helping professions' of counselling, therapy and social work.

Closely allied are other supportive relationships, such as coach and mentor. Again, some elements of these roles will be incorporated into the ministry of regional or national oversight. As I write this, I am the General Secretary of Churches Together in England, the national ecumenical instrument for England. When I started in 2018, I received the gift of three months overlap with my predecessor, Dr David Cornick, before assuming my new responsibilities, and unintentionally, as we discussed the complex world of national ecumenism, he mentored me. It was not intended as such, but it is clear to me that this is what David was offering. When I became General Superintendent for the Central Area of the Baptist Union, I similarly had an overlap with the existing postholder, Roy Freestone. We sat with one another at three meetings of the Union's 'deployment' committee, the National Settlement Team, and he coached me in the role of representing ministers and churches in the Area as churches sought new ministers, and ministers, new pastorates. In a similar fashion I accompanied him to a couple of meetings with the groups of men and women charged by their congregation with seeking a new minister to recommend to their Church Members' Meeting, and learnt the ropes of that task too, coached by Roy.

We might expect those new to roles of regional oversight to be coached and mentored in this way as part of their learning how to fulfil the role and undertake its regular tasks. In 2004, the Episcopal Church in the USA commissioned a course for new bishops, described as a 'formational coaching programme', with a three-year duration.[1] We might also expect that in the early months of occupying such a role, a mentor is assigned to support, guide and assist the new Bishop, Superintendent, Overseer, or whatever title is ascribed. In their turn, they might expect to offer such coaching or mentoring once some years of experience have been gained, and out of which wise mentoring might be offered. That such relationships of support, training and coaching are not universally expected for those new to episcopal roles is surprising, if not shocking.

If you are yourself new to such a role and you have not been offered a mentor, then seek one out – and ask the denomination you serve why such a relationship is not mandatory. Perhaps things will improve for those who follow. But if you have been asked to offer such mentoring and/or coaching to a new occupant of a role of translocal oversight, yet not been offered any training yourself for this important role of mentor, then similarly you might want to ask 'Why not?'

However, what I mainly want to explore here is neither the offering of supervisory oversight to those in regional teams by way of line management, nor the form of pedagogical mentoring and coaching of others new to such roles, but rather the value – indeed, the necessity – of continuing pastoral supervision for all who exercise Christian ministry, from those in pastoral charge of a local church or parish through to all who carry regional or national oversight. Increasingly, it is becoming accepted that pastors or ministers of churches or priests in parishes be recipients of pastoral supervision. The work of Jane Leach and Michael Paterson in promoting this practice has been ground-breaking, and the outworking of this through the Association of Pastoral Supervision and Education (APSE) and the courses associated with it has begun to change the landscape of supervision for ministers (www.pastoralsupervision.org.uk). For instance, the Institute of Pastoral Counselling and Supervision based at the Sherwood Psychotherapy Training Institute in Nottingham offers a course in Reflective Practice and Pastoral Supervision running over an academic year, and a similar course of which I am a tutor is offered by Spurgeon's College in London. In Edinburgh, the Institute of Pastoral Supervision and Reflective Practice offers training in this work, as does a course offered in Cardiff. Still in its infancy, this growing sphere of supportive ministry aspires to become normative for pastoral ministry – and will require many trained and gifted in the practices of supervision. I suspect that many pastors will still view it with some suspicion, or think of it as of use to those who are less spiritual or less gifted than they (the potential 'failures' in ministry or those insufficiently reliant on God alone), but for the majority within a generation or two, practising ministry without appropriate pastoral supervision will seem as unthinkable as ministry without safeguarding checks and training today.

If, indeed, this ministry is an exceptional gift in enabling more effective and professional ministry, valuable in avoiding some of the more destructive practices in ministry that bring such heartache and disrepute, then it makes sense for those with regional and national oversight to both encourage or require it, and to exemplify it by receiving pastoral supervision themselves. This would go a long way towards denying the mistaken opinion that pastoral supervision is only for the novice pastor or for those who have encountered serious failings or difficulties in the course of ministry. It might demonstrate that pastoral supervision is a practice welcomed by the experienced minister and those deemed 'successful' enough to fulfil roles of responsibility in the churches – training incumbents, archdeacons and bishops in the Church of England, Regional Ministers in the Baptist Union or synod moderators for the United Reformed Church. Indeed, the exemplary value of occupying the post of regional overseer and saying to those whom they serve, 'This is of great value', is accompanied by the personal value of remaining a reflective practitioner in *episkope* in order to serve to the best of one's ability in such an office.

A word of personal testimony here: I cannot now conceive of serving as a Baptist Regional Minister, or national Head of Ministry – or, indeed, CTE's General Secretary – without pastoral supervision. When I was in a local pastorate in the 1990s, I carried a small counselling practice and was a member of a supervision group where we took our client work. However, I never really discussed more general pastoral work there, and when I became General Superintendent for the Central Area, and my counselling work ended, I ceased to be in supervision. I was lightly 'line-managed' by the Baptist Union's General Secretary, David Coffey, and I always had recourse to the Head of Ministry, Malcolm Goodspeed, if I had a difficult disciplinary case to handle, but that did not amount to pastoral supervision as it is now understood. From that role of regional oversight, I became Malcolm Goodspeed's successor as Head of the Department of Ministry, and subsequently Ministries Team Leader, as the role was renamed in 2012, and soon found myself carrying a pastoral load of disciplinary cases that became almost overwhelming. Within a couple of years, aware that this was by far the most challenging role I had ever occupied in over 20 years of ministry, I found myself one December morning as close to buckling under overwhelming stress as I have ever been. A long-running case between some vexatious church members and their minister threatened legal action, the accusations were hard to either refute or acknowledge, and the language in the letter received that morning was threatening. It was the day of the Baptist House staff Christmas lunch, and I just could not face going. A close colleague who was aware of the situation sent down my line manager, who promptly sent me home with advice to see my GP – which I did. Within a few days I was ready to return, aware that the much-needed Christmas break had almost arrived. The outcome was much greater sympathy with the many ministers who experience the same stresses, some of whom would sit in my office and describe their own situation, but more importantly for this chapter, I searched for some pastoral supervision with the strong support of my line manager. I found Charles. For the past decade I have seen him almost every six to eight weeks for an hour each time. Throughout the remaining years of national oversight of the Baptist Union's ministers, and on to my most recent role as a minister at Abingdon Baptist Church, we discussed pastoral cases, more general developments in the organization as it affected me, and my own changing role. I continue to see him as I serve in this national ecumenical role. Over those latter years of Baptist Union ministry oversight I certainly carried more challenging pastoral cases than the one that triggered my stress that Christmas. These have included a couple that were characterized by very personal attacks and misunderstandings, and at least one of handling a minister with quite a dangerous narcissistic personality. Through it all, pastoral supervision enabled me to distance my own well-being from the work in a way that I had not previously managed. I gained insights into my own reactions, reflected on my practice and grew in my understanding of the hidden dynamics in conflicted and toxic situations. It saved my ministry.

Perhaps one of the reasons why some find themselves in regional or national roles of responsibility is down to that mixture of holy luck, often called providence, and personal qualities of character and intellect that enable early experience of pastoral ministry to be happy, fulfilling and fruitful. Not that my first pastorate was easy, necessarily, but I was well supported and mentored and grew in experience and confidence. My second pastorate enabled me to continue to grow in a peaceable congregation and extend my experience with chaplaincy and tutoring. I wonder what might have happened if I had encountered intractable difficulties or been inadequately supported. Would I have been approached and asked if I might allow myself to be interviewed for the forthcoming regional post arising from the upcoming vacancy for the Area Superintendent?

And after a fruitful five years in that role, would I have been considered for Head of Ministry had I bungled a situation or two? As I say, holy luck! I now know that pastoral supervision would have deepened those ministries.

I survived without supervision, as many do, but I might have thrived more. I suppose I instinctively made my own supportive networks to carry me through – a close group of colleagues with whom I had been formed for ministry who met regularly, and still do, albeit in a different guise; good conversations about ministry on the Board of Ministry Today UK; regular lunch and honest conversation with a friend in Baptist ministry in the neighbouring town; and much more recently the accountability of the cell of the Order for Baptist Ministry of which I am a part. Some might look at that wide range of supportive relationships and think what a duffer I must be to require them, when others rely on Jesus alone! It is through such support and supervision that God does support me. Those who are too busy, or seem too important for support such as this are, perhaps, just too proudly self-sufficient, a risk I am not prepared to take. I am firmly of the opinion that all who carry pastoral responsibilities as part of their regional or national roles of oversight will benefit from pastoral supervision among the suite of other supportive relationships, such as spiritual direction or peer-group support.

The functions of supervision

It helps to distinguish pastoral supervision from other, more familiar roles. It is not primarily about developing skills like coaching; neither is it about paying attention to personal issues and relationships, such as counselling. It is not necessarily being formed by a practitioner in the same sphere of oversight, which is more like mentoring, nor is it primarily about the spiritual life, which is the province of spiritual direction. It is most certainly not line management, nor is it linked to any performance indicators!

Supervisors can find themselves cast in a helping role that is unsuited to supervision, and identifying that early is an essential task. They might be mistaken for a priest ('Forgive me, Father, I have sinned') or a judge ('I need you to help me find some justice') or a mother ('Please kiss it better and hold me on your lap'). In the language of Transactional Analysis, these transactions are collusive, or crossed, when not identified and named. For instance, the supervisee who needs constant reassurance that everything is OK can find the supervisor's reassurance immediately helpful, but in the longer term it does not promote growth by learning if the supervisee's conduct or practice is never challenged. This is collusive supervision. On the other hand, if the supervisee comes expecting to confess their mistakes or 'sins', and finds only reassurance, they feel misunderstood, or not taken with sufficient seriousness: this is a crossed transaction. Effective supervision avoids collusion and misunderstanding by being 'present' to the supervisee. The listening skill of immediacy can be helpful here.

It is, however, a supportive relationship that enables deep reflection on the tasks that oversight comprises. It empowers continuous learning and shines a lamp on the shadow side of the practitioner. In some ways it will be developmental, with new insights from psychology and theology informing the supervisee, and in other ways it will safeguard the practitioner from abuse of power, ill-judged practice and from too much or too little confidence, either of which can be crippling.

Enabling continuous learning

Just as the initial training of ministers has transitioned from a primarily intellectual task of theological education, through an emphasis on the skills acquisition of theological training to one of vocational development in ministerial formation, so continuing education and learning in ministry has changed. Initially almost entirely absent, in any formal sense, the period after the Second World War saw Continuing Professional Development (CPD) become the norm in the world of work. As the Church became alert to this development, in the wider workplace, so it also moved on to a new expression of integration of personal and professional development, drawing on the insights of the helping professions. So CPD is replaced by CPPD, Continuing Professional and Personal Development, delivered not in workshops, conferences or training courses but embedded in the workplace itself. Many organizations have embraced the 70:20:10 principle: 70 per cent of professional development happens on the job; 10 per cent by attending courses; and 20 per cent by supervision or coaching that connects workplace learning and exterior training. Here the reflective cycle is enabled by supervision that enables action, reflection and reviewing to be held in balance.

This dynamic process has particular power in the context of ministry, where increasing familiarity with the work of formal supervision develops a heightened awareness of an 'internal supervisor', giving the ability to reflect in a live interaction, and not just subsequent to it. Donald Schon (Hawkins and Shohet, 2012, p. 16) defines reflective practice as 'the capacity to reflect on action so as to engage in a process of continuous learning', which is a defining characteristic of professional practice. Reflection-on-action (reflection after the event) develops intuition and enables the practitioner to think on their feet by reflection-in-action.

This notion of the continuing learner is deeply embedded in the Christian idea of the disciple, the one who learns. Christianity understands the role of the disciple as one of growing conformity to Christ, and this is a process of lifelong learning, well beyond even any idea of continuous growth as a professional practitioner.

Supervision as a lamp to light the shadow side

Ministers enter ministry for the best of reasons: a sense of God's call, a desire to effect change for the better, a love of God's people and a passion to see all things under the gracious rule of Christ. Few acknowledge that they might enter ministry to gain power over others, or because their inner world is so fragile that they need the constant reassurance of others' approval within a benign environment where positive regard is mandatory: 'this is my command, that you love one another' (John 15.12).

However, for all the worthy motives, and their public acknowledgement in a selection process, there do lurk beneath the surface, hidden in the subconscious, other drivers of behaviour that emerge under pressure and in conflicted situations. These hidden inner drivers include a lust for power over others, often perceived as conflicting with an expressed sense of powerlessness over events and others. This discrepancy can be exposed in supervision, as can the need to be needed:

> just as our clients need help from us, we need our clients to want help in order to fulfil the self-esteem we gain from our ability to give help. However, we have been brought up to deny our needs but needs in themselves are not harmful. It is just that when they are denied they join the shadows of helping work and manipulate from behind as demands. Demands ask for fulfilment, needs require only expression. (Hillman, 1979, p. 17)

The need to be liked, the desire to heal, the fantasy that we are the Messiah and the fear of insignificance all hide away in the shadow side, and one way of bringing their presence to light is therapy, but even if this has been accomplished in that way, supervision will identify when their malign influence over our practice is close to the surface once again. The ability to recognize these hidden 'scripts' ('I am unlovable unless I meet others' needs'; 'The only way to hold things together is to take control of the situation'; 'I cannot allow myself to fail: I must be perfect') is a shaft of light on to our core beliefs about the world and ourselves, and these are often at odds with the core beliefs we espouse as Christian doctrine, especially when it comes to grace. Supervision is a way of identifying these scripts and learning a different way of behaving. In the process we become less judgemental about others, or reactive to their differing core beliefs.

In all of this we must, however, sound a note of warning. Pastoral supervision is not a fail-safe solution to human wickedness and deviousness. It might be tempting to think that had some of the more high-profile religious figures found guilty of sexual abuse been in pastoral supervision, then their deviant behaviour would have been noticed and their abuse avoided. Perhaps for some this might have been the case, if they had been willing to reveal their inner drives before acting them out – and the supervisor had required they seek appropriate therapeutic help and be closely supervised. However, I suspect that such figures would never reveal that aspect of their personality in supervision, at least. A certain humility towards its efficacy is necessary – it has its important part to play in the suite of supporting and safeguarding relationships that maintain good practice, but standing alone, it is inadequate to the task.

Notwithstanding these concerns, the recent adoption of pastoral supervision for all Methodist ministers arises from the safeguarding context. The Report of Past Cases Review in 2015 made the case for pastoral supervision, which was adopted by the denomination's annual conference in 2017. In the agreed Supervision Policy the Conference affirmed:

> supervision as being an important tool for addressing the weakness identified in the Methodist Church in relation to support and accountability for safe practice ... It was not argued in the 2015 Report that supervision would be a panacea that would on its own eliminate abuse from church life, but that it would be a key tool, alongside others such as a new Code of Conduct for ministers, that would help to change a culture from one which is often one of isolated and vulnerable practice, to one of *accountability*, *support* and more *safety* both for ministers and for those amongst whom they work. (Methodist Church, 2017, 2.1)

Currently, the Methodist Church is rolling out supervision for all its presbyters:

under an interim Supervision Policy to cover the period 2017–2020 rather than under a Final Policy. This is to allow the Methodist Church to proceed by stages; to allow for consultation, feedback and learning; and to separate the period of initial implementation from the processes needed to embed supervision into the life of the Methodist Church for the long term. It is hoped that such an approach will build on the learning that has happened during the last 18 months. (2017, 3.1.1)

Training of District Chairs in pastoral supervision enables them to offer supervision to Circuit Superintendents, who in turn supervise Circuit Ministers. External Supervision for District Chairs is already in place.

This enables the whole community of ordained ministers to be supervised. The report notes that:

the careful attention to boundaries and roles that is needed for supervision to be effective in offering an exploratory and reflective space, even within a context of oversight, itself reinforces the attitudes and skills needed for the safe practice of ministry in which confidentiality is not confused with secrecy and in which power is transparently and responsibly exercised by all concerned. (2017, 3.2.4)

It continues:

The view of the Supervision Working Group is that the most robust form of safety in ministry will arise from the best quality reflection on practice that can be facilitated in supervision; this will involve ministers giving an account of their work in detail and, over time, in rounded enough way to give confidence to the supervisor/minister in oversight that they are working safely and effectively. In our view this kind of reflection is the primary supervising activity. The oversight responsibility is to ensure that good enough supervision is happening and that the issues identified in supervision that need formal action outside the supervision context are appropriately referred. (3.3.7)

To date, this is by far the most thoroughgoing expression of pastoral supervision among a UK denomination of any size, and whether others will follow remains in question. I am not convinced that rolling out supervision through the existing supervisory relationships of District Chair, Circuit Superintendent and then presbyters is the best way, as it can seem to be imposed rather than freely chosen, but it has the virtue of being comprehensive and as rapid a deployment of supervision as could be envisaged.

What is not in question, to my mind, is the value of pastoral supervision for those exercising ministries of regional and national oversight with significant pastoral dimensions, especially as bishop or archdeacon, for instance, but beyond that all who serve in translocal posts would benefit from the skilled delivery of pastoral supervision, not just to assist in pastoral responses to ministries in crisis, for instance, but for every aspect of the ministry of oversight in all of its diversity and complexity.

Note

1 www.episcopalchurch.org/library/article/college-bishops-announces-training-new-bishops (accessed 01.10.2019).

References

Hawkins, Peter and Robin Shohet, 2012, *Supervision in the Helping Professions*, 4th edition, Maidenhead: Open University Press.

Hillman, J., 1979, *Insearch: Psychology and Religion*, Dallas, TX: Spring.

Leach, Jane and Michael Paterson, 2010, *Pastoral Supervision: A Handbook*, London: SCM Press.

Methodist Church UK, 2017, *Reports to Conference 2017. No. 19. Supervision Policy*; www.methodist.org.uk/downloads/conf-2017-19-Supervision-Policy.pdf (accessed 01.10.2019).

Paterson, Michael and Jessica Rose, 2014, *Enriching Ministry: Pastoral Supervision in Practice*, London: SCM Press.

Schon, Donald, 1983, *The Reflective Practitioner*, New York: Basic Books.

19

Translocal Ministry in Post-Christendom[1]

STUART MURRAY

Early in the fourth century the Roman Emperor Constantine identified himself as a Christian and initiated the process of accommodating church and state that would result in the establishment of the sacral society known as Christendom (Kreider, 2002). He quickly recognized that the support of the Church's translocal leaders – the bishops – was key to achieving his aim of constructing a united empire-wide Church, with the help of which he might confront the many social, political and cultural problems that were destabilizing and fragmenting his realm.

Constantine wooed these men through patronage of their interests, extensive financial support for their congregations and ambitious building projects, delegating to them social responsibilities and status beyond their congregations and frequent invitations to dine in imperial surroundings. In 325 he summoned them to Nicaea for an ecumenical council to determine a creedal basis for a united Church – a Church that would no longer be dependent for its cohesion primarily on friendship and mutual respect between churches within which divergent patterns, traditions and emphases flourished.

Translocal ministry was significantly and permanently impacted by what historians call the 'Christendom shift'. The changing focus and functions of fourth-century bishops were early indications of what lay ahead.

Christendom and translocal ministry

The role and authority of bishops had been developing during previous decades, especially the second half of the third century, as churches expanded in size and influence in many parts of the empire. A gradual, though contested movement towards hierarchy, clericalism and institutionalization had been gathering pace, but the Christendom shift exacerbated these tendencies and introduced new elements into the theory and practice of translocal ministry. Identifying and assessing these developments and their legacy will help us discern which remain appropriate as we negotiate the further shift from Christendom to post-Christendom, and which are now problematic.

Among the main effects of the Christendom shift on translocal ministry were the following:

1 As the centre of gravity in the Church shifted away from local congregations towards a translocal institution, fewer decisions about faith and practice were taken locally. Doctrinal discussions took place in translocal gatherings and agreed formulae were imposed on local churches. Church discipline was exercised by translocal leaders and conferences without reference to the congregations to which those placed under discipline belonged. Missionary initiatives were undertaken by individuals or organizations commissioned by and accountable to translocal bodies rather than congregations.

2 The close and long-term relationship between congregations and those who exercised local leadership (Ferguson, 2002, pp. 130–5) was transformed into a serial form of ministry. A clerical caste developed, who exercised local ministry for shorter periods in various contexts before transferring to another as servants of an institutional Church. Local ministry developed into local expressions of what was essentially now a translocal role. Church leaders owed primary allegiance to the translocal church and were deployed locally for periods of service before moving on: sometimes, it seems, mainly to enhance their career.

3 The emergence of a territorial diocesan and, later, parish system within an increasingly bureaucratic Church imposed severe restrictions on translocal ministry that was unauthorized by church authorities. Wandering preachers were perceived – sometimes rightly – as threats to good order rather than welcomed as gifts from the wider Church. Translocal ministry became institutional and restrictive, with bishops defending their territorial rights by excluding other expressions of translocal ministry.

Gradually, as the boundaries of Christendom were established and all within it were assumed to be Christians, translocal ministry lost all vestiges of its earlier missional focus and became thoroughly maintenance-orientated. Those who exercised translocal ministries were responsible for sustaining what was, rather than bringing into being that which was not yet. Only beyond the boundaries of Christendom were missional expressions of translocal ministry feasible or perceived as necessary.

Consequently, the gifts needed for translocal ministry were redefined. The creativity, flexibility and pioneering spirit required for missional forms of translocal ministry were supplanted by the organizational and institutional abilities of those responsible for managing a large, wealthy and socially influential organization. What we might term 'apostolic' and 'prophetic' forms of translocal ministry were regarded as obsolete in an era in which translocal ministry had become essentially pastoral and administrative.

Translocal ministry, then, was both enhanced and restricted by the Christendom shift, as its focus and modus operandi were adapted to the changing context. The legacy of the Christendom era includes structures and ways of thinking about translocal ministry that should be reconsidered as this context changes again and churches from many traditions grapple with the challenges of post-Christendom. Understanding the Christendom era and discerning which elements of its ecclesiology are helpful or disabling in post-Christendom is crucial for developing appropriate expressions of translocal ministry today.

Many are understandably wary of institutional, maintenance-orientated and hierarchical models of ministry. Such expressions of translocal ministry are unlikely to be welcomed or effective. But the way forward is not to jettison translocal ministry or recognize it grudgingly but to discern patterns and practices that will enable it to serve congregations in their emerging mission context.

Translocal ministry on the margins

There are, moreover, other models of translocal ministry from the Christendom era to help us reflect on the underlying issues and work towards a contextually appropriate and ecclesiologically coherent expression of translocal ministry. On the margins, and subject to pressure from both secular and ecclesiastical authorities, were dissident movements whose rejection of the Christendom system was accompanied by creative thinking about many aspects of local church life. Among them this included experimentation with alternative models of translocal ministry.

These groups do not offer a fully fledged theology of translocal ministry or immediately transferable structures and strategies for our very different context, any more than New Testament examples provide a blueprint for contemporary practice. Furthermore, information about most of these movements is limited, since a primary responsibility of the more conventional state church translocal ministers who suppressed them was to eradicate their supposedly heretical writings. However, there are glimpses of such principles and practices operating within medieval and early modern movements, such as the Waldensians, Lollards and Anabaptists,[2] that might stimulate creative thinking about appropriate forms of translocal ministry today. There are also warnings within these movements about the tendency of innovative expressions of translocal ministry to revert to the default forms embodied so powerfully in the dominant Christendom system. Translocal ministry, it seems, is particularly vulnerable to institutional retrenchment and loss of missional dynamism.

What can we learn from models of translocal ministry on the margins?

1 *Translocal ministry can be dynamic.* Waldensians, Lollards and Anabaptists all recognized that their scattered congregations needed to be visited and resourced by those whose experience and gifts equipped them for this task. Some of this activity in the early years appears to have taken place with minimal coordination and without the processes of ordination, training and accreditation required in the state churches. As the movements aged, the normal processes of institutionalization become apparent, with accreditation and training mechanisms emerging to support those involved in translocal ministry – such as the Waldensian 'schools' and their mentoring system for new translocal ministers, or the strategic planning of missionary journeys by Hutterite communities in Moravia and their moving commissioning services for missionaries likely to become martyrs. But by comparison with translocal ministry in the state churches, organization was light and flexible, able to respond to emerging needs and opportunities rather than being locked into rigid structures.

2 *Translocal ministry can be relational.* The Christendom understanding, which exacerbated developing pre-Christendom tendencies of translocal ministry, implied a hierarchy of ministry: local church leaders were inferior in stature and authority to those with translocal responsibility. Not only were the dissidents' instincts against such hierarchical assumptions, but the terms they used to identify translocal ministers consciously challenged hierarchical notions. Waldensians commissioned to translocal ministry were called *barbes*, or 'uncles', in contradistinction to Catholic 'fathers', and Lollards employed the relational and non-hierarchical term 'known men' to designate those who travelled between their communities. The dissidents were suspicious of

honorific titles and favoured the simpler familial terminology of 'brothers and sisters' for translocal ministers and local leaders. A relational understanding of church, which respects congregational integrity and values contextual decision-making, need not be threatened by translocal ministry.

3 *Translocal ministry can be mission-orientated.* The dissident movements appeared threatening to those who were committed to the Christendom system because they challenged the centuries-old assumption that Europe was Christian and so needed pastor-administrators in local and translocal ministry roles. Translocal ministry on the margins certainly included pastoral care and coordinating tasks, but it was primarily concerned with missional activities – evangelizing communities, calling people to repentance, baptizing and catechizing new believers, planting churches, deploying missional resources and pioneering initiatives.

Transgressing parochial and diocesan boundaries, to the dismay of the state churches' translocal overseers, Waldensians, Lollards and Anabaptists offended the settled clergy and maintenance-orientated churches of Christendom. Justus Menius, for instance, expressed Lutheran irritation at translocal Anabaptist missioners, claiming biblical support for his insistence that:

> the Servant of the Gospel does not travel here and there in the land in one church today and another tomorrow, preaching one thing in one and another in the other. But one servant serves with true industry his assigned church and remains with it, leaving other churches to peace and tranquillity. Thereby each church has its own constituted servant and avoids and excludes strange, unlicensed landcombers. (Shenk, 1984, p. 20)

But, for Anabaptists, the mission imperative was regarded as binding on all believers rather than applying only to specialists. It therefore took precedence over ecclesiastical sensibilities and thereby produced a different understanding of translocal ministry. Hans Arbeiter, a Hutterian missionary captured by the authorities in 1568, 'asserted that no earthly magistrate had the right to forbid God's missioners from setting foot on their land, for the earth was the Lord's (Ps. 24.1), and the Lord had called the church to mission' (Shenk, p. 111).

4 *Translocal ministry can be pluriform.* Within the dissident movements many church members, both women and men, were involved in translocal ministry, as individuals or in teams. Nor was there an assumption that ordination was required. Anabaptists often sent out teams of

three, with a preacher accompanied by an assistant and by someone else whose main responsibility was liaising with the churches. It is not always easy to differentiate clearly between those in these dissident groups, or in contemporary church life, who are exercising itinerant ministry and those exercising translocal responsibility. It may be possible to distinguish these, at least in theory, by reference to their level of influence, continuing involvement or strategic oversight, but this is rather less helpful in practice. Many Lollard tradesmen, Waldensian merchants and Anabaptist artisans evangelized in the course of their daily work as they travelled the roads of Europe. Some devoted more and more time to ministry until their trade was secondary and they were as influential among dissident congregations as any bishop in the state churches.

5 *Translocal ministry can be exercised by apostles and prophets.* The activities and roles of those involved in translocal ministry on the margins seem closer to New Testament descriptions of apostles and prophets than the state church models. Nor was there the same reluctance to use these terms as in the state churches or, indeed, in many contemporary churches, where such language is assumed to imply enhanced status or authority. Anabaptists designated some of those who travelled between their congregations 'apostles' and recognized the ministry of 'prophets' who also moved among the churches. Their contemporaneous friendly critic Sebastian Franck wrote about the Anabaptists: 'They wish to imitate apostolic life ... moving about from one place to another, preaching and claiming a great calling and mission.' Some were so convinced of their calling, wrote Franck, that they felt 'themselves responsible for the whole world' (Shenk, p. 64).

The term 'apostle' appears also in Waldensian writings to describe translocal ministers, albeit infrequently, and their contemporaries too compared Waldensian missionaries to New Testament apostles. Although Lollards did not use this term themselves, Anne Hudson, a leading historian of the movement, describes their preachers as 'apostles' and 'prophets' (Hudson, 1988, p. 449).

6 *Translocal ministry can easily revert to inherited models.* The fluid, missional, relational and multifaceted expression of translocal ministry we can see glimpses of in the early years of these dissident movements was susceptible to co-option back into traditional models of ministry. Pressure of persecution discouraged evangelization and resulted in translocal ministry becoming more concerned with survival and maintenance than mission. The growing complexity of developing

movements loaded increasing administrative and pastoral responsibilities on the shoulders of those with translocal roles. Waldensian and Lollard communities, perhaps because they were too widely scattered for greater organization, resisted such institutionalization for many decades, but Anabaptist apostles rather quickly transmuted into Mennonite bishops once the movement began to settle down and a maintenance-orientated role superseded the earlier missional focus.

Translocal ministry in post-Christendom

The emerging culture of post-Christendom in Western society is very different from the Christendom context within which traditional models of translocal ministry were developed and marginal alternatives periodically flourished (Murray, 2004). Learning from this era but refusing to be unduly restricted by it, what issues should we consider as we reflect on the development and renewal of models of translocal ministry today?

Mission-orientation

The most fundamental and pressing issue facing Christians in all traditions is the need for a decisive and thorough paradigm shift from the inherited maintenance-orientation that has shaped our churches to a mission-orientation that will enable us to recalibrate our structures and refine our strategies for a different world. No attempts to reorganize or rebrand translocal ministry will effect more than cosmetic changes unless this shift occurs. This mission-orientation does not denigrate vital maintenance activities or naively oppose 'mission' and 'maintenance', but it insists that maintenance fits within a mission framework, not vice versa.

Like other social organizations, denominations usually begin as movements around a shared vision and gradually develop into institutions. A popular description of this seemingly inevitable process – man, movement, machine, monument, mausoleum – uses non-inclusive language but has a familiar feel for students of church history. However, the normality and seeming inevitability of this process, interpreted by some as maturing, by others as degeneration, does not preclude the possibility of re-imagining a denomination as a movement rather than an institution. Studies of organizational development have discovered processes whereby institutions can be revitalized rather than continuing along the anticipated path towards institutionalization.

In a postmodern and post-Christendom context in which institutions are culturally suspect and the marginalization of Christianity requires a radically different mindset and structure, such revitalization is crucial. How could this be accomplished? We might ask what our churches would look like if they perceived themselves as participating in a movement rather than an institution.

Changing our terminology will certainly not, by itself, achieve this. The language of 'missionary congregations' or 'missional church' has become familiar in recent years and has impacted how denominations and congregations operate, but familiarity with this language can lull us into a false sense of security, imagining that talking in missional terms equates to developing a missionary movement. What is required is an exercise of corporate imagination that has very practical outcomes that can be costed and subject to ongoing monitoring. Nothing less than a radical shift from institutional mode to a movement for mission will suffice in post-Christendom. Translocal forms of ministry have a vital role to play in this imaginative and practical paradigm shift, for this cannot be accomplished at local level alone. But only mission-orientated forms of translocal ministry will be able to make this contribution.

Retraining

All of which suggests that those moving into translocal ministry need not only a process of induction and instruction about institutional issues and working practices in their new roles, but retraining. If men and women commissioned to local forms of ministry are deemed to require training and formation to enhance and reflect on their, often substantial, prior experience of congregational leadership, preaching, pastoral ministry and mission, surely those who move from this local sphere into translocal ministry need such training. Not only has the cultural context within which they were trained for local ministry changed dramatically over the intervening years, so that a refresher course might be useful; but new theological, missiological and pastoral perspectives that have informed the training of new local ministers, to whom they will have responsibilities and with whom they will soon be working, should also be on any retraining agenda. Post-Christendom requires a wholeheartedly missional approach and fresh thinking on a wide range of issues, for which many of those moving into translocal roles were not prepared by their initial training for ministry in institutions and contexts still deeply immersed in Christendom ways of thinking.

Furthermore, in their new translocal ministry, many will encounter different issues and require new skills that were not part of their previous local experience. Some will now be working as members or leaders of staff teams, rather than guiding and coordinating the work of volunteers. Their priorities and the tasks that will occupy much of their time will be different from those with which they were familiar as local ministers. Strategic thinking, mentoring colleagues and local leaders, grappling with disciplinary issues and many other responsibilities require time for equipping and reflection.

Inadequate preparation of translocal ministers can result in disorientation, confusion, overwork, ill-health and unwise intervention in local contexts. Translocal ministers can do much harm as well as a great deal of good. My personal experience of those exercising translocal ministries has been very mixed. Some translocal ministers have been excellent, but I have often been disappointed by the quality of translocal ministry I have encountered, and some in my view have been dangerously incompetent and operating in roles for which they were not gifted or for which they had not been equipped. Effective and sustainable translocal ministry requires an investment in induction training and the provision of ongoing opportunities for skills training, peer mentoring, supervision and theological reflection.

Partnership

One of the lessons emerging from the experience of church planting since the early 1990s has been the importance of partnership between local and translocal leaders in developing mission strategies. Denominations that have relied on local entrepreneurial leadership to initiate church planting have discovered that this will founder without translocal direction and support; it will also result in churches being planted in less strategic contexts. But then, denominations that have attempted to initiate all church planting centrally or regionally have not been able to galvanize local action effectively (Lings and Murray, 2003, pp. 17–19).

What is true of church planting is probably equally true of other aspects of mission and ministry. Neither independently minded congregations that eschew the wider perspective of translocal ministry nor models of translocal ministry that attempt to impose strategies or marginalize local congregational discernment and vision will do. Partnership in non-hierarchical structures that recognize different spheres, rather than levels, of ministry and are rooted in friendship and mutual respect offer better prospects for developing and sustaining the missionary movement needed. A clear and coherent understanding of the potential and purpose of translocal ministry is needed at local church level. In order to facilitate this re-education of local churches, training for local ministry should also incorporate an understanding of the scope and contribution of translocal ministry.

Another partnership issue is the global and multicultural nature of mission today. The institutional separation within some denominations between translocal departments concerned with 'overseas mission' and 'home mission' is anachronistic. In a post-Christendom world in which mission is 'from everywhere to everywhere', this division undermines the effectiveness of both agencies and the churches they serve.

Accountability

One important aspect of partnership to which more attention may need to be given is the accountability of translocal ministers to the local congregation of which they are members or from which they were commissioned to their translocal role. It seems from the New Testament writings that those involved in translocal ministry reported back regularly to their commissioning congregation, as well as conferring with others involved in translocal ministry. Paul certainly consulted with the Jerusalem apostles (Gal. 1.18–2.10), but he and Barnabas spent considerable time reporting to the church in Antioch from which they had been commissioned (Acts 14.26–28).

Missionaries in other cultures regularly return to their home churches for periods of rest, reflection and renewal, where they report on their activities and, at least in some cases, draw on the insights of their home congregation as they discuss issues they are facing. There are indications that Anabaptist apostles were accountable to their commissioning congregations in ways that those involved in translocal ministry today might find beneficial. Such periods of reflection and consultation might further erode any hierarchical dimension of translocal ministry. It might also help to ensure that those involved in translocal ministry are less isolated than at present and less likely to suffer from burnout. It would also encourage them not to lose touch with grassroots congregational life, which can easily happen if their involvement in local churches is primarily as a visiting preacher or pastoral fire-fighter.

Appointment and terminology

A practical implication of all this is that the expectations, job descriptions, skills and priorities of those called into translocal ministry need a thorough overhaul. Putting this fairly bluntly, denominations need to appoint people with pioneering and strategic gifts rather than looking mainly for those with administrative skills or successful local ministries – men and women who are mission-minded, orientated towards envisioning, change-management and risk-taking, rather than supervising stability or managing decline. Having 'a safe pair of hands' or 'knowing the right people' will not suffice!

One term for the kind of role we are envisaging is 'apostolic'. Reflecting on models of church and mission in a changing world, Eddie Gibbs insists:

> in light of the current challenge facing the churches in the West. ... the church needs to move from the Constantinian model – which presumed a churched culture – to an apostolic model designed to penetrate the vast, unchurched segments of society. (Gibbs and Coffey, 2001, p. 181)

This 'apostolic model' implies changes in the way congregations operate, but the catalyst for such local changes may be 'apostolic' forms of translocal ministry.

This does not mean that all translocal ministers must be gifted as apostles, or that this terminology should necessarily be used to describe those who are. The question of terminology may be significant. Will the use of 'apostolic' terminology help or hinder local churches from embracing and benefiting from translocal ministry? If the term worries, confuses or offends local ministers and their churches, is it worth persisting with? On the other hand, if employing a generic term like 'translocal' locks churches into maintenance-orientated models and fails to help them engage with missional challenges or interact with strategic and visionary leadership, maybe 'apostolic' will help signal the changes of priority and ethos that are essential in a post-Christendom era.

Whether the term 'apostolic' is used or not, collapsing all expressions of 'translocal ministry' into 'apostolic ministry' is unhelpful: translocal pastors and administrators, teachers and evangelists will also play important roles. Indeed, the pastoral and organizational abilities that have traditionally been sought in translocal ministers will still be needed by those with 'apostolic' roles, but these abilities will be deployed in new ways and with different priorities. An impressive track record in successful suburban churches may be an inadequate, even unhelpful, qualification or preparation for those called to exercise translocal missional ministry in the urban, postmodern and multicultural contexts that represent the main challenges facing the churches in post-Christendom.

If this is the case for translocal ministry in post-Christendom, there may also be implications for local ministry. Suitable candidates for translocal ministry are likely to be found primarily among those already experienced in local ministry, so what has been suggested regarding the appointment, skills and training of translocal ministers needs also to impact the appointment, skills and training of local ministers. Maybe reflection on the nature of translocal ministry will stimulate renewed thinking about the calling of local ministers and how the churches might perceive their role.

These last reflections may seem to have strayed beyond the subject of this book, but reflection on any aspect of ecclesiology can disrupt accepted notions and priorities in other areas too. The fourth-century Christendom shift impacted many areas of church life, but the changes were felt first among translocal ministers. Perhaps the further shift from Christendom to post-Christendom, which will provoke profound changes in twenty-first-century churches, will also be apparent as clearly as anywhere in the sphere of translocal ministry. And perhaps a renewed expression of translocal ministry will be one of the critical factors in equipping churches to engage effectively with this exciting but challenging new world.

Notes

1 This chapter draws on earlier work in Stuart Murray, 2004, 'Translocal Ministry in Post-Christendom', in Stuart Murray (ed.), *Translocal Ministry: Equipping the Churches for Mission*, Didcot: Baptist Union of Great Britain, pp. 64–74.

2 The Waldensians flourished especially in southern France and northern Italy between the twelfth century and the Reformation era and also spread into German-speaking areas despite sustained persecution. In fourteenth-century England radical followers of John Wyclif were dubbed Lollards and established churches in many parts of the country, some of which survived until the Reformation. Anabaptist communities sprang up in Switzerland, Germany and the Netherlands in the sixteenth century and offered a more radical approach to reformation than their Protestant contemporaries. For a succinct summary of the history and convictions of these movements, see www.anabaptistnetwork.com.

References

Drake, H. A., 2000, *Constantine and the Bishops: The Politics of Intolerance*, Baltimore, MD: Johns Hopkins University Press.
Ferguson, Everett, 2002, 'The Congregationalism of the Early Church', in Daniel Williams, *The Free Church and the Early Church*, Grand Rapids, MI: Eerdmans.
Gibbs, Eddie and Ian Coffey, 2001, *Church Next*, Leicester: IVP.
Hudson, Anne, 1988, *The Premature Reformation*, Oxford: Clarendon Press.
Kreider, Alan (ed.), 2002, *The Origins of Christendom in the West*, Edinburgh: T&T Clark.
Lings, George and Stuart Murray, 2003, *Church Planting: Past, Present and Future*, Cambridge: Grove Books.
Murray, Stuart, 2004, *Post-Christendom*, Carlisle: Paternoster Press.
Shenk, Wilbert (ed.), 1984, *Anabaptism and Mission*, Scottdale: Herald Press.

20

Conclusion:
The Future Trajectory of
Translocal Ministry

PAUL BUTLER

So what might the future trajectory of translocal ministry be in these next few years? In a brief chapter I offer headlines that I believe are all borne out by the contributions made throughout the book and rooted in my own personal journey.

In my current role I cannot but be influenced by the succession in which I stand. First, the great northern saints Aidan and Cuthbert, who are both 'New Monastic' itinerant preachers and healers. Then there are the 'prince bishops', some so engaged in the political life of the nation that it can seem hard to see where the spiritual leadership was exercised. More recently, predecessors like Lightfoot, Westcott, Jenkins, Wright and Welby shape me with their passions for Scripture, prayer, social justice and evangelism.

In the longer reach of my journey there is my first, entirely negative experience of a Church of England bishop at my confirmation, aged 12. I stopped church. The brilliant Christian Union at Kingston Grammar School, and joining a youth group at Staneway Chapel, an Open Brethren Assembly, however, led me to a personal commitment to following Jesus in 1970. In the following years they both nurtured me well. I was profoundly impacted by the early days of the House Church Movement. Gerald Coates, Roger Forster, Bryn Jones and David Tomlinson influenced me greatly. In my mind, at best, the Church of England was decidedly lagging behind what God was doing. Rather reluctantly I found my way back into the Church of England while at Nottingham University. I became an ordinand 'kicking and screaming'. I learnt that a healthy distance from bishops was largely a good thing as generally they were regarded as 'liberal'.

Children's ministry was a key part of my calling from the outset, my engagement with Scripture Union crucial. Dai Lewis became mentor and friend for nearly 40 years.

I married Rosemary, a Baptist. I always saw myself as 'on the edge' so far as the Church of England was concerned. Yet growing contact with bishops made me realize that they were godlier and more significant than I had been led to believe. Peter Selby, then Bishop of Kingston, was incredibly supportive as I moved from curacy into working for Scripture Union. Roger Sainsbury was brilliant as I moved into being Team Rector of Walthamstow. He first made me think that, against all my better judgement, God might call me to be a bishop. So too did my then 'spiritual director', Philip Mohabir. Then, to Rosemary's and my shock, the call came. It has been quite a journey. Five years as Suffragan Bishop of Southampton, four as Diocesan Bishop of Southwell and Nottingham and six years as Bishop of Durham.

My own role as a translocal leader has a specific geographic location in the diocese; an inherited historic role for the north-east; and an expertise or interest role given to me nationally. This latter has included children and young people throughout my episcopal ministry and then, at various times, has covered safeguarding, welfare, refugees and asylum seekers and aspects of international development. Additionally, because of the joys of being part of the Anglican Communion and the friendships that have developed over years, I find myself speaking up for Rwanda and Burundi regularly.

So with that context, here are my headlines.

Continue to grow in significance

Churches Together nationally and more locally have become increasingly aware that relationships matter most. They recognize that organic praying, learning, worshipping and acting together are far more fruitful than overly bureaucratic structures. Translocal leaders can model this. This enables gatherings across the differences of ecclesiology and theology. It also opens up ways of working together. As the Church wakes up more fully to its mission being in a post- or even pre-Christian context, offering leadership across a region is going to be more significant. Supporting one another in different initiatives and seeking to ensure we avoid unhealthy duplication will be key.

Pastoring the pastors

The crucial role of being 'shepherds of God's flock' will grow and become more demanding. In the historic denominations, ministers are finding themselves responsible for more congregations and communities, or in some instances for larger ones. The increasing demand is often unrealistic, and attempts to meet it are sometimes regarded as insufficient. It is often forgotten that translocal ministers also have a pastoral responsibility towards the congregations and communities concerned. Sometimes the dissatisfaction comes because the translocal leader is seeking to balance these 'competing' needs. Those of us called to such roles will need to consider both how we conduct ourselves in this role and what access we have to counsellors, mediators and mentors who can help us fulfil our calling.

Being leaders in evangelism and mission

The Church has always had an evangelistic calling. It also has a responsibility to love the neighbour, and thus engage in mission in its widest forms. In an era in which the very story of Jesus is increasingly less well known, there is an urgent evangelistic task. In a nation and world full of all kinds of need, physical, mental, emotional, social and spiritual, there are abundant opportunities for mission as service. Offering inspiration, encouragement, advice, advocacy and example on a translocal basis will be vital. The nature of the gifting and calling of each leader means that for some this will be direct. For others it may be more indirect. However, all translocal leaders will play a crucial part in supporting church planting and other church growth initiatives. They will be expected to encourage new mission initiatives. Local leaders, congregations and communities want encouragement and advice; they value knowing that their action for the common good has the support of church leaders.

Focal points for unity

When the relative number of active Christian worshippers is reducing, it appears to me likely that small congregations will value having a person, or small team, to whom they will look to represent their wider denomination. Equally, local authorities and others look for those who will act as representatives for the wider church community. In the changing shape of how the unwritten social contract between national and local government, business and the third sector is being rewritten, the faith communities will increasingly be asked to play a role as partners. So the translocal leaders will necessarily have the greater part to play. Indeed, they might discover the advantage in agreeing among themselves how to best represent each other rather than all expecting to turn up to everything.

Deepening relationships

Investment in relationships across the 'denominational' groupings will be essential for the whole Church to live out its witness to the nation. If we really are to be translocal leaders who trust and support one another while encouraging local churches to work well together, then our own relationships must deepen. Giving time to one another in our busy lives will matter. I am deeply grateful to be a part of the North East Church Leaders' group that sees going away together to pray and learn as worthwhile for our whole ministry. From this, the possibility that we can represent one another in wider social engagement grows.

Growing inter-faith relationships

This needs to happen whatever the number of adherents other faiths have in any area. Working together across faiths is not a watering down of any, it is a recognition of mutual respect, of the common good and of the appropriateness of people of faith supporting one another. It will also aid our speaking out clearly together against anti-Semitism, Islamophobia and attacks on all religions, including Christianity. It will help us work together as community sponsors of refugees; on justice for asylum seekers, local housing provision, good education for all and the challenge to build social cohesion.

A prophetic voice for justice for the poorest and most vulnerable

The Church is called to be a prophetic voice and presence, seeking justice for all and with a particular concern for the most vulnerable. This includes children in poverty, the unborn child, the asylum seeker and the vulnerable elderly, especially those with dementia and at risk of abuse. It must also include speaking out together on climate change, particularly on its impact on the poorest in the world. My visits to countries like Burundi and Lesotho highlight the significant impact already on the poorest who rely on subsistence farming.

Geographically defined

The roles will continue to be defined predominantly geographically but there will be a growing number identified more by some relationship or specific function. There is a very long history defining translocal leadership in geographic terms. A Church of England bishop always has a place as a title and most denominations operate with some kind of regional ministry. Yet there has always also been a practice of giving Church of England bishops wider responsibilities relating to specific issues. The Lords Spiritual in the House of Lords operate with 'portfolios'. Newfrontiers is now working on relationships before geography. In the Anglican Church of North America there is a mix of dioceses based on geography and relationship. As part of the Church of England's mutual flourishing there are bishops who are related to on the basis of specific convictions and practices concerning female bishops. There is also now a specific bishop for church planting.

It is my conviction that in the coming decade, while geography will remain primary there will be a growing number of examples of translocal leadership that will be rooted in relationship, theological conviction and/or function.

In England

Specific to England, the globally unique historic role played by Church of England bishops in the life of the nation will continue, or it will experience a sudden and dramatic collapse.

Church of England bishops struggle to remember the unique historic role we play in England. I think other church and faith leaders forget this too. This is coming under renewed questioning and increasing pressure. This is not new. There have been calls for 'disestablishment' at various points throughout the Church of England's history. It is a deeply complex relationship between church and state. Fresh questions will arise when a new monarch is crowned. Questions are rightly posed from the nations of the United Kingdom for whom the Church of England is not a player. My instinct is that there will be further revisions to the relationship but that fundamentally it will remain. However, I do not rule out its sudden and dramatic collapse, the untangling of which might make Brexit look like a relatively easy option.

Conclusion

This whole volume has sought to explore the varied understandings of translocal leadership across the great breadth of church life in the United Kingdom, and inevitably beyond these islands' shores. It has reached back into the scriptural roots of such ministry and its evolution through the early Church's growth, showing how it evolved and developed. It thus has shown how all traditions can claim legitimate succession to this history, but must all do so with due humility, accepting the validity of the views of others. It has helpfully asked a wide variety of writers to explore the thinking and practice of their own tradition. Kindly, it has allowed the Anglican voice to have significant space, including according this bishop the privilege of closing the volume with some reflections on what the near future might hold. I am grateful that my own story draws on some of the breadth of tradition and practice outlined. I continue to learn through the fellowship I enjoy with other translocal leaders, in my region, nationally and internationally.

Translocal leadership has a critical role in the health and well-being of God's kingdom and Church. It plays a vital role in the common good of our nation. May all who are called to exercise it do so:

> as a fellow elder … exercising oversight, not under compulsion, but willingly, as God would have you; not for shameful gain, but eagerly; not domineering over those in your charge, but being examples to the flock. (1 Peter 5.1–3, ESV)

Index

activism *see* evangelism; social justice
Adams, Clive 148
Adeboye, Pastor Enoch 175
Æthelberht 21
African churches *see* Black churches
St Aidan 21, 267
AIDS Care Education Training 173
Aladura International Church 160
Aldred, Rt Revd Dr Joe xix–xx
  diversity or fragmentation? 175–6
All Saint's Church, Stevenage 49
Alpha Course, Holy Trinity, Brompton 33–4
Anabaptists 257–60
Anglican-Methodist Covenant
  episcope and 19, 68, 69
  Mission and Ministry in Covenant 19
Anglican Ordinal 66
Anglican Roman Catholic International Commission (ARCIC) 23–4
St Anselm Community, Lambeth 185
Antony of the desert 186
APEST model 36, 37, 146
Apostolic Church
  history of 156
  translocal practice in 157–8

apostolic ministry
  Constantine model and 264
  early Christianity 3–5, 8
  as *episkope* 9
  Newfrontiers 166–7
  Pioneer and 169–74
  relation to bishops 65
  succession of 108
  translocal ministry 259
  Willow Creek Church and 32–3
'Apostolic Ministry in the New Church Streams' (Virgo) 164–8
Aquinas, St Thomas 64
Arbeiter, Hans 258
archbishops, institutional leadership of 97
archdeacons 94–5, 96
Arles, synod of 21
Ashimolowo, Matthew 160
Askew, Catherine 196
Askew, Pete 194, 195
Assemblies of God churches
  history of 156
  translocal practice in 159–60
  see also Pentecostal Churches
Association of Pastoral Counselling and Supervision 245
Association of the Churches in Christ 48
Atkins, Revd Dr Martyn 228
  'The Methodist Church' 116–24
Atkinson, David 227

St Augustine, Archbishop of
  Canterbury 21, 62
 dispatched by Gregory 213
 Roman Catholic Church
  and 103
Australian Christian Church 35
Australian Stock Exchange good
 practice 35
authority, evangelicalism and 31
Avis, Revd Prof. Paul 25
Azusa Street Pentacostal
 revival 178

Baptism, Eucharist and Ministry
 (World Council of Churches)
 24, 28–9
Baptist Union churches
 in Abingdon 247
 apostolic leadership 130–1
 appointment of clergy 51–2
 care of ministers 127–8
 conflicts and relationships
  131–2
 decentralization xxiii
 'Declaration of Principle' 216
 ecclesiology of 126–7
 ecumenism 133–4
 Faith and Society Team
  Leader 57
 institutional management 128–9
 Local Ecumenical
  Partnerships 48–9
 mission 129–31, 220
 National Settlement Team 244
 ordination of ministers 125–6
 pioneer ministry and church
  planting 132–3
 scholarship and 228–9, 230
 translocal oversight 54–5,
  125–34
'The Baptist Union of Great
 Britain' (Tidball) 125–34

Baring-Gould, R. S.
 'Onward Christian Soldiers' 147
St Barnabas 6, 8, 263
Barton, John 234
Bathsheba 87
Bauckham, Richard 22–3
Bebbington, David 30–1, 38
Beck, Brian 228
Bede, Venerable 21
Benedict XVI, Pope (Joseph
 Ratzinger)
 outside world and bishops
  110–12
 responds to Ignatius on
  bishops 108–13
 writings on bishops 104, 105
Benedictine order, new
 monasticism and 184, 185
Bennett, Dennis
 Nine O'Clock in the Morning
 169
Bennis, Warren 221
Berger, Klaus
 episkopos/presbuteros 176
Bethel Church 31
Bishops in Communion (House of
 Bishops) 29
'The Black Church and
 Episcopacy' (Muir) 175–82
Black churches
 diversity of 175–6
 nongovernmental forms 177
 Pentacostal denominations
  160–1
 women's role in 178–9
Black, Jonathan 158
Blackstone, William 110
Blyth, Myra 229
Boddy, Alexander 156
Bonhoegger, Dietrich 113
Bonser, Henry 56
Book of Common Prayer 64, 65

INDEX

Booth, General William 147
Breen, Mike 36, 37
British Council of Churches 45
Brown, Gordon 20
Bunyan Baptist, Stevenage 48
Burns, Arthur 96
Butler, Rosemary 268
Butler, Rt Revd Paul
 'The Future Trajectory of
  Translocal Ministry' 267–72
 prospects for episkope xxv

Calvin, John 182
Cameron (Sheila) Report
 Episcopal Ministry 28
Carey, Archbishop George 172
Caribbean churches *see* Black
 churches
Carswell, Andrew 36
Catchim, Tim 37
cathedrals 95
Catherine of Aragon 20
Catholic Emancipation Act, 103
Celestial Church of Christ 160
Celtic Christianity
 episcopal figures 21, 62–3
 new monasticism and 185
 Northumbrian Community
  192–9
Champion of the World event
 173
Chan, Simon 181
chancellor, diocesan 96
Charismatic Evangelical Round
 Table 172, 173
Child Sex Abuse inquiry 219
Christ Apostolic Church Mount
 Bethel 160
Christ Faith Tabernacle 181, 182
Christian Union 267
Christianity, early
 bishops and xxi–xxii, 254–6

Christendom 264–5
church fathers 29–30
Constantine establishes 254
Council of Nicaea 254
early ministry 3–5
growth of church 73
monasticism 186
Roman development of 21
tradition and 18
Church of Christ the Cornerstone,
 Milton Keynes 48
Church of Christ the King,
 Stevenage 49
Church of England
 Act of Supremacy 21
 adaptation and change 25
 'apostolic succession' 66
 appointment of clergy 51–2
 Archbishops' Council 97–8
 Bible and theology of episcope
  64–6
 bishops and Synod 29, 66–8
 Canon C on bishops 64, 65
 Church Commissioners 97
 collegiality 55
 difficulty in organizational
  methods 101
 ecumenism and episcope 68–9
 episcope in context of 27–8
 establishment 98–9, 271
 failure and renewal 101–2
 faithful improvisation 99
 Five Guiding Principles 235–8,
  240
 Fresh Expression 172, 185, 189,
  190
 Henry's dissolution of
  monasteries 184
 historical look at bishops 62–3
 historical perspective 20–3
 House of Lords 271
 Houses of 67

275

institutional theory and 99–101
leadership and 93–8, 222
local churches 28
Local Ecumenical Partnerships 48–9
meaning of translocal 94
Mission-Shaped Church report 220
monarchy and 81–3
national translocal ministries 97
orders of 65–6
parish system 83
Pensions Board 97
public identity of bishops 61–2
Queen on role of 90
reason 25–6
scholarship and bishops 226–7, 230
scripture 22, 23–4
scripture, tradition and reason 22–3
secretariats for archbishops 97
social attitude changes and 98
synodical system of 94, 96
three planes of 28
the 'threefold cord' 23–6
tradition 24–5
translocal oversight 55–7
Wesley and 17
women as bishops 232–42
women as priests 233
'Church of England Bishops as Pastor and Evangelist' (Cottrell) 71–9
'Church of England Bishops as Religious and Civic Leaders' (Jones) 81–91
Church of God in Christ 180
Church of Jesus Christ Apostolic 160
Church of the Transfiguration, Stevenage 48
Church Revitalisation Trust 34
Church Times
debate about *Green Report* 26
churches
church planting 262–3
ecclesiological theory xxiv
Churches Together groups 44–5, 47, 53
Enabling Group 49
A Flexible Framework for Local Unity 49
mentoring 244
model for translocal ministry 268
Churches Together in England 180
City Centre Resource Churches 34
Clark, Denis 170
Coates, Anona 169, 170
Coates, Gerald 215, 267
'Personal Reflections from Pioneer' 169–74
Coffey, David 229
'line-manager' 246
'Six Marks of a Missionary Union' 220
Common Worship
ordination and consecration 27–8, 65, 72, 218
community, bishops in communion 29
Conference of European Churches 47
conflict
minister and congregation 219
pastoral supervision and 247
Congregational churches 48
ecumenism 48
United Reformed Church and 136, 137
congregations
conflict and 219
early Christendom 255
Connolly, Billy 74

INDEX

Constantine I the Great 21, 254, 264
context
  C of E episcope 27–30
  evangelism case studies 30–8
  personal experience and 14–16
  threefold chord 23–6
  Wesley's Methodism 16–19
Continuing Professional Development 249
Cornick, Dr David 228, 244
Cottrell, Most Revd Stephen
  'Church of England Bishops as Pastor and Evangelist' 71–9
County Ecumenical Committees 44
Cranmer, Thomas 66
Cray, Rt Revd Graham 57, 172
Crusade for World Revival 173
Cundy, Rt Revd Ian 227
St Cuthbert 21, 62–3, 267
Cyprian of Carthage 24

David, King 87
Davis, Douglas J. 25
deacons 4, 5, 176
deans of cathedrals 95
Delirious 173
diocese
  meaning of translocal 93–4
  structures of 96–7
Dixon, Dr Patrick 173
Donald, James 176
Downs Bible Week 165
Drewery, Benjamin 22–3
Dulles, Avery 102

Ecclesiastical History (Eusebius) 109
ecumenism
  affirmation with distance 47
  C of E episcope and 68–9
  cooperation 51–3
  current views of 44–5
  episkope 50–1
  Lima document 28
  Local Ecumenical Partnerships 48–50
  Methodist Church 117
  movement towards 44–6, 48
  pastoral issues in partnerships 48–9
  resistance/indifference to 46
  Stevenage's churches and 48–9
  structure of 53
  translocal oversight 52, 54–7
education, diocesan work in 97
Edward VI, King 63
Edwards, Jonathan 229
Edwin of Northumbria 63
Elim Pentecostal Church
  history of 156
  translocal practice in 158–9
  see also Pentecostal Churches
Elizabeth I, Queen, bishops and 63, 82
Elizabeth II, Queen
  Anglicanism and other faiths 20
  on Church in national life 90
  oath of homage to 81–2
  Westminster Hall address 30
Episcopacy (Methodist Conference) 19
Episcopal Church, USA 245
Episcopal Ministry (Cameron report) 28
episcope and bishops
  Brown removes PM appointments 20
  characteristics of bishops 179–80
  early church ministry 3–5, 254–6
  Gregory the Great's handbook 213
  hierarchies and 65

277

in the House of Lords 83
meaning of translocal 93-4
ministry of bishops 71-9
monarchialism 106-7
New Testament 9, 176
oath to monarch 81-3
personal, collegial and communal 28-30
St Ignatius on 104, 105-7
succession 29
Episkope and Episcopacy (Methodist Conference) 19
'Episkope and Gender: an Anglican Case Study' (Hollinghurst) 232-43
'Episkope and Supervision' (Goodliff) 244-53
'Episkope and the New Monasticism in the Celtic Tradition: Northumbrian Community' (Searle) 192-9
'Episkope, Identity and Personhood' (Standing) 203-11
Erickson, Millard 177
Ethelbert of Kent 63
Eusebius
  Ecclesiastical History 109
Evagrius of Pontus 30
Evangelical Alliance 30, 45-6
evangelism
  activism 30-1
  bishops mission and 71-9
  consuming audiences of 31
  context of 31-8
  core characteristics of 30-1
  liberal tradition and 85
  new apostolic movements 36-8
  Pioneer 169-74
  translocal leadership in 269
Every Day With Jesus (CWR) 173

Faith, Theology and the Imagination (McIntyre) 86
family and marriage 206-7
Fisher, Archbishop Geoffrey 69
A Flexible Framework for Local Unity in Mission (Churches Together) 49
Forster, Roger 267
Fountain Trust 169
Francis, Rt Revd John 180, 181
Franciscan order 184, 185
Free Churches 57, 69
Freestone, Roy 244-5
Frost, Mike 36
Fusion 173
'The Future Trajectory of Translocal Ministry' (Butler) 267-72

Gather movement 45
Gatiss, Lee 241
gender xxv
Gerald Coates Pioneer (Turner) 172
Gibbs, Eddie 264
Gilead (Robinson) 76
Global Leadership Network *see* Willow Creek Community Church
Goodliff, Revd Dr Paul
  'Contemporary Models of Translocal Ministry' 44-57
  'Episkope and Supervision' 244-53
  scholarship of 228, 229
  'Translocal Ministry and Scholarship' 225-31
Goodspeed, Malcolm 229, 246
Grange Park Church, Northampton 48
Great Ashby Community Church 49

INDEX

Green, Bernard 228–9
Green, Lynn 229
Green (Stephen) Report 25–6, 30
Gregory the Great, Pope (Gregorius Anicius)
  conversion of English 21, 62, 103
  on ministry 76–7, 78
  Pastoral Rule 24, 213
  scholarship 225
  on sentinel's perspective 75
Ground Level 173
Grove Hill Church, Hemel Hempstead 51
Grundy, Malcolm xxiii, 22, 29, 203
Guest, Matthew 25

Habgood, Archbishop, Dr John 85
Hannington, Rt Revd James 57
Hanson, Rt Revd Richard P. C. 23
  Anglican pragmatism 25
  no sense of hierarchy 28
  on tradition of episcopacy 24
Harper, Michael 169
Harries, Rt Revd Richard 57, 227
Hawkins, Peter 250
Hay, Sarah 196
Hayden, Roger 228
Heim, Maximilian Heinrich 109
Henry VIII, King
  bishops and government 22, 63, 82
  dissolution of monasteries 184
  politics over theology 20–1
Hertfordshire Shared Churches, Ltd 51
Higton, Mike 222
Hillsborough Independent Panel 87–91
Hillsong 35–6
Hind, Rt Revd John 227

Hirsch, Alan 36–7
Hollinghurst, Rt Revd Anne
  consecration of 232
  'Episkope and Gender' 232–43
  gender and episkope xxv
Holy Trinity Church, Brompton 33–4
Holy Trinity Church, Stevenage 48
Home Mission Appeal 134
Hooker, Richard 61
  on episcope 24
  Seventh Book of Ecclesiastical Polity 22
HOPE 45
House Church movement 267
  see also Pioneer
House of Bishops 97
Houston, Bobbie 35
Houston, Brian 35–6
Hubbard, Venerable Julian
  'Translocal Ministries ... as Institutional Leadership' 93–102
Hudson, Anne 259
Hughes, Selwyn 173
Human Rights Convention 88–9
humanity under God's authority 111
Hutterite communities 257, 258
Hybels, Bill 31, 32–3

Icthus 173
identity and personhood
  faith and relationship with God 205
  marriage and family of bishops 206–7
  personal character for episkope 213–14
  as religious professional 207–8
  self-appraisal 210–11
  sense of call 208–9

well-being of ministers of oversight 203–4
well-doing for well-being 209–10
St Ignatius of Antioch 24
  secular world and 111
  threefold ministry 176
  writings on bishops 104–7
St Ignatius of Loyola
  new monasticism and 184, 185
Institute of Pastoral Supervision and Reflective Practice 245
institutional theory 99–101
  development of churches 260–1
  leadership 100–1
  organizations and 100
International Church of the Foursquare Gospel 160
International Coalition of Apostolic Leaders (ICAL) 37–8
Irenaeus of Lyon 24
Isabel Mary, Sister 77

St James, Jerusalem church and 7
Jeffreys, George 156, 158
Jenkins, Rt Revd David 65, 226, 267
Jesus Christ
  farewell address 106
  good shepherd 61, 240
  Ignatius equates with bishop 106
  justice and mercy 85
  maleness of 234
  Peter's authority from 109–10
  prayer for disciples as one 45
  prophet, priest and king 64
  representative of 215–16
  understanding of ministry 3–4
  on the unjust judge 87, 90–1
  worldly power and 83–4
Jewel, John 24
St John Chrysostom 109

John Paul II, Pope (Karol Wojtyła)
  Ut Unum Sint 47
John the Faster, Archbishop of Constantinople 213
John, Very Revd Jeffrey 227
Johnson, Bill 31
Jones, Bryn 267
Jones, Keith 229
Jones, Rt Revd James
  '... Bishops as Religious and Civic Leaders' 81–91
Judas Iscariot 9
justice
  Jesus on unjust judge and 87, 90–1
  see also social justice

Kähler, Martin 220
Kasper, Cardinal Walter 178
Kay, Prof. William K. 177
  'Pentacostalism' 155–62
Kaye, Bruce 63
Kendrick, Graham 173
Keyworth, Stephen 229
Kingston Grammar School 267
Kingsway International Christian Centre 160

Lactantius on justice 87
Laloux, Frederic 193
Lambert, Lance 170
Lambeth Conferences 27, 67
Lambeth Quadrilateral 68
Lane, Rt Revd Libby 232
language, terminology of
  'apostolic' 264
Leach, Jane 245
leadership
  C of E roles 93–7
  institutional 100–1
  in mission 269
  organizational models 193
  theology and 221

INDEX

Leo XIII, Pope (Vincenzo Pecci) 103
Lewis, Christopher, Dean of Christ Church, Oxford 227
Lewis, Dai 268
Lightfoot 267
Local Ecumenical Partnerships 48–50, 53
Locke, John 110
Lollards 257–60
Longmeadow Free Church, Stevenage 49
Luther, Martin 225
Lutheran Church, women bishops and 234

McIntyre, John
Faith, Theology and the Imagination 86
McKnight, Scot 33
McNair Scott, Benjamin G. 38
McPherson, Aimee Semple 160
'March for Jesus' movement 173
Marriage Course, Holy Trinity, Brompton 34
Martin-Hanley, Marla 204
Mary I, Queen 63
Mawer, Sir Philip 238
May, Theresa 87
Melania of the desert 186
Mellows, Anthony
Resourcing Bishops 24–5
Menius, Justus 258
Mennonites 260
Methodist Church
  church and oversight 221
  Circuit 116, 118, 119, 121–2
  Conference of 17–18, 116, 118–19, 123
  Connexion 116–120, 123
  Constitution, Practice and Discipline of 118
  in context 14
  Districts 116, 117, 118, 121, 122–3
  episcope and 19, 69, 118–24
  experience and practicality 16–19
  four circles of belonging 116
  the Legal Hundred 19
  Local Ecumenical Partnerships 48–9
  ordained presbyters 116
  ordination and ministry 119, 120–1
  pastoral supervision 244, 251
  safeguarding from abuse 251
  scholarship of leaders 228
  subsidiarity principle 118
  Superintendents 121–2
  translocal oversight 55
  Wesley's movement 16–19
  'The Methodist Church' (Atkins) 116–24
#MeToo movement 33
Miller, Trevor 193, 195
Milton Keynes Mission Partnership 50, 51
ministry
  of bishops 71–9
  blessing 76
  burn-out 263
  itinerant 255
  pastoral care 77–8
  pastoral supervision 244–53
  social justice 75–6
Ministry Today UK 248
mission
  Celtic saints and 197
  conversionism 30–1
  translocal ministry and 220, 258, 260–1, 269
Mission and Ministry in Covenant (Anglican Methodist Covenant) 19

Mission-Shaped Church report 220
Mobsby, Revd Ian
  'Oversight and the New
    Monasticism' 184-91
Mohabir, Philip 268
monasticism
  Abba and Amma 186
  Celtic Northumbrian Community
    192-9
  finances of 188, 189-90
  historical context of 184, 185,
    186
  as lay movement 188-9
  leadership in New communities
    184-91
  use of 'abbot and abbess' 185-6
Moot Community 185, 187
  funding of 190
  leader terminology 186
Morris, Rt Revd Roger 76
Muir, Dr R. David
  'The Black Church and
    Episcopacy' 175-82
Mullally, Rt Rev Sarah 238-9
Murray, Dr Stuart
  'Translocal Ministry in Post-
    Christendom' 254-65
music, Hillsong and 35

Nanus, Burt 221
The Nature of Oversight
  (Methodist Conference) 19
Nee, Watchman 169
Nero, Emperor 84
New Testament
  Christ and men and women 235
  episcope in 9, 176
  gendered roles and 234-5
  no ministry blueprint 23
  translocal ministry and 4-9,
    4-10, 5-8, 256-7
  see also scripture

New Testament Church of
  God 176, 177-8
New Wine Church 38, 182
Newbigin, Lesslie 220
Newfrontiers
  Bible Weeks 165
  Biblically-inspired ministry
    166-7
  developing translocal ministry
    166-8
  origins of 164-6
Nicaea, Council of 27, 107, 254
Nichols, Aidan 107
Nine O'Clock in the Morning
  (Bennett) 169
Noble, John 172
North, Philip 238, 241
Northumbria Community 185,
  192-7

obedience, Ignatius on 106
Ogg, Fredric Austin 213
Onesimus 106
'Onward Christian Soldiers'
  (Baring-Gould) 147
Open Brethren Assembly 267
*The Ordination and Consecration
  of a Bishop*
  liturgy of 27-8
Origen 21
Orthodox churches
  Churches Together and 45
  ecumenism 47
  monastic communities 186
  ordination of women 232, 234
  women in ministry 237
Outler, Albert
  'The Wesleyan Quadrilateral' 18
'Oversight and the New
  Monasticism' (Mobsby)
  184-91

INDEX

parish system, translocal meaning and 93–4
Parker, Commissioner Mike 220
Parochial Church Council 237
Pastoral Rule (Gregory the Great) 24, 213
Paterson, Michael 245
St Paul
  apostleship 8
  on bishops 179, 182
  Damascus Road experience 181
  description of Epaphroditus 8
  early ministry 3
  as envoy 6–7
  equates *episkopos* and *presbuteros* 176
  on governing authorities 84
  itinerant ministry 166
  never a bishop of a place 108
  Pioneer and 171
  reporting to Antioch 263
  we belong to one another 45
Paul, Ian 222
Payne, Ernest 228
Peck, M. Scott 192
Peel, David 228
Pelikan, Jaroslav 225–6
Pentecostal churches
  Black churches 160–1, 175–82
  Churches Together 45
  language of governance 161
  nongovernmental church polity 177
  origins of 156–7
  from overseas 160–1
  theology and legal structure 155
  translocal practice in 157–60, 162
'Pentecostalism: Translocal Leadership' (Kay) 155–62
Percy, Very Revd Martyn xxv, 222
  a community of disagreement 27
on the *Green Report* 26
spiritual *nous* 30
'Personal Reflections from Pioneer' (Coates) 169–74
St Peter
  authority given by Jesus 109–10
  commissioned as bishop 4
  first pope 65
  on oversight 272
  replacing Judas 9
Philippi, overseers and deacons in 4
Phillips, Dr Jacob
  'The Roman Catholic Church' 103–13
Pickard, Stephen 29
Pilate, Pontius 83–4
Pillar, Sarah 196
Pioneer Church 169–72, 187, 188
Pius, IX, Pope (Giovanni Ferretti) *Universalis Ecclesiae* 103
Platten, Stephen, Bishop of Wakefield 227
Podmore, Colin 229
Presbyterian Church 48, 137
presbyters, New Testament 176
Prisons, Bishop to 89–90

Railton, George Scott 147
Ramsey, Michael 229
Ratzinger, Joseph *see* Benedict XVI, Pope
Redeemed Christian Church of God 160, 175–82
Redman, Matt 173
registrar, role in institution 96
Resourcing Bishops (Mellows) 24–5
Richards, Noel 173
Roberts, Alexander 176
Robinson, Marilynne
  Gilead 76

Roman Catholic Church
  Churches Together 45
  communal listening 113
  contraception 112
  diocese in Britain 103
  ecumenism 47
  episcopate as third order 64
  Local Ecumenical
    Partnerships 48–9
  monastic communities 186
  primacy and episcopate 109–10
  St Ignatius on episcopate 104,
    105–7
  threefold role of bishops 29–30
  translocal oversight 55
  Vatican II 29–30
  women in ministry 232, 234,
    237
  world outside and 110–12
'The Roman Catholic Church'
  (Phillips) 103–13
Rominger, Revd Roberta
  The United Reformed Church
  136–44
Ruach City Church 180, 182
Russell, Dr David 228, 229

Sadgrove, Michael 26
Sainsbury, Roger 268
The Salvation Army
  ecumenism 51
  history of 147–8
  leadership structure of 145–6,
    150–2
  mission 147–53, 220
  New Testament and 145–6
  Orders and Regulations 147–8
  spouses 206
  translocal leadership 149–53
Santer, Rt Revd Mark 242
Schauf, Heribert 109
Schohet, Robin 250

Schon, Donald 249
Scott-Joynt, Rt Revd Michael 227
scripture
  basis of episcope 64–5
  biblical theory xxiv
  part of 'threefold cord' 22–4
  Wesleyan Methodism and 18
  see also New Testament
Searle, Revd Roy 185
'Episkope and the New
  Monasticism in the Celtic
  Tradition' 192–9
secular world 110–12, 142
Selby, Rt Revd Peter 227, 268
*Seventh Book of Ecclesiastical
  Polity* (Hooker) 22
sexual abuse, supervision and 251
Seymour, William J. 177, 178
'The Shape of Translocal
  Oversight' (Standing) 231–22
Shervington, David xxiv
Sherwood Psychtherapy Training
  Institute, Nottingham 245
'Six Marks of a Missionary Union'
  (Coffey) 220
social justice
  bearing witness 75–6
  in the parishes 85–1
  The Salvation Army and 146–7
Soul Survivor 38
speaking in tongues 169
St Andrew and St George Church,
  Stevenage 49
St Hugh and St John's Church,
  Stevenage 49
St Mellitus Theological
  College 34
St Nicholas Church, Stevenage 48
St Paul's Theological Centre 34
St Peter's Broadwater, Stevenage
  49
St Thomas' Crookes, Sheffield 37

Standing, Revd Dr Roger 228, 229
  'Episkope, Identity and
    Personhood' 203–11
  'The Shape of Translocal
    Oversight' 213–22
  'Theological Issues' 14–38
Staneway Chapel 267
Stewart, Alister 9, 10
Stoneleigh Bible Week 165
Stott, John 176
Sturge, Mark 180
supervision/mentoring
  continuous learning 249–50
  functions of 248–9
  as a lamp in shadows 250–3
  personal experience without
    244–8
Sutton, Ken 88
Sykes, Rt Revd Stephen 56, 226,
  229

*Talent Management for Future
  Leaders and Leadership
  Development for Bishops and
  Deans* (Green Report) 222
Temple, William 99
Tertullian (Quintus Tertullianus)
  21
The Order of Mission (TOM) 37
Theodora of the desert 186
Theodore of Tarsus, Archbishop
  21
'Theological Issues: Constants in
  Context' (Standing) 14–38
3DMovement 37
Tidball, Revd Dianne
  'The Baptist Union of Great
    Britain' 125–34
St Timothy 166
Tomlinson, David 267
Took, Pat 228
Tozer, A. W. 169

'Translocal Ministries in
  the Church of England as
  Institutional Leadership'
  (Hubbard) 93–102
translocal ministry
  accountability 263
  apostles and prophets 259
  Catholic Church 103–13
  Churches Together example 268
  deeper relationships and unity
    269–70
  dynamic 257
  envoy model 6–7
  future prospects of 267–72
  gender and xxv
  geography of 271
  governance model 7, 9
  inherited models 259–60
  itinerant model 5–6, 7
  mission and 258, 260–1
  models from Christendom
    256–60
  New Testament and 4–10
  partnership with local leaders
    262–3
  pastoring pastors 269
  pluriform 258–9
  post-Christendom 264–5
  relational 257–8
  retraining 261–2
  scholarship and 225–31
  social justice and 270
  terminology 264–5
  theory and xxiv–xxv
'Translocal Ministry and
  Scholarship' (Goodliff) 225–31
'Translocal Ministry in Post-
  Christendom' (Murray) 254–65
translocal oversight
  authority and 216–17
  challenges to roles in 98–9
  churches and 221–2

in context 14–16, 214–17
defining translocal 93–4
definition of xxiv
ecumenism 54–7
evangelicalism and 31–8
institutional leadership 93–102
location 214–15
marginal relations and 217
mission and 220
mutual trust and respect 56
national and local 52
pastoral dimension 218–19
personal character and 203–11, 213–14
practice and experience of xxv
proximity and 215
role of 215–16, 218–19
supervision and 244–53
titles and xxiii
Trinity
  Celtic Community and 194–5
  oneness of 107
Turner, Ralph
  Gerald Coates Pioneer 172
Tutu, Archbishop Desmond 77

United Free Church 228
United Kingdom
  bishops in House of Lords 89
  bishops' oath to monarch 81–3
  Coronation Oath 82–3
  Hillsborough disaster 87–91
United Reformed Church
  Basis of Union 138–9
  Church and Society team 57
  creation of synod moderators 136–8
  ecumenism 48, 143–4
  Local Ecumenical Partnerships 48–9
  origins to present day 136–7
  Reformation spirit of 142
  role of synod moderators 138–41, 143–4
  scholars and 228
  theology and moderators 141–2
  translocal oversight 55
The United Reformed Church: Synod Moderators (Rominger) 136–44
United States, separation of church and state 31
Uriah the Hittite 87

Vineyard movement 31
Virgo, Terry 215
  'Apostolic Ministry in the New Church Streams' 164–8

Wagner, C. Peter
  'New Apostolic Reformation' 37–8
Wagner, Thomas 35–6
Waldensians 257–60
Walker, Simon P. 221
Wallis, Arthur 170
Warren, Rick 31
Weber, Max 216, 217
Week of Prayer for Christian Unity 44, 46
Welby, Archbishop Justin 172, 267
  ecumenism 44
  'man of action' 227–8
Wellspring Community, Peckham 185, 187
Wescott, Rt Revd Brooke Foss 184, 185
Wesley, John
  chain of bishops 23
  Connexion and 18, 117
  itinerant preaching 121
  Methodist movement and 16–19
  personal *episkope* 118–19

watching over one another 116
Westcott, Rt Revd Brooke Foss 267
Whalley, Ernie 229
What Sort of Bishops? (Methodist Conference) 19
Whyte, David 208
William the Conqueror 63
Williams, Apostle Alfred 181
Williams, D. P. 157
Williams, Archbishop Rowan 56, 90, 172
  bishop's connections xxi–xxii
  on the Establishment 20
  scholarship of 226, 227–8
Willow Creek Community Church 31, 32–3
Wimber, John 31
Winter, Revd Prof. Sean F. xxv, 16

women
  the bishop's wife 180
  complexity of episcope 238–40
  first C of E bishops 232
  ministry in Black churches 178–9
  in Northumbria community 196
  theology and episcope 233–5
World Council of Churches
  Baptism, Eucharist and Ministry 24, 28–9
  ecumenism 47
  Lima document 28, 203–4
Worsley, Rt Revd Ruth 232
Wright, Rt Revd Tom 56, 226, 229, 267

Zizendorf, Count Niklaus 18